MW00582388

Student Financial Literacy

Dorothy B. Durband · Sonya L. Britt
Editors

Student Financial Literacy

Campus-Based Program Development

 Springer

Editors
Dorothy B. Durband
Department of Personal Financial Planning
Texas Tech University
Lubbock, TX, USA

Sonya L. Britt
School of Family Studies
and Human Services
Kansas State University
Manhattan, KS, USA

ISBN 978-1-4614-3504-4   e-ISBN 978-1-4614-3505-1 (eBook)
DOI 10.1007/978-1-4614-3505-1
Springer New York Heidelberg Dordrecht London

Library of Congress Control Number: 2012934696

Foreword

New numbers from the College Board show that federal student loan disbursements—the total amount borrowed by students and received by schools—in the 2009–2010 academic years grew about 14% over the previous year to $96.8 billion. At the student level, class of 2009 college seniors carried an average of $25,000 in students loans (College Board 2010). The amount of money students borrow has long been on the rise. With recent economic downfalls, this is even more of a problem than in the past. Nearly 9% of 2009 college graduates had a postgraduation job status of unemployed (Project on Student Debt 2010). Not surprisingly, student loan borrower default rates are also on the rise (US Department of Education 2011).

College students lack an understanding that student aid is really a loan and that they really do not have to take all the money that is made available. Additionally, students lack general money management knowledge and skills. After graduation, these students will find that student loan and credit card debt payments are claiming a good part of their take-home pay, making it challenging for them to support a desirable lifestyle.

To address this and other financial situations experienced by students, financial literacy programs have proliferated on college and university campuses. These programs vary widely in their composition. Some schools offer individual financial counseling services for students, while others provide presentations and workshops relative to personal finance topics. Still, others provide only websites with links to financial content. Some schools offer all of these services. *Student Financial Literacy: Campus-Based Program Development* has primarily been written for individuals directly involved with the formation or enhancement of financial education programs. This book presents the key elements needed in an effective university financial education program and will serve as a much-needed resource for those who want to implement a financial education program or improve an already existing program.

I find *Student Financial Literacy: Campus-Based Program Development* to be unique in many ways; in fact, this book is the first-known resource of its kind. It presents the key components of financial education and counseling centers designed to address the growing concerns associated with high levels of debt and low levels of financial literacy among college students. It is written by people who are not only very knowledgeable about student financial education but who also have hands-on experience in the areas they address. Each chapter includes specific tools and strategies to assist in the foundation or enhancement of a program to improve students' financial knowledge and skills that will ensure their economic stability—both in school and after graduation. Each chapter is supplemented with an extensive list of references, culminating with an appendix that includes annotations of useful websites and a directory of professional associations and conferences.

An impressive array of authors who have been instrumental in establishing financial education and counseling centers of great repute have contributed chapters on various important topics. They offer advice and guidance based on their deep knowledge and extensive hands-on experience in teaching personal finance courses, conducting research, and counseling student clients at financial centers on their campuses. It is wonderful that these experts step forward to share their knowledge and experience in developing and directing their university financial education programs with others.

This book is comprehensive in its coverage of critical topics such as recruiting and training staff, mentoring staff and volunteers, developing staff and volunteer competencies, obtaining support for a program, devising marketing strategies for promoting a program, creating program models, developing research opportunities within a program, and assessing and evaluating program effectiveness.

Student Financial Literacy: Campus-Based Program Development is both timely and comprehensive. It brings together a group of nationally known and very accomplished experts. It provides excellent information on every aspect of what is needed to establish a strong financial education and counseling center on a campus. It is unique in the sense that it addresses an applied concept with evidence from research. I only wish that a book like this had been available to me when I struggled with establishing the financial counseling degree program and a financial counseling clinic at Iowa State University in the early 1980s. Having been through that process, I know that the information provided in every chapter of this book is relevant and valuable. I am very pleased to see that a resource of this quality has been created and made available. There is no doubt in my mind that many people around the country and world will find these materials very useful as they move towards the goal of establishing their own financial education and counseling programs.

Ames, IA, USA   Tahira K. Hira

Preface

You likely chose to read this book for one of the following reasons: (a) you agree that financial education for college students is important and you want to read about how others are doing it; (b) you want to start a program at your college or university; (c) you want to enhance an existing program at your college or university; (d) you want to provide logistical, intellectual, or financial support to a new or existing financial education program at your college or university; or (e) you want to know what all the financial education buzz is about and this looked like a fun read! Regardless of your reason for selecting this book, it is clear that the financial marketplace is becoming more complex with the variety of choices available to college students during school and upon graduation.

State colleges and universities have not historically had a defined role in financial education; however, some universities have reconsidered the role of financial education due to rising tuition costs, changing student demographics, and an uncertain job market (Harnish 2010). There has been a marked increase in the number of financial education programs in both public and private colleges over the past few years, yet the total number of programs is unknown. In a study of financial literacy efforts at 156 large US 4-year public institutions ($n=82$), the majority of respondents (88%) reported that their institutions were involved in "some type of financial literacy training, education, or programming" with three fourths reporting this as a new focus area over the last 5 years (Chamberlain 2011, p. 14). In a survey of 230 financial aid administrators (Student Lending Analytics 2010), 48% of respondents reported that a financial literacy program is offered at their institution. In the same study, 50% of respondents with no programs indicated that their institution had plans to implement a program within the next year. A February 2011 Internet search by the editors resulted in the identification of United States colleges and universities (2-, 4-year, public, and private) with established financial education programs that provide direct financial education to students. Another 75 colleges and universities have nondirect financial education available to students, e.g., a link to an external website. The 75 colleges and universities that provide direct financial education services were surveyed in early 2011 to explore the structure of established programs; results and related advice from the study's participants are discussed in detail in Chap. 2 and are highlighted throughout the book.

Identifying the Need

A frequently cited biennial national survey reveals the need for student financial education. In the most recent administration of the Jump$tart Coalition Survey, the financial literacy level of high school seniors fell to its lowest level ever, with students scoring 48 out of 100% (Mandell 2009). The average score for college students was 62 out of 100%, nearly 15% points above high school seniors. Even though the average score for college students was higher than for high school students, this is not seen as an acceptable grade.

While some promising news is that more states are placing an emphasis on including personal finance in the K-12 curriculum, there are still gaps that exist in exposing students to this content (Council for Economic Education [CEE] 2009). Personal finance is now included in the educational standards of 44 states with 13 states requiring students to take a personal finance course as a requirement for high school graduation (CEE, 2009). In a study of college students from 15 geographically diverse campuses, those from states requiring a high school financial education course had the highest reported financial knowledge levels and were more likely to display positive financial behaviors and dispositions (Gutter et al. 2010).

Regardless of their educational background in personal finance, students frequently begin college without the experience of ever having been solely responsible for their finances even though they will engage in a variety of necessary financial transactions during their years in college (Gutter et al. 2010). Students who do not receive financial education in the K-12 curriculum or do not come from families where money and its management are discussed likely enter higher education institutions at a disadvantage compared to their peers who have had exposure to personal finance information and experience.

Students have expressed a need for financial education at the college and university level. In an exploratory study of current students on two large campuses, many responded that a personal finance course would be helpful or should be required. In the same study, the students were asked what advice they would give to incoming college students. In retrospect, they recommended that incoming freshmen develop thrifty spending and savings habits, make use of a budget, and use credit cards sparingly or not at all; these actions are in line with recommended financial practices (Robb 2011).

An idea for consideration is the option of including students in programs to help other students. This model, used in higher education settings such as resident assistants in university housing and in mentoring or tutoring programs, can be used in a financial education program. Trained and supervised students can serve as paid staff or volunteers to provide financial education services for their peers. Institutions using this type of program delivery offer experiential learning. Students can contribute subject area knowledge and hone their leadership skills in a real world setting.

Looking Forward

As two program directors advised in our study of financial education programs, "if you cannot start big, just start something; the momentum will help grow the program"; just "be persistent and patient in getting your [program] established." As you begin your journey to initiate or improve a financial education program, follow other program directors' advice: Begin with a manageable goal and create a timeline for your short- and long-term goals. The following chapters will provide a comprehensive guide in your respective journey.

Lubbock, TX, USA	Dorothy B. Durband
Manhattan, KS, USA	Sonya L. Britt

References

Chamberlain, L. (2011). Dollars and sense: How colleges and universities promote financial literacy. *NASFAA Student Aid Transcript, 22*(1), 33–36
Council for Economic Education. (2009). *Survey of the states 2009: The state of economic, financial and entrepreneurship education in our nation's schools.* Retrieved March 25, 2011, from http://www.councilforeconed.org/about/survey2009/
Gutter, M., Copur, Z., & Garrison, S. (2010). *Financial capabilities of college students from states with varying financial education policies.* National Endowment for Financial Education. Retrieved March 25, 2011, from http://www.nefe.org/LinkClick.aspx?fileticket=MHmXOsB-QHI%3D&tabid=825
Harnish, T. L. (2010, Fall). *Boosting financial literacy in America: A role for state colleges and universities.* Perspectives, American Association of State Colleges and Universities. Retrieved March 15, 2011, from http://www.aascu.org/policy/perspectives/perspectives_fall10.pdf
Mandell, L. (2009). *The financial literacy of young American adults: Results of the 2008 national Jump$tart coalition survey of high schools students and college students.* Washington, DC: Jump$tart Coalition. Retrieved March 25, 2011, from http://www.jumpstart.org/survey.html
Robb, C. A. (2011). Paying for college: Advice from current students to incoming freshmen. *Family & Consumer Sciences Research Journal, 39*(4), 388–398. Retrieved July 7, 2011, from http://onlinelibrary.wiley.com/doi/10.1111/j.1552-3934.2011.02077.x/abstract
Student Lending Analytics. (2010). *SLA 2010 financial literacy survey.* Retrieved February 3, 2011, from www.studentlendinganalytics.typepad.com/

Acknowledgments

We wish to acknowledge the many individuals who were supportive in the completion of this book. Dr. Tahira Hira had the early vision to implement a financial counseling center at Iowa State University in the 1980s. A national leader in financial literacy education and research, she served as an inspiration for many who have since developed campus-based programs.

The authors' specialties were vital to the success of this project. We are delighted that they share their expertise with you. Several of the chapter authors are former Texas Tech students and volunteers who were instrumental in helping develop the Texas Tech Red to Black® financial education program. Some of them now teach and work in other university financial education programs.

We wish to thank the following individuals for their participation in conducting blind reviews of chapters:

NaRita Anderson, Kansas State University
Swarn Chatterjee, University of Georgia
Amy Cross, Texas Tech University
Julie Cumbie, Kansas State University
John Grable, Kansas State University
Tim Griesdorn, Iowa State University
Katie Horton, Texas Tech University
Jodi Kaus, Kansas State University
Ryan Law, University of Missouri
Nadia Marquez, Texas Tech University
Angela Mazzolini, Texas Tech University
Jeff Nelson, Kansas State University
Ron Sages, Kansas State University

Kathryn White, Mary Eva Bagwell, and Dr. Arthur Durband provided excellent discussion, reviews, and copyediting, all essential elements in the completion of this book.

    Others deserving acknowledgment include Texas Tech University for faculty development leave to produce this book. We wish to thank our financial planning faculty colleagues and students for their encouragement throughout this process. Dr. John Grable was a constant source of inspiration and feedback at every stage of our project. Dean Linda Hoover, Dr. Ralph Ferguson, Dr. Bill Gustafson, Dr. Vickie Hampton, Dr. JoAnn Shroyer, and Dr. Michael Shonrock are recognized for their past and present support of the Red to Black program. Many other individuals too numerous to mention have contributed to the success of the program. Without the experience provided by establishing and maintaining the program, this book project would not have become a reality.

Contents

About the Editors

Dorothy Bagwell Durband, Ph.D., AFC, is an associate professor of personal financial planning at Texas Tech University. Over the past 11 years, she has developed a nationally recognized model financial education program called Red to Black®. At inception, Red to Black was the first program of its kind in Texas and was one of only three known campus financial counseling programs. Red to Black has inspired programs at several universities and Dr. Durband is often called upon to consult when a university is attempting to start their own financial education program. The program has received national exposure by invited presentations and features in *The Chronicle of Higher Education, Business Week, U.S. News and World Report, msnbc.com, and InsideHigherEd.com.* Former Red to Black volunteers have recently been featured in *The Wall Street Journal* and *Business Week.* She received her Ph.D. from Virginia Tech in resource management with a specialization in family financial management. She earned an M.S. degree from Texas Woman's University and a B.S. degree from Louisiana State University. Dr. Durband teaches undergraduate and graduate courses in financial planning. Her teaching areas are money relationships, counseling and communication skills, pro bono financial planning, and research fund development. She received the Texas Tech Alumni Association New Faculty award in 2004 and the Texas Tech President's Excellence in Teaching Award in 2006. Her research interests are primarily centered on the attributes and behaviors of individuals and families with regard to their personal finances. She currently serves as a member of the board of the Financial Therapy Association and the Personal Finance Employee Education Foundation.

Sonya Britt, Ph.D., CFP®, AFC, is an assistant professor of personal financial planning and doctoral program coordinator at Kansas State University. She teaches courses in the undergraduate and doctoral degree programs, including advanced personal financial planning, family and consumer economics, advanced research methods, and advanced statistics. As a graduate student at Texas Tech University, Britt served as the assistant director of the Red to Black® peer financial counseling center for students and community members. Britt is now actively involved in the Kansas State University peer financial counseling program, Powercat Financial

Counseling, where she conducts research on college students' financial literacy. Britt has been invited to speak at national and international events for her work in financial literacy. As founding president of the Financial Therapy Association—an international association of practitioners and academicians—Britt enjoys the opportunity to combine her skills in marriage and family therapy with her talents in financial planning. Britt's groundbreaking research in the field of financial therapy has been featured in the *Wall Street Journal* and *New York Times*, along with other publications.

Contributors

Suzanne Bartholomae, PhD Department of Human Development and Family Science, The Ohio State University, Columbus, OH, USA

Mary M. Bell, PhD candidate School of Family Studies and Human Services, Kansas State University, Manhattan, KS, USA

Sonya L. Britt, PhD Institute of Personal Financial Planning, School of Family Studies and Human Services, Kansas State University, Manhattan, KS, USA

Swarn Chatterjee, PhD Department of Housing and Consumer Economics, University of Georgia, Athens, GA, USA

De′Arno D. De′Armond, PhD Department of Management, Marketing, and General Business, West Texas A&M University, Canyon, TX, USA

Dorothy B. Durband, PhD Department of Personal Financial Planning, Texas Tech University, Lubbock, TX, USA

Jonathan J. Fox, PhD Department of Consumer Science, The Ohio State University, Columbus, OH, USA

Jamie Lynn Garrett, MDiv, MBA Department of Finance, Real Estate and Business Law, Hattiesburg, MS, USA

Joseph Goetz, PhD Department of Housing and Consumer Economics, University of Georgia, Athens, GA, USA

John E. Grable, PhD Institute of Personal Financial Planning, School of Family Studies and Human Services, Kansas State University, Manhattan, KS, USA

Timothy Griesdorn, PhD Department of Human Development and Family Studies, Iowa State University, Ames, IA, USA

A. William Gustafson, PhD Department of Personal Financial Planning, Texas Tech University, Lubbock, TX, USA

Ryan E. Halley, PhD School of Business, George Fox University, Newberg, OR, USA

Sandra J. Huston, PhD Department of Personal Financial Planning, Texas Tech University, Lubbock, TX, USA

So-hyun Joo, PhD Department of Consumer Studies, Ewha Womans University, Seodaemun-Gu, Seoul, South Korea

Jodi Kaus, JD Powercat Financial Counseling, Kansas State University, Manhattan, KS, USA

Ryan Law, MS Office for Financial Success, University of Missouri-Columbia, Columbia, MO, USA

Angela L. Mazzolini, MS student Department of Personal Financial Planning, Texas Tech University, Lubbock, TX, USA

Jason McGarraugh, MS Neal Financial Group, Houston, TX, USA

Lance Palmer, PhD Department of Housing and Consumer Economics, University of Georgia, Athens, GA, USA

Kate S. Trombitas, MA Financial Education, NSLP, Worthington, OH, USA

Chapter 1
The Case for Financial Education Programs

Dorothy B. Durband and Sonya L. Britt

Introduction

One method of addressing personal finances among students of higher education is through college- and university-based financial education programs. In recent years, there has been a growth in the number of these programs, which vary widely in their composition. Some schools offer individual financial counseling services for students, while others provide presentations and workshops relative to personal finance topics; others provide websites with links to financial content. And some schools offer all of these services! Throughout this book, we refer to all as financial education programs. This includes financial counseling, financial planning, and financial literacy programs designed to help students with their money matters while they are affiliated with an institution of higher education. The term *education* is defined by the Merriam Webster dictionary as "knowledge and development, resulting from an educational process"; *literacy* is defined as being literate or "able to read and write" or "having knowledge or competence." In other words, education tends to refer to a certain level of understanding, whereas literacy is the ability to use or apply knowledge. Obtaining follow-up information from students is very difficult due to their high turnover rate (primarily a result of graduation), frequent moves, etc., so measuring literacy is much harder than delivering education. Although some programs are able to obtain literacy data, it is more likely that most programs operate from an

D.B. Durband, Ph.D. (✉)
Department of Personal Financial Planning, Texas Tech University,
15th Street & Akron, Room 262, Lubbock, TX 79409, USA
e-mail: dottie.durband@ttu.edu

S.L. Britt, Ph.D.
Institute of Personal Financial Planning, School of Family Studies and Human Services,
Kansas State University, 317 Justin Hall, Manhattan, KS 66506, USA
e-mail: sbritt@k-state.edu

D.B. Durband and S.L. Britt (eds.), *Student Financial Literacy:*
Campus-Based Program Development, DOI 10.1007/978-1-4614-3505-1_1,
© Springer Science+Business Media New York 2012

educational standpoint which is the rationale for using the term *financial education programs* throughout this book. Furthermore, we understand that the word *campus* can describe a number of settings. It might mean a physical location like a residential college, a building for a downtown university, or even a satellite campus. We will therefore be sharing content that can be applied to several types of campuses.

We have often been called upon to consult when an individual is attempting to start a financial education program at another institution and desires information on where to begin the process, which is one of the main reasons for producing this book. Our consultations have included campus visits and dissemination of information via webcasts, phone conferences, and email exchanges to share program design and delivery methods. Many exciting programs have developed over the past 10 years as a result. Given the frequency of requests we have received, it is our belief that this book is both timely and necessary in order to share the information desired with a larger audience. This book is the first known resource of its kind.

Reasons to Offer a Program

A college or university setting offers the opportunity to educate students at important decision points during their life to help them "avoid mistakes and missed opportunities" (Lerman and Bell 2006). Consider just a few of these decision points in the life cycle of a student: choosing a major, financing an education, establishing credit, renting an apartment or home, paying for major purchases, reviewing job offers, and choosing health-care coverage or a retirement plan. Many young people are vulnerable when it comes to making important financial decisions. Challenges students face while in the process of assimilating to a campus community may include escalating tuition costs, being presented with various unforeseeable expenses, and the use of financial aid packages and credit cards or other loan products. Within these decision points and others are opportunities and challenges that can be addressed by a financial education program.

Some students may experience difficulty at decision points in their life because of a lack of experience or knowledge and also because of the amount of information that is available. Multiple sources of information exist in a rapidly changing environment. Unfamiliar financial terminology and numerous complex financial products and related documents can be daunting for students and nonstudents alike. So in some cases, "what is lacking is not information but rather the ability to interpret the information" (Lerman and Bell 2006, p. 5). A financial education program can fulfill the role of translator to assist students in making informed decisions.

A focus on personal finance offers the opportunity for problem prevention and early intervention. It is easy to make a case for this by simply observing trends and personal financial outcomes in adult populations, e.g., low savings rates, lack of retirement preparedness, and/or debt and default levels. College students make decisions that have lasting financial implications for years to come, and many of them recognize this. A cursory search of your campus newspaper is likely to reveal a plea from students for financial education resources at your college or university.

Financial wellness is a component of overall well-being and a status of financial health (Joo 2008). Many universities have wellness programs or wellness centers that promote the integration of health and wellness to enhance their students' physical and emotional health. Joo contends that to become financially healthy, individuals need to demonstrate desirable behaviors in cash management, credit and debt management, planning for events during the life cycle, and consumerism. All or most of these are behaviors that students will exhibit. Therefore, why not include personal finance in an existing university wellness program?

While financial education efforts have been shown to be effective in some groups (e.g., Bernheim et al. 2001; Danes and Haberman 2004, 2007; Lusardi 2003), they have had mixed results among others (e.g., Cole and Shastry 2009; Xiao et al. 2010). Despite this, there is still much that we do not know about students. A program in a higher education institution provides a means to learn about students' financial management practices, knowledge, and attitudes. A financial education program can provide important evidence-based outcomes to the university and the community.

Financial education programs can be easily designed to reflect university missions of outreach, research, and teaching while at the same time helping students become more financially sophisticated. Expanding financial literacy is not the only goal of financial education programs. These programs are also in line with college and university goals to increase student retention rates and limit delayed graduation or academic interruption of students due to financial reasons. Financial education programs may best serve their students by providing access to important resources, such as emergency loans offered by the college or university, affordable housing, or directions to a food bank.

Universities who invest in future generations through a financial education program will foster the transfer of financial knowledge and skills likely resulting in financially independent and responsible alumni. Loan default prevention and timely graduation are two outcomes that are of great importance in higher education.

To find an article in a school newspaper highlighting the need and desire for student financial literacy is not difficult. Building a program from the ground up is challenging and not as easy as simply identifying the need. As will be illustrated throughout this book, other matters must be addressed when initiating a financial education program including recruiting and training of staff members, obtaining support, determining programming content, developing marketing strategies, forming partnerships, and evaluating processes and outcomes. Before delving into the specifics of beginning a program, it is important to have an understanding of the issues faced by today's college students. As advised by a program director surveyed for this book (Durband and Britt 2011), research must be done in your institution to answer the following questions:

- What is the quantity of student loan debt among your students?
- What is the quantity in dollars that the Financial Aid Office is processing in student loans?

- What is the default rate for your graduates?
- Are your students citing money-related issues as reasons for them leaving the university?
- Are money-related questions on any existing surveys or questionnaires being distributed to students? If "yes," what are the findings?

Potential Uses of This Book

This book fills an important need in helping college and university administrators, faculty, and staff who seek a guide for use in establishing financial education programs for college students. Our goal is to share practices and resources based on our experience in developing and directing one of the first university financial education programs. Our contributing authors are content experts representing all aspects of a program. In the chapters that follow, they share a collection of practice, research, and knowledge that will help you in implementing and sustaining an effective program at your institution.

Despite frequently cited recommendations for offering financial education to audiences such as college students, a one-size-fits-all financial education program is not recommended (Lusardi et al. 2010) nor is one-time education since learning is a continuous process and each person has a unique financial literacy context (Beck and Neiser 2009). Consider the makeup of the students at your institution and their cultural backgrounds, programs of study, and classifications, not to mention their financial socialization, their preferences for the use of technology, and their learning styles. The financial education needs of a first-year student may be very different from a transfer student or an international student, so tailoring a program to the specific needs of the target learners will be important.

Financial Help-Seeking Among College Students

When determining the type of financial education programming to offer, it is also important to consider who is most likely to seek financial education services. This is just what a group of Kansas State University researchers did. The researchers collected data from a group of students who sought help from the on-campus financial education program and a group of non-help seekers to determine what factors influenced the financial education program's clients to seek help (Britt et al. 2011). The help seekers were older and carried higher credit card debt but similar amounts of installment debt. The help seekers had lower net worth, were less prepared for a $1,000 financial emergency, had lower financial and income satisfaction, and reported lower levels of financial knowledge. The help seekers reported only slightly higher financial stress than the non-help seekers.

Britt et al.'s (2011) decision tree revealed that five significant variables can be used to anticipate who is likely to seek on-campus financial counseling: (a) perceived net worth, (b) mental health, (c) age, (d) financial knowledge, and (e) income. In general, help seekers are older with a lower asset base, less satisfaction with income, less knowledge, and elevated levels of stress and depression.

The perception of a low net worth could be influenced by the overall amount of debt a student has, including credit cards, installment loans, and student loans. The other possibility is that high net worth respondents have a lack of debt, which may be the result of parental payment of college tuition and college expenses. These students are likely to have a strong support system for financial advice and therefore do not require the use of a financial counseling center now or perhaps in the future. The perceived lack of financial knowledge among help seekers is a positive sign that financial counseling centers may be attracting those students who feel they need more information regarding personal finances. If the intention to start an on-campus center is to help students with low financial literacy, then the results from this study suggest that this strategy may be effective.

When a financial emergency arises, the tendency to use credit (i.e., credit cards) drastically increases if sufficient cash is not available to cover the necessary expenses. These findings may work in tandem since a person not able to meet a financial emergency must find alternative cash sources (which are likely to charge high rates of interest and fees), leading to dissatisfaction with their financial situation. This, in turn, may cause anxiety, fear, and depression.

As students mature and approach graduation, they begin to gain a more realistic grasp of their personal financial realities. The students' evaluation of their personal financial situation as they look to enter the "real world" may drive them to seek help. Other external factors might also be motivating help-seeking behavior, such as self-reflection. As one begins to interview for jobs, separate from parental support, or perhaps make plans to get married and take on the financial dependency of a family, the realization that there is more to be learned may surface. Additionally, age may simply be associated with experience. Some older students have amassed more debt in the latter part of their postsecondary education than the former and thus have more debt to pay off creating a sense of urgency to seek financial guidance. They have gained experience through behavior that prompts a help-seeking response.

Book Overview

This book presents key components and effective strategies needed in a college or university financial education program; it is a unique guide for those interested in starting a program or for others desiring to enhance aspects of an existing program. The chapters provide distinct components with a common thread between them. Experts in financial education share their knowledge as your program development team in this book. Due to the size and space of any book project, one can never hope to include all of the relevant experts in any particular field; however, program directors of all known college and university financial education programs were invited to convey their expertise and experience through a survey conducted prior to publishing (Durband and Britt 2011). There are likely other emerging programs that were unidentifiable by an Internet search at the time of the survey.

Chapter 2 highlights the current state of financial education programs. Dr. John Grable, Ryan Law, and Jodi Kaus present the program model survey results conducted for this book by the editors (Durband and Britt 2011). John is a university financial planning program director and was instrumental in starting the financial education program at his school. Ryan and Jodi are the directors of their respective schools' financial education programs. In addition to presenting the results of the survey, the trio reviews and discusses financial education program models and best practices for programs.

Guidance on how to staff a financial education program is presented in Chap. 3. The primary author, Dr. Ryan Halley has experience as a financial consultant and assistant director of a campus financial education program. Drs. Dorothy Durband and Sonya Britt assist Ryan in comparing and contrasting the various staffing options that may be used in a program. The trio extends the topic into training of financial education staff in Chap. 4. Mentorship can help with transitions inherent in a college setting as detailed in Chap. 4 written by the same authors. The chapter provides a description of recommended competencies for staff and volunteers in financial education programs. Knowledge and skills necessary and desirable for those who provide services to student clients are offered.

No program can exist without ongoing support. Chapter 5, authored by Drs. Dorothy Durband and Bill Gustafson, addresses this critical aspect of a program. Bill served as program director of one of the original 20 CFP-Board-registered programs for 14 years. He has acquired an immense amount of knowledge that addresses program support and sustainability. The authors offer advice on how to identify supporters and persons that may help secure space for operating a financial education program.

Chapter 6 focuses on content and delivery in programming. Drs. Joseph Goetz and Lance Palmer have practical and educational experience in financial education programming for students. These authors outline programming content efforts and the process of program delivery. Examples of the most popular requests for individual sessions and group presentations are given as well as innovative and/or interdisciplinary approaches to offering services.

Encouraging students to attend and participate in your programming efforts necessitates a solid marketing strategy. These guidelines are provided in Chap. 7. Mary Bell, a Certified Financial Planner™, practitioner has worked with the Department of Defense and the US Department of Agriculture to assist military and military dependents to further their financial education during their military experience. Jason McGarraugh is also a Certified Financial Planner™ practitioner whose teaching of financial planning extends from working with students to working with practitioners in Singapore. Dr. De'Arno De'Armond teaches marketing courses, so he brings skilled focus in marketing strategies to the chapter. Defining your target population and finding creative ways and places to promote your program will result in a positive outcome for your program.

The goal of Chap. 8 is to present strategies for developing partnerships in and around the institution and community. Drs. Sonya Britt and Joseph Goetz focus on the benefits of partnerships, who can potentially be involved, and how to establish, maintain, and terminate partnerships. A sample memorandum of understanding illustrates the mechanisms of forming a partnership.

The goal of most college or university financial education programs is to enhance the financial literacy of students. Dr. Sandra Huston provides a mechanism for assessing financial literacy in Chap. 9. Sandra recently led a team of faculty and students in creating the Financial Literacy Assessment for Adults. In this chapter, she defines financial literacy, justifies the need for an assessment of financial literacy, highlights the process of developing an assessment, and shares the key findings of the Financial Literacy Assessment.

Some colleges and universities have a research component in their financial education program. Others may desire to begin collecting program outcomes. Chapter 10 showcases research opportunities within programs. Dr. So-hyun Joo has published numerous scholarly papers and book chapters. Dr. Swarn Chatterjee is proficient in the study of consumer and household economic behavior and the economic integration of immigrants. Together So-hyun and Swarn explain why we need to conduct research with financial education programs and summarize the areas of research interest with college students and financial matters within the last 20 years. They conclude with direction on future research needs.

A key element of interest for administrators and funders of financial education programs is evaluation data, and in Chap. 11, Drs. Jonathan Fox and Suzanne Bartholomae and Kate Trombitas describe how to effectively evaluate a program. Each of them has extensive experience in program evaluation.

The last chapter ends with an overview of three national certification programs that staff may obtain to enhance their knowledge and skills and provide credibility to the program. This final chapter will discuss certifications relevant to program staff, including students. Angela Mazzolini writes about the Accredited Financial Counselor designation history, purpose, background on current certificants, education and practice requirements, and code of ethics. Mary Bell describes the same areas for the Certified Financial Planner™ designation as Angela does for the Accredited Financial Counselor designation. Finally, Dr. Timothy Griesdorn, who has experience in teaching financial counseling and working in a university financial education program, discusses the key concepts of the Certified Retirement Counselor® designation.

An important aspect of this book is the wide extent of resources provided in the Appendix. Jamie Lynn Garrett has worked for several agencies in providing financial education services to a broad range of audiences. She annotates useful websites, software, professional associations, and conferences in the appendix.

Getting Started

We hope that you will use this book to build the foundation of a new financial education program or find ways to build upon an existing foundation. The chapter authors were carefully selected to deliver timely and practical information. In general, the book is written for individuals involved with the formation of a financial education program for college and university students. However, it can also be used by colleagues, administrators, and general supporters of financial education who want services to be offered to students.

Your job as the reader is to determine what role you can play. Have you conducted a needs assessment? What assistance from colleagues, other departments, or your administration will you need in beginning a program? Are there campus connections that you can make as you begin this process? Are there opportunities for you to collect research data to examine student behaviors, attitudes, knowledge, and actions related to personal finances? What resources are needed to keep a program sustainable? This book will help you answer these questions and can serve as the go-to resource for beginning or enhancing your successful program.

References

Beck, T., & Neiser, B. (2009, Summer). Learning and growing: Lessons learned in financial education. *Federal Reserve Bank of San Francisco Community Investments Online, 21*(2). Retrieved October 29, 2011, from http://www.frbsf.org/publications/community/investments/0908/index. html.

Bernheim, B. D., Garrett, D. M., & Maki, D. M. (2001). Education and saving: The long-term effects of high school financial curriculum mandates. *Journal of Public Economics, 80*(3), 435–65.

Britt, S. L., Grable, J. E., Cumbie, J., Cupples, S., Henegar, J., Schindler, K., & Archuleta, K. L. (2011). Student financial counseling: A study of a clinical and non-clinical sample. *Journal of Personal Finance, 10*(2), 95–121.

Cole, S., & Shastry, G. K. (2009). *Smart money: The effect of education, cognitive ability, and financial literacy on financial market participation. HBS Working Paper Number: 09-071.* Retrieved October 29, 2011, from http://www.hbs.edu/research/pdf/09-071.pdf.

Danes, S. M., & Haberman, H. (2004). *Evaluation of the NEFE high school financial planning program 2003-2004.* Denver, CO: National Endowment for Financial Education. Retrieved October 29, 2011, from http://hsfpp.nefe.org/loadFile.cfm?contentid=273.

Danes, S. M., & Haberman, H. R. (2007). Teen financial knowledge, self-efficacy, and behavior: A gendered view. *Financial Counseling and Planning, 18*(1), 48–60.

Durband, D. B., & Britt, S. (2011). Perspectives on university financial education programs: Research survey highlights. Unpublished raw data.

Education. (2011). *Merriam-Webster.com.* Retrieved May 12, 2011, from http://www.merriam-webster.com/dictionary/.

Joo, S. (2008). Personal financial wellness. In J. J. Xiao (Ed.), *Handbook of consumer finance research* (pp. 21–34). New York: Springer.

Lerman, R. I., & Bell, E. (2006). *Financial literacy strategies: Where do we go from here?* The Urban Institute Opportunity and Ownership Project Report No. 1.

Literacy. (2011). *Merriam-Webster.com.* Retrieved May 12, 2011, from http://www.merriam-webster.com/dictionary/.

Lusardi, A. (2003). *Saving and the effectiveness of financial education. Pension Research Council WP2003-14.* Retrieved October 29, 2011, from http://papers.ssrn.com/sol3/papers. cfm?abstract_id=476022.

Lusardi, A., Mitchell, O. S., & Curto, V. (2010). Financial literacy among the young. *Journal of Consumer Affairs, 44*(2), 358–380. doi:10.1111/j.1745-6606.2010.01173.x.

Xiao, J. J., Serido, J., & Shim, S. (2010). *Financial education, financial knowledge and risky credit behavior of college students. Networks Financial Institute Working Paper 2010-WP-05.* Terre Haute, IN: Networks Financial Institute.

Chapter 2
An Overview of University Financial Education Programs

John E. Grable, Ryan Law, and Jodi Kaus

The Need for Financial Education Programs

The growth in debt levels among young people in the United States, particularly among college students, has been well documented. According to Sallie Mae, as reported by Jassim and Taylor (2010), 21% of all college students hold credit card balances between $3,000 and $7,000, with an estimated 84% of students holding at least one credit card. Upon graduation, the average senior leaves college with $4,100 in credit card debt. Credit cards are just one type of debt held by young people. Goetz et al. (2011) noted that today's college student is likely to graduate with multiple forms of debt, including car loans, student loans, credit cards, and other liabilities, such as payday loans, title loans, and, on occasion, mortgage debt. When combined into one figure, it is not uncommon for a graduating senior to graduate from college with debt in the high five figures (e.g., $80,000 or more).

Financial stress is an issue both at the beginning and end of a student's academic career. According to Borden et al. (2008) and Goetz et al. (2011), few students entering college are prepared to manage their financial situation or to make effective financial decisions. The situation does not improve as a student progresses towards degree

J.E. Grable, Ph.D. (✉)
Institute of Personal Financial Planning, School of Family Studies and Human Services,
Kansas State University, 318 Justin Hall, Manhattan, KS 66506, USA
e-mail: jgrable@k-state.edu

R. Law, M.S.
Office for Financial Success, University of Missouri-Columbia,
239 Stanley Hall, Columbia, MO 65211, USA
e-mail: lawr@missouri.edu

J. Kaus, J.D.
Powercat Financial Counseling, Kansas State University, 809 Student Union,
Manhattan, KS 66506, USA
e-mail: jkaus@k-state.edu

D.B. Durband and S.L. Britt (eds.), *Student Financial Literacy:*
Campus-Based Program Development, DOI 10.1007/978-1-4614-3505-1_2,
© Springer Science+Business Media New York 2012

completion. Few colleges and universities provide a formal means for obtaining important personal finance knowledge and experience. Besides a small number of personal finance courses—few of which are required for all students—most college students today graduate without ever discussing or making optimal financial decisions at the personal or household level.

This lack of financial education stands in stark contrast to other common behavioral intervention or support programs on college and university campuses. Palmer et al. (2010) noted that it is somewhat paradoxical that drug and alcohol education and intervention programs are prevalent on campuses but financial education programs are lacking. Of course, the ramifications of drug and alcohol use are immediate, with student outcomes known to college and university administrators. Outcomes associated with financial distress associated with suboptimal financial management skills are neither immediately apparent nor generally life threatening. In some respects, it is easier for college and university administrators to look the other way when it comes to providing education and intervention services for those college students facing financial stress and questions.

The subtlety of financial stress may hide the threat associated with a lack of financial management skills, but a more detailed look at the issue shows that financial stress is a topic that deserves greater attention among college and university administrators. Nearly every study that has tested the association between financial stress and college student outcomes has arrived at the same conclusion; namely, there is a profile of financially at-risk students that matches general at-risk student populations. Palmer et al. (2010) identified the most vulnerable groups who tend to be adversely affected by financial stress: (a) low-income students, (b) women, (c) first-generation students, and (c) minorities. On nearly all college and university campuses, student retention efforts tend to focus on one or more of these groups. However, few institutional retention efforts include aspects of financial education as a tool to promote college completion.

Financial stress, particularly among at-risk students, promotes (a) low academic performance, (b) student attrition, and (c) lower levels of wellness (Palmer et al. 2010; Pinto et al. 2001). The impact of financial stress, caused by low levels of financial management skill, has later life implications as well. Palmer and his associates noted that high debt levels often reduce a graduate's flexibility upon entering the workforce. Specifically, "decisions about marriage, family, and home purchase may be adversely affected" (2010). Increasingly, employers, rental agencies, and insurance companies use credit scores as a screening tool. Those with low scores are often shut out of opportunities available to those with higher credit scores.

Although the impacts of financial stress, resulting from weak financial management skills, low financial literacy, and increasing debt burdens, are more subtle than outcomes associated with activities typically seen in college and university intervention programs (e.g., drugs/alcohol, sexually transmitted diseases, weight management), a strong argument can and has been made that colleges and universities "should provide financial tools and education to help students develop appropriate financial management skills" (Palmer et al. 2010) as a way to increase student wellness and reduce student attrition. Unfortunately, the evidence, to date, has not been compelling enough for large numbers of college and university administrators to take action on a wide scale. There are relatively few centers, intervention services, or educational programs designed exclusively to help students increase their financial literacy and skills.

Financial Education Programs: A National Review

The study of student financial stress, literacy, knowledge, and behavior is a relatively recent phenomenon. As such, it is not surprising that the earliest financial education program was established in 1986 at Iowa State University. It took seven additional years before the second program was started, and another three years before the third program was established. In 2010, however, four financial education centers were opened. The information that follows was obtained from a national survey of on-campus financial education programs. The survey was commissioned for this book by researchers at Texas Tech University and Kansas State University (Durband and Britt 2011) to learn more about how existing educational programs and centers are organized, marketed, managed, and funded. An Internet search revealed that at least 150 colleges and universities have publically available websites marketing some type of financial education program for students. Seventy-five of those programs that provide direct one-on-one or group presentations to students were surveyed for use in this book and chapter. Of those, 30 programs responded to the survey. Survey results are presented below.

Providing Services

Programs on college and university campuses tend to be somewhat eclectic. At some institutions, services are contracted out to third-party agencies with oversight by a campus-wide committee. It is most typical, however, for services to be provided by counseling staff and peer counselors. At many colleges and universities that have a Certified Financial Planner Board of Standards, Inc. registered program, students majoring in financial planning and counseling often volunteer to provide services to other students. This model provides students studying financial planning and counseling with applied experience while meeting the ever-increasing demand for services among general student populations.

Financial education programs are almost always housed in a specific college. Most typically, financial education programs are housed in human sciences/ecology units; however, there are a few programs within colleges of business administration. Peer counselors in the human sciences/ecology programs have typically been taught about the family dynamics surrounding money issues, whereas peer counselors working from a business or economic education model tend to focus on more technical issues involving money, including investment management and tax planning. Programs that blend a human sciences/ecology perspective with a traditional business perspective can be quite successful.

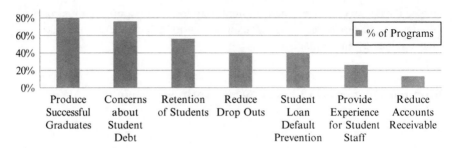

Fig. 2.1 Reasons for initiating on-campus programs

Reasons for Program Implementation

As shown in Fig. 2.1, there are a number of reasons colleges and universities implement financial education as an outreach service to students and community members. The impetus for program initiation varies, as many of those responding to the survey indicated more than one reason for program development. Eighty percent of respondents reported that their program was initiated to help produce financially successful graduates. Concerns about student debt levels were reported by 76% and retention of students by 56% of programs. Other reported reasons for initiation included reducing the number of students who drop out (40%), student loan default prevention (40%), and to provide experiential learning for student staff (26%). Though not one of the survey items, open-ended responses indicated two financial education programs were initiated due to requests from students, while another institution reported that their institution requires financial education for students. This is likely to be an increasing trend in the future as more states begin to require financial education on academic campuses.

Delivery Methods

Although delivery methods are diverse, financial education programs are typically provided using one-on-one, telephone, and/or live web counseling (reported by 76% of programs). Group methods (e.g., seminars, workshops, and credit or noncredit courses) are provided by 100% of campus financial education programs. Two-thirds of programs provide mass delivery methods, including seminars, radio programs, flyers, television, DVDs/CDs, blogs, podcasts, YouTube® videos, and e-mail messages. Overall, most respondents (96%) reported using a classroom style for their programming. More than half (66%) reported using small group discussion, with less than half (40%) using interactive activities such as board games or online entertainment. Frequently cited methods used are shown in Fig. 2.2.

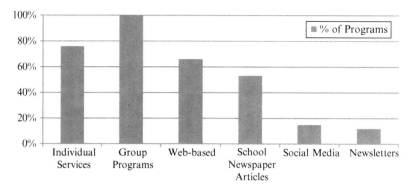

Fig. 2.2 Most common delivery methods

Requested Educational Topics

When asked about frequently requested topics for group programs, the top choices were cash management/budgeting and establishing and maintaining credit (reported by 86% of the sample) as shown in Fig. 2.3. Seventy percent of those responding listed reviewing credit reports and credit scores as a requested topic, followed by a little more than half (56%) reporting student loan repayment. It should be noted that in addition to students, university faculty, staff, and administrators often also request group programs.

Although mass outreach efforts are a commonly used method associated with on-campus financial education programs, there is an increasing trend towards one-on-one counseling, provided either by paid staff or peer counselors. Figure 2.4 shows the frequently requested topics for one-on-one financial counseling. The most frequently requested individual counseling topics, as reported by respondents, were cash management/budgeting (70%) and student loan repayment (70%).

Location of Services

The survey also asked respondents about the various places where financial education programs are provided on campuses. The most frequently cited locations were information sessions at student orientation: new student orientation (71%), transfer student orientation (29%), graduate student orientation (23%), and international student orientation (16%). Respondents reported less frequent delivery of services during financial aid entrance counseling (13%) and during financial aid exit counseling (19%). Student service offices are also a place where students receive financial information, education, and counseling. These services include student health/wellness centers (19%), career services (19%), and student counseling centers (13%). A little less than half of the respondents (42%) reported that services are provided through printed material provided at the locations mentioned above. Full information regarding where services are provided is shown in Fig. 2.5.

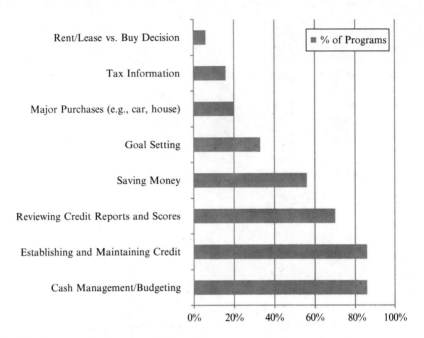

Fig. 2.3 Most requested group workshop topics

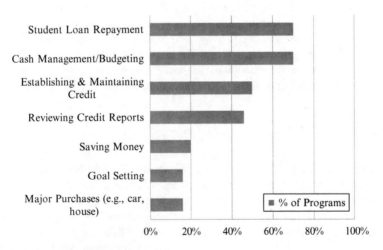

Fig. 2.4 Most requested one-on-one topics

The physical location for financial education programs varies across campuses as well. The two most frequently cited locations are in an academic building (36%) or a Financial Aid office (26%). Other campus locations are shown in Fig. 2.6.

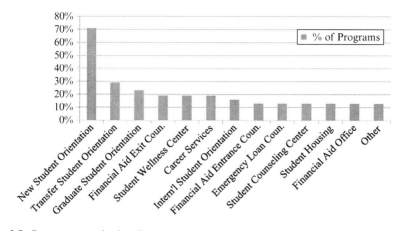

Fig. 2.5 On-campus service locations

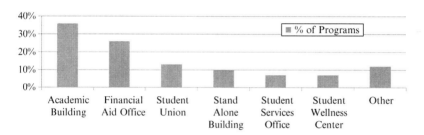

Fig. 2.6 Common program locations

Marketing Issues

Marketing services is an important task for those involved in developing and promoting programs. As shown in Fig. 2.7, the methods reported as most effective include word of mouth (86%), mass e-mail announcements (50%), information provided through a booth or table (46%), and information provided in a brochure or flyer (46%).

Charging for Services

An important topic of discussion among program directors and college and university administrators is funding. The survey asked respondents to indicate if they charge for their financial education program services. Few programs charge for services, as long as the client is a student (86%). Nonstudents may pay a fee, but it is important to note that only about 40% of programs offer services to nonstudents.

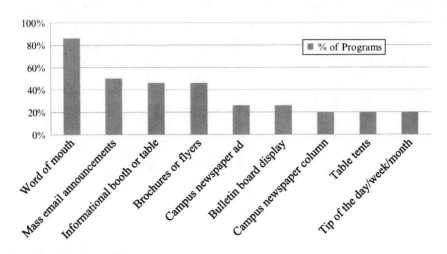

Fig. 2.7 Effective marketing methods

Regional Distribution of Programs

A majority of programs (83% of the sample) are located in 4-year public universities. Fewer programs (10%) are in 4-year private universities, and just a few (6.7%) are located in 2-year public institutions. In terms of region, a great many programs are concentrated at institutions in the South (43%), Midwest (36%), Northeast (10%), and West (10%).

Practicum Experience for Peer Counselors

Financial counseling programs offer important opportunities to gain practical client-advisor experience for those serving as peer counselors. The majority of programs offer ongoing training and practicum experience for student financial counselors (84%). Twenty-six percent of programs require one or more credit-based courses before participating in the program, while 48% of programs have no course prerequisites. The training is provided by a diverse group of individuals, including faculty (48%), financial aid officers (45%), and external professionals (42%). The content covered during training includes personal finance information (81%), presentation skills (68%), counseling skills (68%), confidentiality (68%), policies and procedures (61%), and recordkeeping (58%) as shown in Fig. 2.8.

Outcome Assessments

The majority of programs collect immediate impact evaluation data including participant satisfaction, change in attitudes, knowledge, or skills (68%) and program

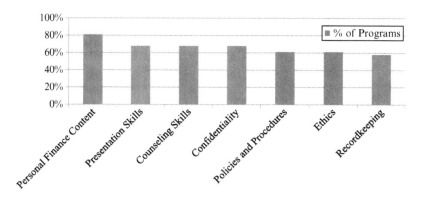

Fig. 2.8 Training topics

improvement evaluation data including participant rating of instructors, educational materials, and overall program strengths and weaknesses (61%). Fewer programs engage in intermediate (32%) and long-term (23%) impact evaluation procedures.

Staff Size

The average number of staff members is three full-time (with a range of 0–35 full-time staff employed), two part-time (with a range of 0–8), and five volunteers (with a range of 0–35) with activities ranging from management and training to providing direct services by both full-time and part-time staff.

The most commonly reported educational level of staff members was a master's degree for full-time staff (35%). The most common educational level was enrollment in an undergraduate program for part-time staff members (38%).

Academic Training for Staff

Survey respondents were asked to indicate an academic college affiliation for any of their staff members. As shown in Fig. 2.9, 29% of the staff members working in a program or center were not affiliated with any academic college. Of those affiliated with an academic college, 26% represented units in Human Sciences/Ecology, followed by Business (23%) and Education (23%).

Staffing Issues

Staff positions tend to be permanently funded (39%), contracted annually (25%), or contracted by a frequency other than 1 year (18%). Eighteen percent of respondents

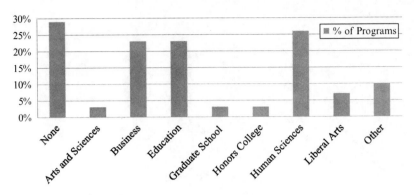

Fig. 2.9 Academic affiliation of financial education programs

either did not answer this question or indicated that it did not apply to them, as shown in Fig. 2.10.

Ongoing Funding Issues

The operating funds for financial education programs surveyed are shown in Fig. 2.11. One-third of the programs receive part of their support from grants. Approximately one-quarter of the programs receive their support, in part, from an academic unit, student affairs, student fees or tuition, or a financial aid office. Fewer programs receive money from donations and fund-raising efforts. Nineteen percent of programs receive partial support from unidentified sources. In addition to direct support, 90% of programs also receive institutional in-kind support in the form of office space, equipment, printing, supplies, and web support. Forty-eight percent of programs receive noninstitutional in-kind support.

Summary

The survey results presented above appear throughout the book as they relate to a particular chapter topic. The findings are representative of 2- and 4-year public and private colleges and universities that offer in-person financial education services for students. Now that basic demographic information is known about existing programs, it is necessary to consider how services are generally provided.

Fig. 2.10   Source of staff funding

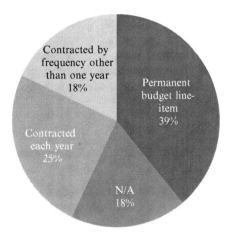

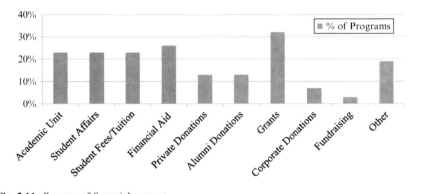

Fig. 2.11   Sources of financial support

Program Structures

There are two basic structures for providing financial education, according to the
Get Financially Fit: Financial Education Toolkit produced by the American Council
on Consumer Interests (Federal Reserve Bank of New York n.d.):

1. Financial education/counseling centers with two subcategories

   • Peer-to-peer programs
   • Programs delivered by financial professionals

2. Distance learning programs

   There is not one perfect delivery structure. Existing programs incorporate different structures for unique reasons, including funding, time, and expertise. Further, a

program that starts out with one structure may decide to use an altered approach as the program grows, or the program may decide to use an eclectic approach incorporating more than one method (see Goetz et al. 2011). The following sections highlight commonly used delivery methods, while discussing opportunities and challenges associated with each approach.

Financial Education/Counseling Centers

For definitional clarity, a financial education or counseling center, as used in this narrative, is an established site on campus, such as a student financial wellness center, a debt counseling clinic, a center for economic and financial education, or financial education training clinic. A director or staff member may oversee this type of clinic. Generally, counseling is provided by students or financial professionals.

Some benefits of having an established site on campus include the opportunity for multiple campus and off-campus partners to come together in collaborative efforts. For example, a director might convene an advisory board of both on- and off-campus partners, such as a member from the financial aid office, someone from student advising, a local credit union and/or bank member, faculty members, deans, or other key stakeholders.

A financial education or counseling center can also offer clinical experiences for graduate and/or undergraduate students, similar to a marriage and family therapy clinical center on campus. Some of the challenges associated with this type of delivery method, or any type of financial education and counseling offered on campus, include encouraging students to visit the center *before* they have a financial crisis, getting the word out to students and others that the center is available, and obtaining sufficient funding to cover center expenses and staff needs.

Peer-to-Peer Programs

A peer-to-peer program is one in which student employees or volunteers provide services. Such services provided typically include one-on-one financial counseling, group counseling, and group presentations. Some programs provide counseling for students only, while others offer services to anyone in the community.

For this type of program to be successful, it is important that peer counselors are properly trained and have the needed expertise to provide competent counsel. For example, peer counselors may be required to complete a series of classes, be in a certain major, interview for a position, and attend periodic training sessions on important topics. Some programs also require peer counselors to demonstrate competencies in a supervised clinical setting prior to working with clients.

Depending on funding and the number of students interested in being a peer counselor, a determination needs to be made as to whether counselors will be compensated (e.g., through salary, honoraria, or a scholarship). For example, paid counselors may tend to be more dependable than volunteers. On the other hand, programs that rely on volunteers typically attract students who have an altruistic desire to share their expertise with other students. Both volunteers and paid employees earn a valuable résumé item as they begin to interview for positions, as they have a hands-on, real world experience.

Lacey Mitchell, a former student peer counselor at her university, summed up her experiences being a counselor:

> Being a financial counselor was an amazing experience. When I look back at my four years at Mizzou nothing I was involved in brings me as much joy as being a part of the Office for Financial Success (OFS). Being involved in this organization helped me to uncover my true passion for helping people with their everyday financial situations. There is nothing more fulfilling to me than helping others to achieve their financial goals! I was able to portray this passion when I began the interview process prior to graduation. With the OFS on my resume, every interview was filled with questions about the services we provided to students. The OFS provided a way for me and my colleagues to stand out in a very tough job market. How many college seniors can say they were a part of an organization that provided one-on-one financial counseling to other students? Essentially the OFS provided an environment for us to learn skills that are essential in the financial planning world, while gaining real world experience and doing something we love! I can't think of anything else like it (L. Mitchell, November 17, 2010, personal communication).

Along with the benefits of peer-to-peer programs, there are some challenges, including a possible lack of expertise, supervision and training of students, turnover of students, and staffing issues. The lack of expertise can be overcome through training, but without adequate supervision, it can be difficult to monitor how well peer counselors are doing and the quality of the advice they are providing. Having experienced counselors work with newer counselors can help, along with having a way for a supervisor to monitor counseling sessions, either through some type of observation room or recording sessions. (Both scenarios need to be done with the consent of the person being counseled). Turnover of students will always be an issue that requires continual recruitment of new counselors.

Programs Delivered by Financial Professionals

Programming delivered by financial professionals, financial aid officers, student loan providers, or other financial services professionals typically occurs through workshops, seminars, and other clinical activities. For example, at the University of Georgia, volunteers—one from marriage and family therapy and one from financial planning—meet with clientele. This dual program approach provides a collaborative environment that enhances client outcomes and student peer counseling experience. Most often, these delivery methods operate with one or two full-time paid internal professional staff members who provide the financial education services. Other approaches include inviting financial professionals from the community to provide the services. For example, one large public university has started a service where a Certified Financial Planner (CFP®) certificant from the community offers counseling services.

One benefit of this delivery approach is the quality of advice the students (or others being counseled) receive. If experts are delivering the advice, then the advice should be of the highest quality. Another benefit is that if someone from the community is engaged in providing counseling, the partnership may blossom into other opportunities within the community. Challenges include finding off-campus partners that support the mission of the program, finding the right financial experts that can offer the financial counseling, and avoiding partners who simply want to promote their services and products.

Distance Learning Programs

Examples of distance learning programs include websites or other online programs, courses offered via correspondence, or self-study courses or workbooks. Through these types of programs, more students can be reached. Colleges and universities can offer services from a distance via technology, which may appeal to students. Further, distance programs usually require less staffing needs than other types of counseling, and information can be obtained when the client is ready for change—anytime, day or night.

Unfortunately, distance learning does not usually give students and counselors direct contact with each other. Additionally, it may be difficult documenting a program's impact. It can also be difficult to find the staff or financial resources needed to establish and maintain a program.

Effective Practices

Since the overwhelming majority of financial education programs are self-selected by students rather than required courses, encouraging and obtaining student use of these services is critical. Several universities have found unique ways to break down various barriers that may prevent students from using services. Some colleges and universities are creatively engaging students and marketing their financial education programs to enhance their success. Both new and existing programs can benefit from highlighting effective practices currently being used by others. The following discussion describes some of these barrier-breaking methods.

Location

The number one best practice advice is akin to the real estate business; a key to successful student utilization of a program is location, location, location! A well-thought-out strategy for the physical location of a financial education program is critical to its success. Both the delivery of the educational programming and the physical location of the program are generally more effective if offered in a student-friendly locale.

Two of the newly established programs surveyed for this book have had immediate success in part due to their office locations being in their campus student unions. However, even the smallest nuances of a program's design can have an impact on student usage. The front door of one center opens directly to the concourse area adjacent to a food court in the student union. As a result, this center has experienced success with students merely walking in to their office to ask a quick money question. The other newly established program, on the other hand, is located inside a larger suite of student service offices with a receptionist, which requires students to check-in. A receptionist in this way acts as a "gatekeeper" that students must pass through to seek help; thus, walk-in traffic at the second university has been insignificant despite targeted marketing initiatives. A creative solution for this program may be to initiate a *walk-up* option at a tabling event in the union concourse where students could readily access a counselor to ask a quick money question or to schedule an appointment for more assistance.

Eliminate Barriers

Financial programs must continue to creatively reduce as many barriers as possible preventing students from seeking their services. In general, students want to learn more about personal finance topics, but often feel they do not have the time to access help. Campuses may have a population of students for which this is a particular concern. For example, at one large Midwestern university, veterinary medicine students are committed to courses and labs all day on the farthest edge of the main campus. Therefore, the university's financial education program has turned to Skype-to-Skype online financial counseling to provide convenient access to its services from any location. As a result, even geographically dispersed students can receive financial counseling in a virtual environment.

Providing convenient access to financial counseling services is a key factor when working with students. Some financial education programs do so by offering financial education via online *webinars* where students can learn while in their own personal environment. Other programs record their financial education programs. They then embed recordings within their websites for students to access anytime it is convenient for them.

Outreach

In regard to best practices in the area of service, 100% of the respondents to the survey of financial education programs indicated that they offered group education via seminars, workshops, or course offerings. Students are more apt to be present to receive financial education when it is delivered in a location where students are captive and open to learning new information. Thus, tagging on a financial education component to an orientation type lecture or immediately following a compulsory course is the next best thing to requiring counseling services and education. For example, several financial education programs successfully deliver annual financial education presentations at campus orientation sessions, reaching hundreds, if not thousands, of students this way. It is from these broad outreach efforts that individual students may take the next step of seeking one-on-one financial counseling for their particular situation.

Student Involvement

The national increase in interest in financial education has resulted in the implementation of a variety of different program models at colleges and universities. While no single model is preferred, the peer educator model presents a variety of effective and innovative practices others can draw from. *Students Helping Students: A Guide for Peer Educators on College Campuses* summarizes several research studies, indicating peer educators have been found to be effective (Newton and Ender 2010). From sharing learning styles and generational perspectives to the premise that students are influenced by their peers, studies have shown peer educators are effective helpers (e.g., Newton and Ender 2010). In a sense, peer educators can offer a positive spin on the age-old behavior of peer pressure by modeling positive financial conduct for fellow students. As one faculty member working with a newly launched peer-to-peer university program noted:

> This is such a great tool for students. Students teaching students the basics of how to handle their money while they journey through college is the ultimate student experience. We have found that 95 percent of the students surveyed on campus want to learn and know more about money while they are in college. The Peer Educators can speak freely with the students during their appointment and even share their own real life money experiences. The Peer Educators are the best teachers! I think that our Peer Educators are making a difference and changing lives every day in our office—one student at time!

For one-on-one financial education services in peer-to-peer programs, personal financial planning or business majors typically act as peer financial counselors, as they possess the technical, substantive financial knowledge required of the position. However, best practices involve grassroots initiatives, including all types of students that can create synergy around a financial education program on a campus, giving students true ownership in its success. Creating a student organization where the talents of all interested students can be employed has been a very successful approach when building a leading program. For example, students in public relations and marketing may join the center's student organization to give and get experience in marketing initiatives, which, in turn, helps build the financial program. A student organization would be a campus group typically registered with student government and entitled to privileges such as funding opportunities, use of campus meeting space, assistance with fund-raising activities, and other support. Having the student organization host interactive events such as "Thrifty Gifting" and "Spring Break! NOT Spring Broke" makes learning about personal finance fun for students. Additional tips and ideas about marketing efforts for a financial education program are presented in Chap. 7.

Student-driven financial education programs provide an exciting opportunity for colleges and universities. In addition to hosting interactive financial events, members of the organization can serve as ambassadors across campus helping identify needs that students in the peer educator role may not become aware of otherwise. Allowing a student organization to support the marketing efforts of the program also allows the peer educators to focus on their specific roles without overburdening them with additional responsibilities. As one program coordinator indicated, "Our student organization's role is to generate awareness so that our peer counselors are kept busy with client appointments."

Behavior Change

Many student financial education programs find that changing the knowledge, attitudes, and behavior of students in regard to money management is the key to success, both individually and on a program level. One student money management program has found an effective strategy for beginning the process of financial behavior change. According to the Director of this program:

> Getting the students involved with estimating and tracking their expenses before their first appointment with our trained Peer Educators is a great asset to the students. I think that this process really gets them in touch with the Latté Factor®. The Latté Factor is [comprised of] the small things that students spend money on every day. For example, that $2.50 cup of coffee a student has to have every morning eventually adds up to big dollars over time. Most students do not know where their money goes on a daily basis and this process puts them in touch with their spending habits. The students are really grateful for engaging them in this learning progress. The positive feedback from the students that visit our office is very rewarding.

Summary

In summary, colleges and universities that are in the first stages of instituting a financial education program, with services designed for direct student contact, face many choices in the way the program can be established, delivered, and grown. Each program is (and should be) as unique as each individual institution. What works at one college or university may not be feasible at another. However, effective strategies and techniques for the design of a new program can be drawn from among the most successful practices, as exhibited by existing education programs.

In the end, any reasonably well-thought-out, funded, and managed educational program should be well received, especially by at-risk students. Programs like those discussed in this chapter can help students persist in school by promoting academic performance, decision-making skills, and financial wellness. If a program can be incorporated into the behavioral intervention and support framework of a campus, then it is likely that the financial stress of a wide number of students will be reduced. Although there is no single best approach to the design and delivery of educational programming, as long as the goal remains to provide students with the financial tools and techniques to improve financial management skills, the overall financial capabilities of graduates will improve. This is a goal that students, parents, administrators, and other stakeholders all share in common.

References

Borden, L. M., Lee, S., Serido, J., & Collins, D. (2008). Does participation in a financial workshop change financial knowledge, attitudes, and behavior of college students? *Journal of Family and Economic Issue, 29*, 23–40.

Durband, D. B., & Britt, S. L. (2011). *Perspectives on university financial education programs: Research survey highlights.* Unpublished raw data.

Federal Reserve Bank of New York. (n.d.). *Get financially fit: financial education toolkit.* Retrieved October 29, 2011, from http://www.newyorkfed.org/regional/Fin%20Ed%20Toolkit%20 for%20College%20Campuses.pdf.

Goetz, J., Durband, D., Halley, R., & Davis, K. (2011). A peer-based financial planning & education service program: An innovative pedagogic approach. *Journal of College Teaching & Learning, 8*(4), 7–14.

Jassim, A. A., & Taylor, J. C. (2010). College students' credit card usage and debt. *Competition Forum, 8*(1), 101–110.

Newton, F. B., & Ender, S. C. (2010). *Students helping students: A guide for peer educators on college campuses* (2nd ed.). San Francisco: Jossey-Bass.

Palmer, L., Bliss, D. L., Goetz, J. W., & Moorman, D. (2010). Helping undergraduates discover the value of a dollar through self-monitoring. *American Journal of Business Education, 3*, 103–108.

Pinto, M. B., Parente, D. H., & Palmer, T. S. (2001). College student performance and credit card usage. *Journal of College Student Development, 42*(1), 49–58.

Chapter 3
Staffing and Recruiting Considerations for Financial Education Programs

Ryan E. Halley, Dorothy B. Durband, and Sonya L. Britt

Introduction

A program is only as good as the people who staff it. There are a number of fundamental staffing decisions that must be made when developing a campus financial education program. In this chapter, we discuss staffing and recruiting procedures that can be used within a financial education program.

It takes a team of devoted individuals to make a financial education program viable. Work needs to be done on multiple levels, ranging from strategic planning to determination of staff structure and functions. There are a variety of individuals who can serve as a support team for your financial education program. From within the university, potential options include administrators, professional staff, faculty, and students. External options include local financial services professionals, mental health clinicians, and other professionals. Likely categories for a support team include the following: (a) executive director, (b) program director(s), (c) clerical staff, (d) mentors, and (e) counselors/educators. The roles and responsibilities of each potential support member are discussed in detail below. As you are reading, keep in mind that one person could serve in one or more positions.

R.E. Halley, Ph.D. (✉)
School of Business, George Fox University,
414 North Meridian Street #6263, Newberg, OR 97132, USA
e-mail: halleyr@georgefox.edu

D.B. Durband, Ph.D.
Department of Personal Financial Planning, Texas Tech University,
15th Street & Akron, Room 262, Lubbock, TX 79409, USA
e-mail: dottie.durband@ttu.edu

S.L. Britt, Ph.D.
Institute of Personal Financial Planning, School of Family Studies
and Human Services, Kansas State University, 317 Justin Hall, Manhattan, KS 66506, USA
e-mail: sbritt@k-state.edu

D.B. Durband and S.L. Britt (eds.), *Student Financial Literacy:*
Campus-Based Program Development, DOI 10.1007/978-1-4614-3505-1_3,
© Springer Science+Business Media New York 2012

Executive Director

Roles/Responsibilities

A solid program with a sustainable future needs a vision. The individual who serves as the visionary may conduct much of the initial work in launching a program and will function in an executive role. Big questions that will need to be posed and answered include: Who is the target audience for the program's services? How will these services be structured (e.g., pro bono, fee for service, or sliding scale charge)? Who are the important decision makers on campus who need to be convinced of the program's importance? Are there other partner programs on campus that could serve as valuable collaborators in either planning (e.g., advisory capacity) or providing services? How will the program integrate with the existing campus culture? How will the program be funded? How will the program be staffed? Where will key services be provided? What is the vision of the program 3, 5, and 10 years from its inception? What are the steps necessary to move closer to the vision? In addition to these formational questions, the executive administrator should continue to drive the program forward by staying connected with other decision makers on campus.

Selection Criteria

The executive director should have experience in financial services or a related profession and be well versed in knowledge of available campus and off-campus resources. This individual needs to know the intricacies of the higher education institutional structure and have connections on campus. Developing a working relationship with university administration will help ensure continued support for your financial education program. Creativity in fund-raising and budget planning are also assets necessary for this position.

Program Director(s)

Roles/Responsibilities

A crucial role in any program is the leadership position responsible for carrying out the central features of the mission. The director needs to recruit, interview, and hire a competent program staff. Program staff may include financial educators, counselors, and clerical support. This position will also include locating the possible venues that exist within the campus and the community where financial education can be offered, deciding topics to address in financial education and who will develop these presentations, and designing methods to evaluate, train, and mentor educators.

Once a qualified staff has been selected, the director needs to work diligently to train and orient the staff to the work that they will be conducting. This director must work with the executive director to execute effective methods for marketing and publicizing the services of the program (see Chap. 7). This individual will also be heavily involved in the programming work (see Chap. 6) that outlines the features of the services available.

In addition, this individual will be responsible for determining the quantity of staff necessary, formulating the process for client intake, working with the executive director to establish an appropriate location on campus to conduct services, and developing program policies and procedures including record keeping, ethics, confidentiality, safety, and liability reduction.

Selection Criteria

The program director needs to have experience in financial services; university experience in student services is also helpful. This individual should work effectively with others, including facilitating staff training and providing ongoing staff mentoring. Effective communication skills and leadership capabilities are strong assets. The ability to work well in crisis situations is also a necessary attribute.

Clerical Staff

Roles/Responsibilities

The clerical support staff serves a vital role within the program model. Clerical staff will become the face of the program; most prospective clients or educational program audiences will interact with this person/team initially. Depending on the size of the program, having one primary clerical staff member may be preferred. The more people involved in this function, the more difficult it may be to ensure organization, follow-through, confidentiality, and adherence to established procedure.

As previously mentioned, all services begin with contact with the clerical support staff. Through a phone call, an email, or a face-to-face meeting, a prospective client or a contact for an educational program will initiate an inquiry. The clerical support staff needs to quickly respond to each of these inquiries and determine if and how the program can best meet the presented need(s). The clerical staff will likely be contacted by individuals requiring immediate assistance; therefore, the ability to remain calm and effective in the face of crisis is of paramount importance.

Selection Criteria

The clerical position requires someone who demonstrates strong professional skills such as organization, confidentiality, and relational skills. Effective communication is necessary, as is the ability to work well in crisis situations and changing circumstances. This individual (or team) will need to have a good working relationship with other staff members, as his or her role will primarily encompass collecting and delivering information to these persons and carefully following procedures that have been established by program directors.

Mentors

Roles/Responsibilities

There will typically be an experienced, as well as inexperienced, staff base. The mentoring of inexperienced staff may be successfully accomplished by senior staff members and may result in higher client satisfaction ratings. Mentoring could consist of joining a financial educator in presentations or observing a financial counseling session (with client permission) with a more seasoned counselor. Another approach could be having the senior staff member periodically accompany the less experienced staff member during a session or meeting to discuss previous sessions or to focus on questions that have arisen. If the program uses a peer model, experienced students can serve as mentors for new students.

Selection Criteria

Mentors should demonstrate proficiency in working as a financial counselor, an educator, or both. These individuals should be collaborative, energetic, good recruiters, and actively engaged in providing services. Mentors play a key role in attracting, developing, and retaining critical staff members.

Financial Counselors and Educators

Roles/Responsibilities

Financial counselors and educators conduct the central tasks that drive the program's mission. These individuals provide individual and group financial counseling or may be involved in delivering personal finance information to a variety of audiences in an educational format. Counselors may be involved solely in personal contact with clients, be focused on providing educational content, or may be cross-trained to conduct a combination of both individual and group programming.

Financial counselors and educators will most likely work with a schedule that is provided by the clerical staff. Counselors can either work during specified time periods each week (e.g., Monday and Wednesday from 3:00 pm until 5:00 pm) or they can work a set number of hours each week based upon a mutually beneficial arrangement with a client or program scheduler. These are factors that need to be decided by the directors of the program, as they directly influence the procedures that the clerical staff will follow when contacted by a new or returning client. The availability of accessible space for client meetings could play a large role in determining the preferred method of counselor/client meeting times.

Selection Criteria

Financial counselors must be skilled at interpersonal communication and conduct themselves in a professional manner. Requiring coursework in financial counseling and helping relationships for student financial counselors and educators is a simple way to ensure staff are skilled in interpersonal communication. Nonstudent financial counselors and educators may be required to submit proof of taking such coursework or having equivalent training in working directly with people in high stress situations. Staff must have the best interest of their clients at heart and be able to work effectively in stressful situations.

Financial educators need to be comfortable with and passionate about the personal finance topics they present. They must also communicate well publicly and be able to respond effectively to questions from an audience.

Staff Demands

Securing financial resources is an important part of launching the program. While raising money is helpful, saving money is equally important. One way to save significant resources is to find creative ways to staff the program. As with most organizations, human resources are the most expensive assets. Ideas to make this work are illustrated below.

Full-Time Needs

Depending on the size of the program (including the number of staff members within the program, the size of the respective institution, and the volume of counseling/education), the executive director, program director(s), and clerical staff could be full-time or part-time. The executive director may be a faculty or staff member of the respective institution or a practicing clinician from the community. Directors may have shared appointments in academic or student services units, be graduate part-time instructors, or be graduate assistants with workload being determined primarily by the details set forth in the assistantship guidelines. Depending on funding, the two most likely full-time candidates would be the clerical staff member and the program director.

Part-Time Needs

The financial counselors/educators will most likely be working on a part-time basis. If a peer program model is used, the staff will most likely be full-time students providing services on a part-time basis.

One of the larger benefits of developing a campus-based program is that the program has access to a student staff base. If the structure of the institution permits, both graduate and undergraduate students may be involved. If a campus is fortunate enough to have a program in financial planning, counseling, marriage and family therapy, business, or social work, it is likely that there will be significant synergies between the content of classroom instruction and the required knowledge, skills, and experience needed to be a successful financial counselor or educator.

According to social learning theory (Sloane and Zimmer 1993), students may learn best from models they see as similar to themselves; therefore, using peer educators who are similar to the target audience may improve the likelihood of students receiving the intended message. In addition, peer educators tend to serve as role models and activists on campus, sharing countless teachable moments with other students. The use of peer education models is increasingly common within higher educational institutions to offer varied student services (Goetz et al. 2011; Newton and Ender 2010).

While it is possible to compensate students financially for their time devoted to the program, it is also possible to provide other incentives such as work-related experience, resume enhancement, class credit, and credit toward certain professional certifications. Methods of compensation include hourly wages, honoraria, and scholarships. Creativity is necessary in considering various options, and the use of volunteers or campus-funded staff is beneficial in stretching a limited budget.

Other Staff Considerations

While the formation of a staffing plan is paramount, the specific details can be challenging since staff planning hinges on several different variables. In addition to the specific items above, program administrators will want to consider the following items:

- Financial resources available
- In-kind resources available
- Types of services that the program desires to offer
- Level of staff content expertise (i.e., Is there a degree or certificate program at the institution as a resource?)
- Type and size of facility where services will take place
- Size and scope of the program (i.e., Who is the program's target audience? Will the program focus its services to students or will it extend its efforts to the larger community?)
- Other programs on campus with which the program could collaborate

These points are addressed in other chapters throughout the book. During the process of building or expanding your financial education program, be sure to check in with legal services or higher administration to be certain you are in compliance with university regulations. The authors of this chapter have not been involved with a university program that requires errors and omissions insurance, although it is possible that your university may require liability insurance, particularly if you are working with individuals outside of the university.

Staff Recruitment

Following the development of a well-designed staffing plan, it becomes essential to implement recruiting efforts to fill the staff positions. Since staff will be working with highly private financial data, it may be wise to obtain a credit report or a background check on staff members. Once quality staff members have been identified, there are a few different considerations to think about. If student employees or volunteers are going to make up a portion of the staff base, a strategy for pro bono work is critical. In order to recruit a volunteer staff, incentives and marketing need to be a focus.

Possible incentives to attract current students include the ability to attain course credit for an undergraduate or graduate course, practicum, or internship. This would lead toward fulfilling degree requirements and the possibility of earning work experience hours for professional credentials. Examples include the Certified Financial Planner™ and the Accredited Financial Counselor designations (see Chap. 12 for a discussion of these designations). In addition, students preparing for careers in the financial services profession or other helping professions are granted the opportunity to gain practical experience and application of their classroom knowledge.

Some methods of recruiting are more overt and are designed to be informational. At the very least, holding an informational session and inviting interested parties to attend is an initial way to build interest and momentum in the program. In this session, potential volunteers may learn about the financial education program as well as position descriptions and program expectations. Closely related to this is the idea of inviting potential volunteers to program events or internal training events so they can learn about the program while being engaged with current staff.

There are other, more subtle, ways of recruiting staff members for a financial education program. If a financial education program has ties to a degree program, the financial education that the program offers to campus constituents is a recruiting tool to the degree program and then subsequently to student volunteering. Current staff members are probably the best source of recruiting. An energetic, passionate, and fun-loving group of student staff members will naturally attract other members. Some recruiting efforts can take place in the classroom. If the executive director or program director has a teaching appointment, he or she can selectively recruit students out of his or her classes. Staff members may visit classes to recruit others.

A sample application used with volunteer undergraduate and graduate students is shown in Fig. 3.1. The application may be posted on your program's website, if applicable, for completing online or for printing. This sample application may be modified for use with others, such as paid staff or nonstudent volunteers. You may wish to add your volunteer requirements or desirable volunteer skills (e.g., bilingual, computer skills) to this application.

Two of the authors have worked with programs that have a points-based system for tracking volunteer activities. With this system, volunteers must obtain a number of preassigned points each semester. A designated staff member keeps a log of volunteer points, and volunteers are also highly encouraged to keep track of their own points. One point may be awarded for providing services to clients such as a financial counseling session, conducting a seminar or presentation, copresenting a workshop, or working at a booth for a campus event (e.g., fairs, orientations, and homecomings). Other ways to earn points are through attendance at the financial education program's continuing education, reading a personal finance book and briefly reporting on it at continuing education, writing an article for the campus newspaper, developing a new presentation, or completing self-study for one or more national certification programs (see Chap. 12 for a discussion of certification programs). At the midpoint of the semester, the program coordinator reminds student volunteers of their accumulated points. The benefits of a points system are keeping volunteers motivated and accountable. At the end of the semester, outstanding volunteers are recognized for going above and beyond the points system.

Campus Financial Education Program Application

The [_____] program is accepting applications from [_____] to fill volunteer positions in the fall and spring semesters. Eligibility requirements for Peer Financial Planners are as follows:

- Completion of defined coursework (specific to program)
- Completion of the financial education training program (specific to program)

Responsibilities of Peer Financial Planners:
- Provide presentations on personal finance topics to classes and student organizations
- Recommend alternatives and solutions to help students with their personal finances
- Attend monthly continuing education (CE) training sessions

Benefits of Volunteering for the Financial Education Program:
- Use your classroom skills and knowledge to educate students and the community about their personal finances
- Apply volunteer hours toward partial fulfillment of national accreditation program's experience requirements
- Obtain experience working under the direction of a nationally recognized program

Date: _____ Expected Graduation Date: _____

Name: _____

Local Address: _____

Apt. Number: _____ City, State, Zip: _____

Local Phone Number: _____

Email: _____

Are you available to work during the:

_____Academic Year   _____Summer   _____Both   (Check all that apply)

Have you taken the following classes (Insert applicable classes below):

Other relevant classes that you have taken (e.g., Counseling, Marriage & Family Therapy):
_____

Do you work on campus? _____ Yes _____ No ____Average number of hours/week
Do you work off campus? _____ Yes _____ No____Average number of hours/week

Hours and days available to work as a volunteer (or the applicant may attach their printed school and/or work schedule):_____

Are you bilingual? If so, what languages do you speak?_____

Please attach a current resume and a list of references.
We will contact you to schedule an interview.

Fig. 3.1 Sample program application

Summary

Developing a staffing model for a campus-based financial education program is paramount, while being both complex and rewarding. Careful attention needs to be devoted to staff planning, recruiting, and selection. There is no script for a best practices method for staffing. However, the information contained in this chapter is intended to provide an overview of the various components of staff planning that should be addressed as well as to provide recommended details for inclusion within each section. The success of a financial education program is largely made up of the people who staff it. Thoroughly executing the staffing plan provides a strong foundation on which to build an impactful program.

References

Goetz, J., Durband, D. B., Halley, R., & Davis, K. (2011). A peer-based financial planning and education service program: An innovative pedagogic approach. *Journal of College Teaching & Learning, 8*(4), 7–14. Retrieved September 20, 2011, from http://journals.cluteonline.com/index.php/TLC/article/view/4195.
Newton, F. B., & Ender, S. C. (2010). *Students helping students: A guide for peer educators on college campuses* (2nd ed.). San Francisco, CA: Wiley.
Sloane, B. C., & Zimmer, C. G. (1993). The power of peer health education. *Journal of American College Health, 41*, 241–245.

Chapter 4
Training and Development of Financial Education Program Staff

Sonya L. Britt, Ryan E. Halley, and Dorothy B. Durband

Training

The previous chapter discussed possible staff positions you will want to recruit for your financial education program. The focus of this chapter is the training and development of your staff. You may buy skills through hiring or you may develop skills through providing internal training and development programs for staff (Olian et al. 1998). Key questions to ask when considering training for program staff are posed here: What types of training support your financial education program's mission? What changes in the external environment (e.g., knowledge or financial) demand training and development of your staff members? Which of your staff members need training and development and how much do they need? What staff tasks need improvement through training and development? How can experienced program staff be used to mentor new student staff members? To begin answering these questions, we report the expert advice of existing program directors surveyed for this book.

As shown in Fig. 4.1, full-time and part-time financial education staff members do not always spend their work time doing the same tasks, meaning different training programs may be needed for various levels of staff members. Full-time financial

S.L. Britt, Ph.D. (✉)
Institute of Personal Financial Planning, School of Family Studies and Human Services,
Kansas State University, 317 Justin Hall, Manhattan, KS 66506, USA
e-mail: sbritt@k-state.edu

R.E. Halley, Ph.D.
School of Business, George Fox University,
414 North Meridian Street #6263, Newberg, OR 97132, USA
e-mail: halleyr@georgefox.edu

D.B. Durband, Ph.D.
Department of Personal Financial Planning, Texas Tech University,
15th Street & Akron, Room 262, Lubbock, TX 79409, USA
e-mail: dottie.durband@ttu.edu

D.B. Durband and S.L. Britt (eds.), *Student Financial Literacy:*
Campus-Based Program Development, DOI 10.1007/978-1-4614-3505-1_4,
© Springer Science+Business Media New York 2012

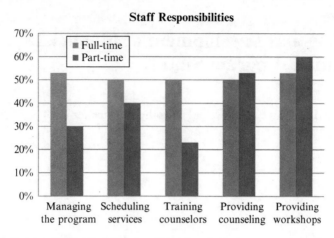

Fig. 4.1 Staff responsibilities by full-time and part-time status

education program staff members tend to serve as directors and clerical staff members, which is consistent with the support team categories presented in Chap. 3. Part-time financial education program staff members tend to fill the roles of financial counselors and educators.

The remainder of this chapter will present recommendations for necessary and desirable competencies, training content, and training format considerations.

Core Competencies

Staff members must possess some level of fundamental skills and knowledge to be effective in providing financial education program services. This section addresses what we believe to be the core competencies for financial education program staff members who provide financial counseling or education services. The general competency areas are basic financial knowledge, interpersonal skills, university policies and procedures, support resources available to students, and presentation skills.

Basic Financial Knowledge

A perusal of any introduction to personal financial planning university-level textbook reveals coverage of the following broad topics:

- Overview of the financial planning process
- Time value of money
- Cash management
- Credit management

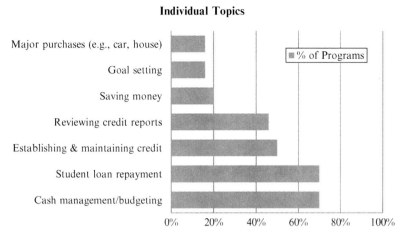

Fig. 4.2   Frequently requested individual financial counseling topics

- Major purchases
- Tax planning
- Insurance planning
- Investment basics
- Retirement planning
- Estate planning

These content concentrations tend to reflect the most commonly requested program topics for campus financial education programs as found in the recent survey of existing financial education programs surveyed for this book (Durband and Britt 2011). The study found that 81% of respondents include personal finance content within their training program for their financial education program staff. Figure 4.2 illustrates the most frequently requested topics for one-on-one financial counseling within the financial education programs. The most frequently requested topics for individual counseling were cash management/budgeting (70%) and student loan repayment (70%).

The most frequently requested topics for group workshops include cash management/budgeting and establishing and maintaining credit, both reported by 86% of the sample (see Fig. 4.3). Seventy percent of the sample listed reviewing credit reports and credit scores as a requested topic, followed by a little more than half (56%) reporting student loan repayment. In addition to students, university faculty, staff, and administrators will also request group programs for their classes or for campus organizations.

Interpersonal Skills

After a basic understanding of financial knowledge is assured, the next step is becoming confident that staff members have adequate interpersonal skills. A college or university course in helping relationships or counseling skills would likely

Group Topics

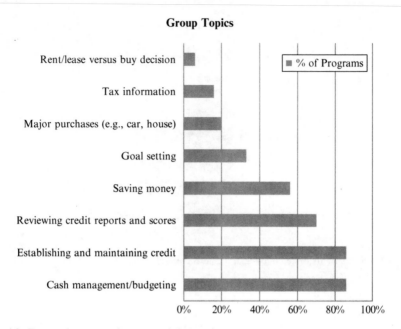

Fig. 4.3 Frequently requested group workshop topics

strengthen the interpersonal skills needed by financial education program staff members. Noncredit courses, online courses, workshops, or books may also be an option, depending on your available resources.

University and Program Policies and Procedures

The third basic competency needed from financial education program staff is an understanding of university policies and procedures. Reviewing existing policies and procedures will promote organizational awareness and convey the responsibilities, structure, and rules of one's college or university to staff members. In addition, staff members need to be well informed on your internal program policies and procedures.

Resources Available to Students

Universities are known for the numerous free and low-cost services they offer to students. Given the immense amount of resources available, students may need help finding the best resource to meet their needs. Your financial education program staff needs to know enough about the other services on campus to make a referral, if needed. Additional information about making referrals is provided below.

Training Content

This section will discuss specific training methods and procedures. It seems logical to conclude that staff members need a working knowledge of items covered in an introduction to personal finance course, although it is surprising to note that only 26% of programs polled in our study for this book require a for-credit course prerequisite for staff members or volunteers. The majority of programs surveyed for this book offer ongoing training for their staff members (84%). The training is provided by a diverse group of individuals including faculty for 48% of programs, financial aid officers for 45% of programs, and external professionals for 42% of programs. A few programs indicated that they do not provide training because their services are provided by external professionals.

In the survey of existing financial education programs, respondents were asked to indicate partners who provide training for their staff. As shown in Fig. 4.4, faculty members are the most frequently called upon group to provide training. Other sources include financial aid office professionals and external professionals (i.e., other financial counselors).

Current financial education program directors are covering the basic competencies among other key topics (see Fig. 4.5). Specifically, 81% of programs train on personal finance content, 68% of programs train staff on presentation and counseling skills, as well as confidentiality issues, 61% of programs train their staff on policies and procedures and ethics, and 58% cover recordkeeping in the training process.

Figure 4.5 displays how complex and multifaceted the role and responsibilities of a financial education program staff member can be. A comprehensive list of staff competencies is provided in Tables 4.1 and 4.2, and some of these are discussed in detail in the following section. In addition to personal finance content, it will be necessary for staff to be trained on other issues, such as how to give quality presentations and how to conduct a financial counseling session.

Referrals

There may come a time in the course of providing services when it is appropriate for the financial counselor to refer a client to another source. One of the most important aspects of training financial counselors is to help them determine when a referral is needed. The program staff should be trained on guidelines that would indicate a need to refer a client for further assistance outside of the financial counseling setting. Some of the warning signs that might be present include:

- Dissatisfaction with one's major or with college itself.
- Multiple class absences.
- Marked seclusion and unwillingness to communicate.
- Outbursts of unexplained crying or anger.

Fig. 4.4 Sources providing training for financial education program staff

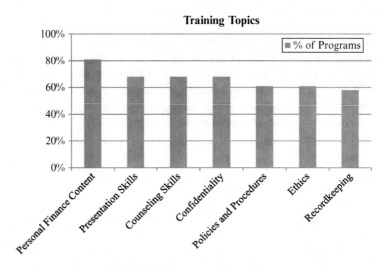

Fig. 4.5 Topics covered in financial education training programs

- Excessive fatigue, lethargy, depressed mood.
- Increased activity levels (e.g., incessant talking, irritability, physical restlessness, disruptive behavior).
- Any form of physical aggression or violence.
- Noticeable change in dress or personal hygiene.

Table 4.1   What financial education staff members should be able to do

Understand their roles and responsibilities
Maintain client privacy and confidentiality
Follow ethical principles
Establish client relationships
Build trust and rapport
Demonstrate empathy
Recognize nonverbal messages
Demonstrate interviewing and listening skills
Manage client expectations
Maintain boundaries
Problem solve
Let clients solve their own problems
Handle difficult questions for which they do not know the answer
Resolve conflicts
Manage crises
Exercise discretion
Keep good records
Educate clients on sound money management principles
Assist clients in exploring their values, attitudes, beliefs, and behaviors around money
Guide clients in achieving financial goals
Defuse anger
Provide tools and resources for clients
Identify alternatives

Table 4.2   What financial education staff members should know

How to greet a client for the first time
Cultural differences in working with clients
Campus support resources that are available for students
How to make a referral to another resource
How to handle a crisis situation
Personal safety indicators
Internal program policies and procedures
College or university policies and procedures
The scope and boundaries of their position

- Extreme suspiciousness or irrational feeling of persecution.
- Nonsensical conversation, indications of being markedly out of touch with reality.
- Consistently missed appointments.
- Death or serious illness of family member or friend.
- Difficulties in relationships (e.g., marital problems, breakup with significant other).
- Roommate or family problems.
- Signs of intoxication or being "hung over."
- Detached, non-caring, and/or manipulative behavior.

- Statements of feeling that life in not worth living or that problems cannot be solved.
- Any reference to personal consideration of harm to self or others. Immediate referral is necessary (Newton and Ender 2010; Texas Tech University n.d.).

The financial counselor should be instructed to use personal judgment when assessing the above signs. Financial counseling typically involves working with students who have financial difficulties and are often under substantial stress as a result of these circumstances. It is not uncommon for a client to cry during a session or to mention that other areas of life are suffering because of financial stress (e.g., poor academic performance). It is important for the financial counselor to exhibit discretion in assessing each client and to be able to distinguish the "range of normal" from those signs that indicate that the client needs additional help. Staff member training on the topic of referrals should provide instruction on the specific steps of referring. These steps would include:

1. Describe to the client why there is a need for additional assistance. Articulate why you feel it is necessary or desirable to make a referral.
2. Demonstrate a nonjudgmental attitude. Provide only concrete descriptions of client behaviors, thoughts, and speech that indicate the need for a referral.
3. Be clear about what services you can provide and what services you cannot.
4. Support the client by suggesting that help-seeking behavior is healthy and a sign of strength.
5. Acknowledge any fears or anxiety that the client may express about further counseling.
6. Leave the option open for the client to accept or refuse further counseling. Give the client time to think the suggestion over.
7. Volunteer to help the client make the initial contact (i.e., provide a phone number and offer the use of the office phone). The client should make the initial contact if at all possible.
8. Encourage the client to check-in with you to see if they followed your recommendation.

Safety

Staff should always be made aware of the need for exercising safety. There should also be appropriate training on campus and/or program safety resources. Some general safety procedures include:

- Setting boundaries for giving personal phone numbers to clients
- Using an office phone for calling clients versus a personal phone
- Positioning the financial counselor's chair nearest the door when in session
- Leaving the room or terminating the session if the financial counselor feels unsafe at any time
- Developing a code phrase that a staff member can use to call for assistance

Campus Financial Education Program Name

I hereby agree that I will maintain the confidentiality of clients and that I will not disclose any personally identifiable client information. I will respect client privacy and the confidentiality of the client/financial counselor relationship. Such matter will not be discussed outside of the [Program name] supervisory staff.

By signing this agreement, I agree to fulfill in good faith the confidentiality requirement set forward herein and be strictly guided by this agreement in all my activities related to [Program Name].

Printed Name: _____
Signature: _____
Date: _____

Fig. 4.6 Confidentiality agreement

- Knowing who else is present at the facility and where they can be found (e.g., a supervisor)
- Never conducting a private counseling session in a place where there is no assistance close by
- Knowing the number for campus police or finding out if your facility has a police/emergency call button

Client Confidentiality

Clients need to know that there is a strong commitment to maintaining the confidentiality of the information they share. A confidential client file should be established and maintained in a safe place within the reach of only authorized staff members. Information discussed in counseling sessions remains confidential unless the client indicates in writing that he or she wishes the information to be communicated to a specific person outside of the program. If a parent, friend, roommate, employer, or family member requests information about a client, the program cannot state whether a student has been to an appointment or not nor can they release any session information.

A formal policy and procedures manual is highly recommended. If you are developing a program, some counseling policies that you should consider include confidentiality and ethics. All staff members must sign a confidentiality agreement before providing any counseling. A sample confidentiality agreement for staff is provided in Fig. 4.6.

In terms of location, all individual sessions must be performed in a private office. Prior to service delivery, the financial counselor must have the client sign a counseling consent form. Clients and their counseling sessions are not discussed outside the program office with anyone at any time. It is recommended that financial counselors are given an opportunity to discuss their case load with a supervisor on a regular basis. This may be organized through regular supervisory meetings or a practicum. A sample consent form for a university financial education program with student volunteers in a teaching program is provided in Fig. 4.7.

I voluntarily consent to receive financial counseling services from the [   ]
Program. I understand that services will be provided by a student of the [   ]
program under the supervision of the [   ] staff or faculty. Additionally,
I understand that a faculty member may be involved in the supervision process. I
further understand that Name of University is a teaching institution and I agree to
be part of the teaching program.

I understand that the student providing financial information is *not a licensed
financial professional* and cannot recommend any investments, insurance, nor provide
legal advice. If I feel that I need legal advice, I will contact Student Legal Services or
an attorney.

*Confidentiality is an important aspect of the counseling process, and we will carefully
guard the information you entrust to us. There are three situations, however, when it
may be necessary for us to share certain information with others: when a counselor is
uncertain of how to address a particular problem and needs to seek advice from a
supervisor; when there is a clear indication that someone may be harmed unless others
intervene; or when it becomes necessary to seek the assistance of others in the
community to help you (with your permission). Please be assured that our counselors
strongly prefer not to disclose personal information to others, and they will make every
effort to help you find ways to resolve a problem as privately as possible.*

In the course of [Program Name] providing financial counseling services to me, it may
be necessary for my counselor to discuss my financial information with his/her
supervisor and creditors to whom I owe money.

I understand the educational purpose and potential of questionnaires and supervision
of my financial counseling sessions and I voluntarily consent and agree to their use.

By my signature (or the signature of my guardian) below, I do hereby release,
indemnify, and hold harmless Name of University, its Board of Regents, University
officers, agents and employees, and students of the [   ] program from any and all
liability of any type whatsoever arising from any acts or omissions, negligent or
otherwise, by said [University] officers, agents, employees, volunteers, or students
relating to the [   ] Program.

If I have any questions or concerns now or in the future, I understand that I should
consult with my financial counselor or the Director of the Program (phone number).
I certify that this form has been fully explained to me, that I have read it or had it
read to me*, and that I understand its contents.

Client (1)	Client (2)
Date	* Translator / Counselor

Fig. 4.7 Counseling consent and release

When a financial counselor is not sure how to handle a particular situation, it
should be discussed only with a supervisor. Information is not released to anyone,
including faculty, administration, parents, or creditors without written consent from
the client. The only exception to confidentiality would be when a counselor suspects
immediate threat of the client's harm to self or others. In this instance, the counselor
is to notify his or her supervisor and the authorities when there is imminent risk to
the client's physical health or safety.

Ethics

It can be helpful to support the program's ethical stance by incorporating a code of conduct or adhering to a code of ethics by an outside source. Compliance with the ethical standards set forth by an organization is crucial. An ethics agreement is recommended. For illustrative purposes, we use the Association for Financial Counseling and Planning Education (AFCPE) Code of Ethics. Accredited Financial Counselors:

- Take responsibility for conducting themselves in a credible manner, striving for excellence in providing services with competence, diligence, promptness, and care to the best of their abilities
- Continue to grow in professional practice, keeping abreast of industry developments and striving to improve professional competence through continuing education
- Exhibit personal and professional honesty and integrity in advising and counseling clients
- Maintain high standards of ethical conduct according to the objectives of the institution with which they are affiliated
- Recognize their limitations, referring clients when appropriate
- Respect client privacy and the confidentiality of the client-counselor relationship in all matters pertaining to the course of professional service and revealing client information of any kind to others only with the expressed consent of the client
- Establish compensation that is fair and reasonable and assist clients in finding other services if their fees are not affordable (AFCPE 2009, reprinted with permission)

Having an ethics training program and requiring staff to sign a code of ethics can go a long way in conveying the importance of confidentiality and ethics and in creating uniform standards throughout the program.

Training Manual

The various topics of the training can be reinforced through assembling a training program and manual. Each of the aforementioned training topics should be covered in the training manual; the importance of such a document cannot be overstressed. For example, a training manual clearly circumscribes what guidance can and cannot be given to clients, which is imperative to address liability concerns. Staff members should be cognizant of the boundaries of their responsibilities (e.g., confidentiality) and of limitations on the financial information they give to clients (e.g., investment education and general advising rather than specific mutual fund recommendations). Finding ways to incorporate continuous learning opportunities through on-the-job training may be beneficial.

Training Format

The level of training required for staff will be driven primarily by the type of individuals who are hired or recruited to provide services (e.g., internal or external professionals or students), as well as the type of academic programs that are available. If financial planning programs are offered at the respective institution, students in these programs will likely take an introductory course in financial planning and possibly a financial counseling or communication skills course. According to Certified Financial Planner Board of Standard's website (CFP Board, n.d.), at the time of publication, there are 326 CFP Board-registered financial planning programs across certificate, undergraduate, and graduate programs. These are most frequently located in academic units of human sciences or business. The skills and knowledge acquired in these courses foster substantial preparation for work as a financial counselor.

If no related-content academic program exists and a peer-to-peer model is chosen, the degree of training required increases substantially. A resource for training if no academic program exists is an online credit or noncredit program or workshop from another college or university. For additional training, one might choose to enroll in a national certification exam (discussed in Chap. 12).

Training Duration

A one-time training workshop is not recommended. Financial services are rapidly changing, so staff members (particularly those working directly with clients) need to stay abreast of relevant regulations and pertinent news. A common method for providing the initial training is through a credit-based course at your college or university. A quarter of the programs surveyed for this book require a credit-based course before staff members or volunteers are allowed to provide services to clients. Recommended courses for this requirement include introduction to personal financial planning, financial counseling, and/or a helping relationships course. Keep in mind that financial counseling may not be (and probably is not) entirely financially driven. Regardless of the personal finance content familiarity of staff, new program recruits need interpersonal skills training prior to facilitating client sessions or presentations. This training would typically cover topics such as program policies, procedural measures, expectations of staff or volunteers, technology usage, facilitator-client role plays, case studies, touring of facilities, emergency protocol, liability issues, presentation tips and outlines, and common difficult scenarios and questions from clients. Knowledge of financial content is a necessary prerequisite, but communication skills and procedural understanding are equally as important in providing diligent services.

Outside of requiring a credit-based course, one-time training may also include half-day or full-day training for new staff members on the content, process, and procedures of financial counseling. The program director does not need to lecture the staff members for several hours to be effective; use interactive learning to best capture the audience. Bringing experts in to talk about different subjects is an enjoyable way for staff members to learn about topics common to your financial education program. For instance, inviting a financial aid officer in to talk about their role within the university and common questions they receive from students would help prepare financial counselors and educators for questions they are likely to hear.

We recommend you mimic the practices of existing programs and offer ongoing training for your staff members. Periodic continuing education and training seminars are recommended to reinforce content or introduce new content. It allows for presentation of changes in the external environment (e.g., legislation changes affecting higher education and consumer finances). Requiring continuing education is an expectation of most professional associations and is good practice for life after college for any students you may have on staff. Ways to enhance the professional development of staff members include inviting guests to speak, requiring distance education courses, and participating in webinars, teleclasses, or podcasts. We encourage you to check with your college librarian for other training resources that may be available through your institution. Sources of webinars include professional associations, state guaranty agencies, and nonprofit and governmental organizations. Attendance at local, state, or regional conferences is also encouraged. The Appendix provides a list of some professional associations that host national conferences. In addition, some universities may allow faculty and staff to take credit or noncredit courses as an employee benefit. These benefits may consist of tuition reimbursement, tuition waivers, and/or the opportunity to audit courses.

Continuing education serves to keep staff and volunteers apprised of the evolving laws that affect consumer financial decision-making and acts as a tool to allow the individual staff members to learn from each other's experiences. For example, client cases and presentation experiences may be discussed and used as a tool for learning. By meeting frequently and sharing previous experiences with each other, the entire staff is able to stay abreast of the financial issues that are most relevant to the student population. If a volunteer is unable to attend an established number of continuing education trainings, it may be beneficial to have him or her perform alternative service duties to stay current in the key role responsibilities.

Frequent continuing education is beneficial for several reasons: (a) it creates a sense of program unity; (b) each staff member can be exposed to the sessions of the larger whole instead of solely their own clients' situations; (c) current concerns can be addressed on a systematic, continuous basis; and (d) directors can monitor the needs of the staff. If meeting weekly, for example, it is helpful to have a portion of each training session devoted to staff debriefing. Financial counselors are given the opportunity to share lessons learned from previous sessions and to learn from one another. Having staff members write a tip of the week for the general student population is an effective way for leadership to provide relevant, timely content that they must first research on their own. As an example, "The tax due date is approaching! Have you claimed the educational credits you may be entitled to receive? If you are paying for college with cash or loans, you may be eligible! Schedule an appointment with Your Financial Education Program's Name to learn more!" These tips can then be shared through various outlets: Your website, blog, social media, e-mail, or newsletters.

Teaching Methods

Now that you have ideas on how to structure your initial training and/or continuing education, it is time to consider how that education will be delivered. A variety of teaching methods can be employed as a means of staff training. Methods employed will depend on factors such as your training objectives and resource or time availability. Some of the more successful methods reported by current financial education program directors include the following:

- Invite guest speakers who are experts on topics relevant to both financial counseling and education. Local experts, video chats, conference calls, and webinars may be scheduled for speakers who cannot present in person.
- Have "lunch and learn" meetings where staff members bring their lunch and share stories on what is going well or is challenging for them. The problem-based learning model (Duch et al. 2001) can be used with client case analysis, which allows opportunities for the counselors to share their experiences with other staff members. Together, they can brainstorm alternative approaches to the situations presented.
- Use tools such as Google Docs, Facebook, and blogs to create web forums where questions can be answered and strategies and techniques can be shared with staff members in your program and other programs.
- Permit the opportunity for staff members to train the rest of the staff on certain topics. This method allows the presenting member to become an expert on a topic and the go-to source for future questions on this topic. It also helps staff members obtain more experience presenting to an audience.

Presentation Training

Many of the training topics previously mentioned are aimed at financial counselors who deliver individual client sessions. However, most financial education programs also offer group outreach in the form of presentations. In order to facilitate the development of competent and confident presenters who feel equipped to deliver professional presentations, ongoing training should also be offered for this staff or volunteer group. Items for inclusion in presentation training can be grouped around two major themes: presentation preparation and presentation execution.

Presentation Preparation Training Topics

Being forward thinking is absolutely critical for group presentations. The first element is to ensure that details regarding the presentation (requested time, location, contact person, length, topic(s), particulars about the audience, how many will be in attendance) are checked once and checked twice the day of or a day before the presentation. Program directors surveyed for this book also enforced the necessity of being prepared. Room or time changes are not at all uncommon in a college setting.

Visiting the presentation room prior to the presentation enables the presenter to determine the setup of the room (e.g., auditorium, classroom, boardroom, u-shaped, rounds) and the amenities (e.g., chalk/whiteboards, podium). A visit also allows the presenter to note what equipment will be needed (e.g., laptop, projector, remote clicker, laser pointer, microphone). If using a computer already in the room, security features may prevent the presenter from accessing it without assistance. The presenter may also want to check for wireless connectivity. Be sure to build in extra time before the presentation to address any last minute technical difficulties. The best advice we can offer is to prepare for the worst. Bring a printed copy of the presentation that you can refer to in the event the electronic copy fails.

Another more micro-level training topic is to remind presenters that they need to rehearse their presentation. If using computer visuals, check website URLs and video links to make sure they are working. Be sure the room has audio so any videos that are used can be heard. There is nothing more annoying than a presenter who is unprepared. Respect the audiences' time. A 30-minute presentation should last 25 minutes with 5 minutes for questions from the audience. Also, if handouts will be used, be sure to account for the time necessary to distribute the handouts to the audience. Finally, especially for student presenters, it is wise to have a dress code for presentations. Some programs provide shirts for staff and students to wear during program events. These can be in school colors or with a program name or logo.

A final recommendation for presentation preparation is to think about many of the frequently asked questions that may be received in a presentation. Talk with other presenters and ask them about questions they have received. It is recommended that presenters have answers prepared for some of the most frequently asked questions about the financial education program and personal finance matters.

Presentation Execution

During the presentation, as mentioned above, the speaker should plan to arrive early. Although the presenter should have prepared for technical difficulties, it is hard to predict what new issues might arise.

Presentation training needs to include time for presenters to practice their *elevator speech*, which is a brief 1- to 2-minute introduction of who they are, what the financial education program does, and why they are involved with the financial education program. The more presenters practice their introduction, the smoother the delivery.

Next, presenters should come prepared with an icebreaker or energizer that allows them to create rapport with the audience. This could be a quiz or a game. During the presentation, tell stories. Audiences prefer to hear personal stories or other practical applications of the material that is being presented (Kotter 2008). Chapter 6 of this book provides ideas for financial education programming content.

Questions are a good way to engage an audience. Ask questions throughout the presentation to gauge the audience's level of knowledge and comprehension and call for the audience's questions either during or after the presentation. Respond effectively to questions from the audience. If an answer is not known, simply be honest with the audience. Tell the inquirer that an answer will be found and communicated to the inquirer after the presentation.

One of the best ways to improve presentation techniques is to instill more confidence in the presenter. An effective way to do this is to educate presenters on the topics that will be included in presentations. This can be accomplished through formal coursework, continuing education sessions, attendance and presentations at regional and national conferences, and one-on-one training with the presenter. Another resource to enhance presentation and speaking skills is a Toastmasters club, some of which can be found on a college campus (Sterman n.d.) The more knowledgeable the presenter, the more likely he or she will be in demonstrating confidence and polished presentation skills.

Tough Questions Training

The importance of giving accurate information in an increasingly complex world of personal finance is paramount. One helpful method for staff is to revolve the content of continuing education training around the tough questions that get asked by clients. It is in financial education practitioners' best interest to be prepared to effectively answer these tough questions. The more comfortable staff members are with the most frequently asked questions, the more confidence that will be portrayed in the individual session and the more likely the staff member will be comfortable with questions from a group presentation audience.

TQT (tough questions training) is a problem-based method grounded in experiential learning theory to help financial educators and counselors effectively answer questions. At the foundation of experiential learning lies the belief that learning takes place when a person is actively involved with an experience (Kolb 1984), which is an integral step in the TQT process. The response of a presenter to difficult questions can either promote or hinder a strong rapport with an audience. Myths and misinformation are commonly associated with personal financial information, consequently making the wide array of questions potentially posed quite challenging.

The TQT method allows program staff to apply what they have learned in their training and leads to an informal mentoring process. TQT may also be used as an ongoing refresher training method for experienced financial counselors and educators by addressing the most current questions asked by audiences. The questions used are generated from ongoing experience with clients. Current and accurate information concerning financial issues is critical, as is the consideration of the needs of a particular audience. Utilizing the TQT approach results in multiple benefits. First, the process builds collaboration among trainees. Through the group process, opportunities for future training and development are revealed. When TQT is used as a continuous training process, constant feedback for quality assurance is provided. The process of discussing strategies for answering difficult questions fosters learning for educators and counselors. The art of handling difficult questions with multiple approaches is acquired and honed through the TQT method. Lastly, self-confidence is experienced among financial counselors and educators as they become better equipped (Goetz et al. 2004).

Mentoring

A mentoring program is a way to gain transfer of knowledge and skills within a group (Mason and Bailey 2003). A student staff member or volunteer can be paired with a returning student staff member or volunteer, a nonstudent, or other staff member in a mentoring program.

Because there are some aspects of financial counseling that are best learned through experience, new staff members should have the opportunity to observe their mentors in active financial counseling sessions and, therefore, receive hands-on training without feeling overwhelmed. In some programs affiliated with clinical training programs, rooms may have equipment for recording sessions so that supervisors can review and provide feedback to trainees. Alternatively, the rooms may be designed for observation capabilities to assist in training and mentoring.

Some beneficial requirements of a mentoring program might include:

1. Before new program staff will be assigned clients, they must observe at least one of their mentors' sessions.

   - The mentor will have the added responsibility of meeting with the new student staff member and discussing the session that was observed. A record of the meeting should be turned in to the program director once the meeting is adjourned. An observation write-up might include the following: What was the presenting problem? What are the solutions that were generated by the client? By the financial counselor? What were the techniques the mentor used? Why did he or she choose those techniques? What are other techniques that could have been used? What were some general observations of the session? Are there any questions the new counselor may have?

2. After the new staff member has begun to offer program services, it is advantageous to have a required meeting with the mentor every 2 weeks. The mentor should take notes from the meeting, including:

   - When did the meeting take place? What questions did the new financial counselor have? What suggestions did the mentor make? What other information does the mentor deem relevant?

3. The mentor should also observe at least two of the new staff member's first few sessions. This will allow the mentor to evaluate the mentee's progress, as well as serve as an extra resource during those sessions.

Summary

This chapter covered the nuts and bolts of training financial education program staff. Training must be oriented around the role of your various staff members; training clerical staff on presentation skills is probably not an efficient use of time, but training all staff on confidentiality is essential. Other basic competencies needed for staff members include financial knowledge, interpersonal skills, university policies and procedures, and support resources available to students. Training staff members on these core competencies can occur over the course of a day or an entire academic quarter or semester. Common trainers include university faculty members, financial aid office staff, and external financial counselors.

Training for staff members who work directly with clients should revolve around the key issues clients bring to individual financial counseling or common questions asked at group presentations. Cash management/budgeting is the most frequently requested topic for individual and group financial counseling and education sessions. Budgeting can be made fun by having students give examples of the most ridiculous item they can think of to plan for in a budget. Other programming ideas are provided in Chap. 6.

Finally, seasoned staff members provide a valuable mechanism for developing newer student staff by transferring their learning and experiences through a formal mentoring program. Actively learning by observing peers giving presentations or providing individual financial counseling is an effective way of teaching new staff members. We encourage you to utilize the methods and resources presented in this chapter to develop your own training program and accompanying training manual.

References

Association for Financial Counseling and Planning Education. (2009). *AFCPE counselor code of ethics*. Denver, CO: Association for Financial Counseling and Planning Education.

Certified Financial Planner Board of Standards. (n.d.). *List of CFP Board-Registered programs*. Retrieved August 1, 2011, from http://www.cfp.net/become/programs.asp.

Duch, B. J., Grosh, S. E., & Allen, D. E. (Eds.). (2001). *The power of problem-based learning: A practical "how to" for teaching undergraduate courses*. Sterling, VA: Stylus Publishing.

Durband, D. B., & Britt, S. L. (2011). *Perspectives on university financial education programs: Research survey highlights*. Unpublished raw data.

Goetz, J., Bagwell, D., & Halley, R. (2004). Tough questions for student financial educators. In *Proceedings of the Association for Financial Counseling and Planning Education*, Denver, CO.

Kolb, D. A. (1984). *Experiential learning*. Englewood Cliffs, NJ: Prentice Hall.

Kotter, J. P. (2008). *A sense of urgency*. Boston, MA: Harvard Business Press.

Mason, C., & Bailey, E. (2003). Benefits and pitfalls of mentoring. *Proceedings of the Society for technical communication 50th annual conference* (pp. 6–10). Retrieved October 26, 2011, from http://www.faculty.english.ttu.edu/barker/5377/Mentoring/BenefitsAndPitfallsMasonandBailey.pdf.

Newton, F. B., & Ender, S. C. (2010). *Students helping students: A guide for peer educators on college campuses* (2nd ed.). San Francisco, CA: Jossey Bass.

Olian, J. D., Durham, C. C., Kristoff, A. L., Brown, K. G., Pierce, R. M., & Kunder, L. (1998). Designing management training and development for competitive advantage: Lessons from the best. *Human Resource Planning, 21*(1), 21–31.

Sterman, P. (n.d.). *Communicating on campus: From California to Dubai, college clubs enrich academic life.* Retrieved September 12, 2011, from http://www.toastmasters.org/MainMenuCategories/WhyJoin/SuccessStories/CommCampus.aspx.

Texas Tech University. (n.d.). *Students in distress.* Retrieved September 10, 2011, from http://www.depts.ttu.edu/dos/studentsindistress/CAQ.aspx.

Chapter 5
Obtaining Financial Education Program Support

Dorothy B. Durband and A. William Gustafson

Introduction

Finding support for a financial education program can be challenging in light of current events in the university environment. Yet, several trends point to the need for supporting financial education initiatives in higher education. Many state legislatures are pressuring higher education to improve graduation rates (Cook and Pullaro 2010). Several states (in the case of public institutions) are demanding greater accountability with regard to student matriculation rates. Studies have shown that financial issues are one of the top reasons for dropping out of college (Johnson et al. 2009) and first-generation college students may struggle with financial issues as well as lack of a parental mentor (Noel-Levitz 2011; Terenzini et al. 1996).

A financial education program is an obvious mechanism for decreasing or preventing the financial stress of students and should be seen by higher education administration as a worthwhile use of university monies. Financial education program staff members need to be visible and active in communication with university administration to secure current and future funding. Individual and business donors are also likely to be interested in the success of a program at their alma mater or local university and support your goals as long as they understand your purpose.

Defining Your Purpose

This section identifies and discusses a variety of topics associated with the basics of envisioning and implementing a financial support program, including issues such as program recognition by higher education administration for both on- and off-campus

D.B. Durband, Ph.D. (✉) • A.W. Gustafson, Ph.D.
Department of Personal Financial Planning, Texas Tech University,
15th Street & Akron, Room 262, Lubbock, TX 79409, USA
e-mail: dottie.durband@ttu.edu; bill.gustafson@ttu.edu

D.B. Durband and S.L. Britt (eds.), *Student Financial Literacy:*
Campus-Based Program Development, DOI 10.1007/978-1-4614-3505-1_5,
© Springer Science+Business Media New York 2012

benefits. If you are reading this, you have recognized the need for student financial education outside the classroom environment in your institution. Your purpose will vary by your intent in the operation of the financial education program. Whether it is financial or in-kind, this chapter will provide you with ideas to obtain support for your program. Key questions to ask and answer are (a) What is your immediate or potential capacity to carry out the program's purpose? (b) How can you align what you need in terms of financial education program support with the strategic goals of your university?

Recognize that the potential for a successful entity is exciting and this will likely be reflected by others in your college or university, especially if the purpose(s) directly benefits operational issues. Your institution's administrators may see the need for a financial education program to supplement or support an existing student services or academic unit. For example, your program may provide assistance to the financial aid office or scholarship office in working with enrolled students regarding their use of funds for educational expenses; or you may be asked to supervise a program as part your faculty appointment. Another scenario is that a student government administrator could show support for a program that directly benefits students through allocating student government funds and/or student fees.

It is wise to consider the benefits that a financial education program could bring to your college or university when developing your purpose and specific goals for your unit. It is also important to match those goals to your unit's capabilities to insure that they can deliver the services without excessive additional workload. It is highly doubtful that in times of static (or declining) budgets, a student services unit, department, or academic program will be given additional full-time equivalents (FTE) specifically for the purpose of financial education program operation. University faculty members, especially those trying to attain tenure, need to consider the congruity of purpose and goals of the academic unit with those tenure criteria used by their institution (e.g., teaching, research, service). It is possible to conduct research related to student financial issues as well as develop research or service-related grant proposals related to a financial education program. Grants and publications are usually a path to tenure. If you are affiliated with an academic unit, consider training students as program personnel. Not only is this a valuable opportunity to have students help their fellow students, the use of volunteers will also help control program costs.

We suggest the use of an advisory council that meets periodically to provide guidance or support for your program in key areas such as fund-raising, obtaining space, and developing or promoting your program. Ideally, advisory council members are stakeholders selected from administrative, student services, and academic units. Possible members could be administrators, faculty, staff, students, and alumni or friends of the university.

Determining the Need for a Financial Education Program

Perhaps you have already determined the need for your financial education program. According to a program director surveyed for this book (Durband and Britt 2011), "You need to [obtain] a personal 'face' for financial literacy on your campus along with knowing national research findings." Maybe you have read reports or studies that provide support for this need. You may also wish to consider personal observations, anecdotal evidence, or student trends in your institution or state (e.g., student loan usage, student loan default rates, emergency loan requests). Are there institutional reports of student studies available? If you have not yet familiarized yourself with the literature, Chap. 10 provides a summary of research findings and presents research opportunities for financial education programs. If you have a research appointment, consider conducting a study to identify outcomes such as student needs, risk factors, and behaviors. Interviews, focus groups, and surveys are methods of potential data collection. Reflect on the possibilities that exist for data collection: new student orientation, classes, events in the dorms, student organization meetings, and other campus locations. Are there existing surveys of students to which you can add items of interest? If you do not have a research appointment, can you collaborate with another unit or a faculty member to help you collect data? You will want to obtain institutional approval for any research conducted directly with human subjects due to federal regulations (Department of Health and Human Services [DHHS] 2004).

Types of Support

Both on- and off-campus sources should be considered for program support. In addition to your institution, consider individuals (e.g., alumni and friends of the university); businesses; public grantmaking charities; private, corporate, and community foundations; governmental agencies; and membership associations as potential funding resources for your program. Funding may be in the form of a grant, contract, matching gift, sponsored program, sponsored research project, local or state line item, gift, or donation. Chapter 2 provides a summary of the types of support received by financial education programs surveyed for this book.

Companies can benefit from either donating services or equipment to your program or could provide those at a reduced cost. Aside from any tax benefits they may be entitled to as a result of a donation, this gift can result in increased visibility for that organization. In instances such as these, however, it is important to fully consider the implications or perceptions that these donations may create. It may not be in your organization's best interests to be perceived as promoting any one company or organization through your outreach. It is important to remain cognizant of any potential conflicts or misperceptions that may arise through these relationships.

Regarding the development of grant proposals, many colleges and universities have staff members who specialize in this area and could assist you in writing. These staff may be found in units such as research services, student affairs, development, or institutional advancement. Proposal writing for research funding is frequently an expectation for faculty tenure and promotion so you may also consider collaborating with other faculty members to write a grant proposal for research or outreach related to your program. "The presence of a well-known researcher's name on a proposal can be very helpful because reviewers have confidence in known quantities and often confer that same confidence on collaborators" (Locke et al. 2007, p. 160). In addition, a multitude of resources exists on how to develop grant proposals. Consider contacting your university librarian for references and funding databases. Another great place to start is the Foundation Center website and its network of funding information centers located in educational institutions, community foundations, and public libraries nationwide (Foundation Center n.d.). From the website or one of their information centers, you will be able to determine the guidelines and availability of institutional, local, regional, or national funding sources.

General line-items for a program operating budget include personnel salaries (e.g., 9- or 12-month appointments), fringe benefits, equipment, physical space costs, utilities, travel, telecommunications, printing, advertising, and office supplies. If you are employing students, you will also need to factor in undergraduate hourly wages, graduate student assistantships or stipends, graduate tuition and fees, and fringe benefits.

Physical space is an important asset to secure for your financial education program. The location of a program is a matter that should be thoughtfully considered. If you desire higher visibility, use of space (if available) will attract students to visit the building for your services. Sometimes clinical space appropriate for academic programs such as psychology or marriage and family therapy can be shared. Multifunctional office space could be used by several student services that schedule individual appointments with students. Examples include career services, student legal services, and the student counseling center. Presentations or workshops can be hosted in classrooms, seminar rooms, a computer lab, a private dining room, a common area or lounge of a residence hall, the library, or rooms in the student union. Furniture may often be appropriated from surplus property warehouses on university campuses. In some cases, businesses can make donations (e.g., computers, printers, software) to a financial education program knowing that access to equipment will assist in educating students using up-to-date technology. If you have an interior design program in your university, their students or faculty can be enlisted for the design of your program office. Students in an art or design program can be excellent sources to consult about elements such as furniture, lighting, color, accessories, and artwork; they may even provide some of their own designs for you to display.

An important area that may be overlooked is marketing and promotional materials. (For an in-depth discussion of marketing strategies, see Chap. 7). A consideration for creating materials is to have a technical and professional editor take on your program as a project. Web design may also be provided through a technical and professional editing class. Some senior level and graduate classes will have students write grant proposals for community organizations as assignments. Student editors can review printed materials such as a grant proposal, brochure, or website. An additional idea is to work with a marketing class for assistance in developing a marketing plan for your program.

If your unit has the ability and the faculty or staff commitment to deliver services to the community surrounding your university, the political and financial benefits from external supporters can be substantial. Support from local government or a local business or nonprofit organization in the form of financial help and possible use of centralized space to deliver services could be negotiated. Both public and private nonprofit organizations actively seek volunteers to assist citizens with financial issues that can include such matters as paying utility bills to avoid cessation of services. Community organizations can also provide opportunities for collaboration, as financial services and counseling are a perpetual concern for many underserved groups without access to paid services.

Institutional Support

The following sections address how institutional sources can support your financial education program. Institutional supporters could range from university administration to faculty and staff to students. The development of a vision that enhances institutional success and builds upon your existing academic or student services goals can earn support from administrators who see a direct benefit to units under their purview. One of the program directors surveyed for this book conveyed that an important factor in your success will be identifying and securing an advocate among your university's senior administrators. This person "will become an invaluable ally to secure the necessary funding to initiate financial literacy programming." At one university in the southwest, the Vice President for Student Affairs had student housing and dining as one of his responsibilities. Each semester he received a list with a significant number of names of students that he was going to be forced to dismiss from the university due to nonpayment of housing and dining fees. At the same time, faculty in the personal financial planning program wanted to develop a clinic/outreach model to help students, faculty, and staff with financial issues ranging from debt management to retirement planning. The administrator eventually gave startup funds to the financial planning program to develop a unit that directly benefited his office by lowering the number of students who fell into nonpayment status. Meanwhile, the faculty were able to conduct research, give students hands-on experience, and build political support for the growth of the financial education program.

Administrative structures vary from institution to institution, but many administrators who should be interested in the collaborative possibilities are directly involved with academic affairs (e.g., Office of the President, Office of the Provost, Dean of Student Life or Student Affairs, and Graduate School). For instance, student borrowers have reported delaying decisions to enroll in graduate school because of the amount of debt accumulated during pursuit of the undergraduate degree (Jendrick and Lynch 2007; Millett 2003). Student affairs administrators may be a source of seed funding in the early stages of a program. Many student affairs units may be responsible for entities with names such as student support services, enrollment management, financial aid, and the business office/bursar. All of these units deal with negative effects from a lack of student financial literacy and the resultant financial problems that lead to dropping out of school or taking a longer time to matriculate. Opportunities may exist for direct support from student government. If you have student volunteers providing financial education services to other students, you may be eligible to register as a student organization or club. Colleges and universities allow their registered student organizations to apply for funding for programs, specific projects, and activities. Some academic units may also provide funds available for student organizations that fall under their control.

Support (either political or financial) from your student body will usually secure visibility within the campus newspaper, which can benefit the financial education program in referrals for services and in recruiting volunteers. Coverage in the student newspaper or on the college or university radio station may also benefit the academic program (if applicable) through recruiting new majors.

A relationship may be established with your university's media relations office. Financial education program staff may be contacted as experts for interviews from local and national media personnel writing stories on personal finance content. This is an excellent means for continuous program recognition by administrators and students.

Depending on the structure of the institution and working relationships across colleges and departments, faculty and department leaders can be very supportive. For instance, a financial counseling clinic can cooperate with a tax clinic in an accounting unit and, if present, can also collaborate with a law clinic. Through this type of approach, academic unit administrators can strengthen institutional unity, and students from two or more disciplines can benefit from learning skills sets from each program. If your university is a land-grant institution ("The Land-Grant Tradition" 2008) and you have Cooperative Extension (USDA n.d.), which has a specific focus on outreach, you have the opportunity for faculty/professional interaction, research, and internship experience with another unit.

External Support

University alumni can provide another funding opportunity for a financial education program. Visit with your institution's development office to let them know of your interest in cultivating alumni and friends of the university in your fund-raising. Your university development or external relations office maintains a mailing list of current and prospective donors. Alumni events are a great place to meet prospective donors and share information about your program. You can obtain details about these events through your institution's external relations office. Of course, financial stability is a necessary component of graduates having the ability to give back to their alma mater, but research suggests financial capability is not the only reason alums choose to donate or not donate to their university. According to a study of non-donors, Wastyn (2009) found that non-donors evaluated the cost-benefit relationship of their college education. If the benefit they received exceeded the costs of attending, they were more likely to consider giving back to the university. Students who receive the added benefit of an on-campus financial education program are likely to report a profit, if you will, from attending that particular college or university. Even non-donors reported they would likely give to a "legitimate college need that resonated with their college experience" (p. 105), especially if it were a small amount. Based on the results of Wastyn's study, it seems probable that financial education programs could be in part funded by past users of the program. Satisfaction with university student services offices has been shown to be related to alumni giving (Jendrick and Lynch 2007).

Just as we recommend you teach your staff to prepare an elevator speech, i.e., a brief 1- to 2-minute introduction of who they are, what the financial education program does, and why they are involved with the financial education program, we recommend a similar speech be developed to present to potential supporters. Keep in mind that not all support is financial in nature. Maintain a list of the types of support that might be used in order to be prepared to talk to potential supporters at any moment.

Summary

In this chapter, we provide recommendations for on- and off-campus resources for funding and support for a financial education program. Defining the purpose and communicating it to higher education administration is a first step. Financial education program staff members need to be visible and active in communication with university administration and external sources, when applicable, to secure current and future funding. The visibility of a program both within and outside the college or university is an important part of achieving your goals and enhancing outcomes. These outcomes may lead to startup funding and sustained support from internal and external sources.

References

Cook, B., & Pullaro, N. (2010). *College graduation rates: Behind the numbers.* American Council on Education Center for Policy Analysis. Retrieved September 27, 2011, from http://www.acenet.edu.

Durband, D. B., & Britt, S. L. (2011). *Perspectives on university financial education programs: Research survey highlights.* Unpublished raw data.

Foundation Center. (n.d.) *About the foundation center.* Retrieved October 15, 2011, from http://foundationcenter.org/.

Jendrick, M. P., & Lynch, J. M. (2007). *Report on student debt and alumni giving.* American Student Assistance. Retrieved September 30, 2011, from http://www.asa.org/pdfs/corporate/report_on_student_debt_and_alumni_giving.pdf.

Johnson, J., Rochkind, J., Ott, A. N., & DuPont, S. (2009). *With their whole lives ahead of them. A public agenda report for the Bill and Melinda Gates Foundation.* Retrieved October 25, 2011, from http://www.publicagenda.org/files/pdf/theirwholelivesaheadofthem.pdf.

Locke, L. L., Spirduso, W. W., & Silverman, S. J. (2007). *Proposals that work: A guide for planning dissertations and grant proposals.* Thousand Oaks, CA: Sage.

Millett, C. M. (2003). How undergraduate loan debt affects application and enrollment in graduate or first professional school. *The Journal of Higher Education, 74*(4), 386–427.

National Association of State Universities and Land-Grant Colleges. (2008). *The land-grant tradition.* Retrieved September 27, 2011, from http://www.aplu.org/.

Noel-Levitz. (2011). *Forty percent of first-generation students have "very distracting" and "troublesome" financial problems.* Retrieved October 20, 2011, from http://blog.noellevitz. com/2011/02/15/first-generation-college-students-financial-insecurity/.

Terenzini, P. T., Springer, L., Yaeger, P. M., & Nora, A. (1996). First-generation college students: Characteristics, experiences, and cognitive development. *Research in Higher Education, 37*(1), 1–22. Retrieved October 28, 2011, from http://www.jstor.org.

U.S. Department of Health and Human Services. (2004). *Human subject regulations decision charts.* Retrieved October 29, 2011, from http://www.hhs.gov/ohrp/policy/checklists/decision-charts.html.

United States Department of Agriculture. (n.d.) *About us: Cooperative extension system offices.* Retrieved October 20, 2011, from http://www.csrees.usda.gov/Extension/.

Wastyn, M. L. (2009). Why alumni don't give: A qualitative study of what motivates non-donors to higher education. *International Journal of Educational Advancement, 9,* 96–108.

Chapter 6
Content and Delivery in Financial Education Programs

Joseph Goetz and Lance Palmer

Introduction

The delivery of financial education programming content, as well as the content itself, requires regular revision and updating to be most effective with various target audiences. The financial content presented and how that material is presented are two of the most important factors in the development of a successful program. A plethora of excellent, publically available content exists for building slideshow presentations, handouts, and websites on common topics most pertinent to various college student populations. To make mention of specific content is space prohibitive; therefore, much of this information is provided in outline form for purposes of obtaining a broad perspective on potential topics to include in your educational programming. The majority of this chapter focuses on innovative programming content and content delivery that is not likely available elsewhere. This chapter is also designed to complement the other chapters available within this text.

Programming Content Resources

A number of learning perspectives and theories support many of the recommendations for programming mentioned in this chapter. For example, there is substantial evidence supporting the benefits of experiential learning, or the transformation of experience into learning. Experiential learning is an umbrella concept that includes techniques such as service-learning, case studies, and implementation exercises. Higher levels of learning are often found through evaluating and creating. Thus, for the purposes of this chapter and the recommendations found within, the integration

J. Goetz, Ph.D. (✉) • L. Palmer, Ph.D.
Department of Housing and Consumer Economics, University of Georgia,
205 Dawson Hall, Athens, GA 30602, USA
e-mail: goetz@uga.edu; lpalmer@fcs.uga.edu

D.B. Durband and S.L. Britt (eds.), *Student Financial Literacy:*
Campus-Based Program Development, DOI 10.1007/978-1-4614-3505-1_6,
© Springer Science+Business Media New York 2012

of exercises requiring higher levels of thinking into financial education programming is assumed to increase effectiveness. With that said, the authors fully recognize the need for further experimental and longitudinal research work to provide valuable information on what is working and how one particular strategy may be more or less effective than another financial education strategy.

As previously mentioned, there is a host of materials available for use at no cost, including curricula, podcasts, videos, and fact sheets. The majority of these resources are available through Cooperative Extension (see www.extension.org) and the National Endowment for Financial Education (NEFE). More specifically, available through NEFE is the *Financial Education Clearinghouse* (see www.nefe.org), which provides a seemingly endless amount of valuable content for financial education programming. As stated by NEFE, the "primary function of the Clearinghouse is to assist community organizations in finding appropriate materials to implement financial literacy programs for underserved populations." The Clearinghouse primarily functions to identify financial literacy curricula and provide facilitator and learner materials and related educational resources that help the underserved and serve as a financial education resource for individuals seeking self-help materials on a variety of money management topics.

Another resource that should be on the top of your list is campus-based financial education programs already in existence. Many of these university programs referenced throughout this book are more than willing to share their stories and products with other colleges and universities. A couple of the programs at the University of Georgia are discussed in greater detail later this chapter.

Again, do not start from scratch when developing and planning the content for your financial education programming. Building from the ground up makes little sense when there are so many valuable resources already publically available. You will, however, want to customize programming content to your campus and students. Furthermore, you should periodically modify and update your programming content to be consistent with the changing laws associated with personal financial management, as well as new research findings from areas such as behavioral economics, financial decision-making, and college students' financial behavior. All of the aforementioned resources may be of particular value to a new program director who does not have the time nor the capacity to develop original materials.

Outline of Potential Program Content

The outline below is a list of topics the authors developed for college student financial education programming. The appropriateness of each topic depends on the college life cycle stage of the student. As previously mentioned, the complete write-up of the content and content delivery for each topic is not possible given space limitations. The purpose of this list is to make readers aware of the wide spectrum of potential topics to include in financial education programming. The ordering of the topics outlined below may also inform the development of training modules for financial education staff. The authors do expand on a number of these topics later in this chapter.

- Financial goal development
- Students' money relationship

  - Money socialization, money scripts, attitudes toward money
  - Assessing and promoting readiness for change
  - Relational financial factors (parental assistance, conflict with partner)

- Cash flow planning/budgeting

  - Methods of tracking spending
  - Spending targets
  - Reframing exercises (values-based spending, promoting a future orientation)

- Establishing and improving credit

  - Reviewing credit report
  - Developing a credit score plan
  - Identity theft prevention

- Managing debt

  - Types of debt (unsecured vs. secured, student loans, credit cards, auto)
  - Student loan debt
  - Debt prioritization

    - Debt vulnerability (secured-unsecured)
    - Debt history
    - Debt cost

  - Developing a debt reduction plan
  - Negotiating with creditor

- Saving and investing

  - Getting started saving
  - Getting started investing

- Tax education

  - Tax credits (e.g., EITC, saver's credit)
  - Tax filing assistance

- Job selection

  - Employee benefit comparison in job selection
  - Employee benefit selections

- Planning for expenses after college

  - Risk management (health, life, auto, home, umbrella, disability)
  - Renter rights

- – Home purchase
- – Automobile purchase
- • Premarital financial counseling
  - – Comingling of funds (joint accounts, separation of accounts)
  - – Financial socialization (money scripts, attitudes toward money)
  - – Development of plan for cash flow management

Outline of Potential Program Delivery Mechanisms

Campuses can provide delivery of financial education in various ways. There is significant support for a peer-based model for content delivery (see Chap. 8). Thus, one decision is whether to utilize students as providers of financial education. Another decision is how that financial information will be delivered by students or other professional staff. In many campus programs, professional staff members or external speakers deliver the content for financial education programming. University staff members, such as a financial aid officer, student affairs professional, or financial planner, could organize the delivery of financial education programming or provide the education themselves. Alternatively, external speakers who are national experts in certain areas such as student loan debt, financial motivation, and personal financial planning for young adults could provide the programming. External speakers might also include locally based financial planners and bankers as part of a speaker series; this arrangement is low cost while providing meaningful financial education.

Previous research (Goetz et al. 2011a) which utilized a random sample of college students, has documented that students are interested in receiving financial education and counseling through multiple delivery formats, including seminars, online methods, and counseling centers. More specifically, this study examined associations between students' characteristics and their interest in three financial education delivery methods: a counseling center, the Internet, and workshops. The fact that there was substantial interest among undergraduate students in some form of financial education is in itself informative and congruent with previous findings (Lyons 2004; Lyons and Hunt 2004). In terms of delivery mechanism, the strongest interest was in online resources, followed by workshops, and then financial counseling centers. However, substantial interest in all three analyzed delivery methods suggests colleges and universities should implement a multipronged approach to financial education programming and financial counseling. The fact that the different delivery methods appeared to be complementary in nature corroborates this notion. In other words, students who had previously completed a personal finance course were much more likely to express interest in additional financial education. It may be that students who acquire a certain level of personal finance knowledge possess heightened awareness of the utility that can be derived from further financial education or assistance and thus are more likely to seek out additional knowledge and support across financial education delivery methods.

The strong interest in accessing online resources may be a result of students' increasing comfort with technology as well as the flexibility associated with this type of instructional approach. Although there was a strong interest in online financial education, this delivery model may lack effectiveness. For example, previous research has indicated high attrition rates for education programs provided solely online (Angelino et al. 2007). Thus, future research should differentiate the goals of providing online resources and levels of technological delivery if online courses are offered (e.g., interactive vs. passive education). Furthermore, some students, particularly African American students, report significantly greater interest in receiving financial education at a campus-based financial counseling center (Goetz et al. 2011a, b). For these reasons, universities that provide financial education content via multiple delivery mechanisms will likely be more effective in reaching students.

Within these different delivery mechanisms exist opportunities for innovative and interdisciplinary approaches to offering financial information and counseling:

(a) Social networking
(b) Study groups
(c) Book club discussions
(d) Financial health checkups
(e) Wellness fair booth, NAPFA money bus tour (tour has concluded)
(f) Game show competitive format
(g) Courses in personal finance (credit, noncredit)
(h) Investment clubs

- Campus-based promotional campaigns

    - For example, *What's My Score* (credit score education campaign)

- Interdisciplinary Programming

    - Jointly with student legal services (e.g., students facing debt collection, garnishments, and fines)
    - Jointly with financial aid office (e.g., student loan planning, repayment, and human capital planning)
    - Jointly with housing and residential life (e.g., budgeting, housing, and transportation costs)
    - Jointly with health education (e.g., correlation between high-risk health behavior and high-risk financial behavior)
    - Jointly with nutrition education (e.g., how to eat healthy on a low budget for off-campus students)
    - Jointly with relationship counseling (e.g., component of premarital counseling)

Some researchers have suggested financial education through campus-based promotional campaigns. Gartner and Schiltz (2005) reported a successful *What's My*

Score credit score education campaign on a college campus. Adams and Moore (2007) suggested promoting financial education awareness in conjunction with health education, as students with high-risk financial behavior also exhibit high-risk health behavior. Promotional campaigns to educate college students about the negative consequences of irresponsible borrowing may also be effective (Braunsberger et al. 2004).

Students as a Target Audience

Increasing costs of higher education along with decreasing financial aid in the form of grants and tuition waivers have forced more students to rely on student loans and credit cards for financing their education (Lyons 2008). In fact, the proportion of students taking out education loans has increased to almost two-thirds of all students over the past couple decades (Garcia 2008a). Furthermore, students who are borrowing are borrowing more. Although spending on education is a great investment in human capital, high amounts of debts can adversely affect financial stability, at least within a short time horizon (Yilmazer and DeVaney 2005).

Students are taking on more debt in multiple forms, including car loans, student loans, and credit cards. Most undergraduate students (84%) have at least one credit card, and about half of all students have at least four (Sallie Mae 2009). Survey data indicate a 46% increase in credit card debt among college students since 2004 (Sallie Mae 2009), and about half of new college graduates revolve a balance on one or more credit cards (American Council on Education 2006). The high use of credit cards often leads to incongruence between students' levels of income and amount of credit available to them. This proves problematic if a student is predisposed to overspending or lacks other financial resources (Chen and Volpe 1998). This relationship is further complicated when considering students' lack of financial management experience, escalating tuition costs, and other unforeseeable expenses. Consequently, many students are graduating with low credit scores, typically due to high levels of credit card debt and poor payment histories. Poor credit scores can impact employment opportunities. Housing choices may also be limited by poor credit scores since leasing and mortgage companies rely heavily on credit scores. A poor credit history can even lead to higher insurance premiums (Insurance Information Institute 2011).

Research has shown there are some groups of students who are financially at risk for acquiring high levels of debt and mismanaging credit. Another trend on college campuses includes an increase in the number of financially independent students. This results in more students working to cover college expenses. These groups include women and minorities, low-income students, first-generation students, and financially independent students (Lyons 2004). Of students who did not complete their college degrees, 43% of white students and 70% of minority students reported that debt prevented them from staying in school (Nellie Mae 1998). Thus, it may make sense to target certain subpopulations of students.

The programming content should be consistent with the academic level of the student audience. For example, a focus on evaluating employee benefits for students' first professional job would not make sense for an audience of freshmen. Conversely, a seminar on navigating the financial challenges of a college student would not be ideal for a group of seniors. The obvious point here is that programming should include timely content that students will find most relevant to their lives. Presenting standard financial education programs to all students, regardless of their year in college, will likely lead to less than optimal results. Brenda Cude, a University of Georgia professor of consumer economics, has illustrated this point quite well. Cude has developed a one-credit-hour financial life skills course for freshmen and a one-credit-hour financial life skills course for seniors; the content of these two courses varies substantially based on the students' stage in life. Other examples of timeliness and relevance include making programming on the topic of taxes available for the months preceding April 15 (the infamous tax-filing deadline), teaching freshmen how to choose their first credit card, providing seniors and graduate students with training in managing student loan debt or investing in retirement plans, and emphasizing premarital financial education counseling for recently engaged students. All of these are examples of delivering financial education in moments of time that students are more receptive to acting on this education. Other examples of how timeliness can increase engagement in educational content include smart shopping modules implemented prior to holiday seasons or smart travel planning prior to spring break. That said, there are also topics that transcend age or year in school and are always quite relevant, such as general budgeting, saving, investing, and credit score planning.

Action Plans

The authors have noticed that with traditional financial education programs, most participants leave without having written anything down. A seemingly simple, yet very effective, tool is to create a one-page *action plan template*. This template includes a column for the participants to list individual goals that coincide with the topics being discussed during the program. Other columns are labeled as *action steps* (to reach goals) and *timeline* (i.e., a specific date is listed). Based on goal-setting theory (Locke and Latham 1990), audience members will be more likely to implement behavior changes with this strategy. You may be familiar with the SMART acronym in the goal development process, which was derived in part from Locke's work; goals (or actions) should be *specific, measurable, attainable, relevant, and time-bound*. Encouraging the transformation of increased knowledge into actionable steps should be considered a best practice in all financial education programming.

Financial Empowerment

It is important to note that students who receive financial education may derive numerous benefits beyond the expected increase in financial knowledge and increased financial well-being. There are other not-so-obvious benefits to effective financial education. These include a student feeling empowered to change a current behavior that will affect her future. A student growing up in an impoverished family may experience the empowerment that financial knowledge can bring in helping him/her understand how to one day break his/her family out of the cycle of poverty. Students can learn that even people making a modest salary can develop wealth and financial independence. Furthermore, research substantiates that the sharing of financial information often translates into the reduction of current financial problems and the prevention of future concerns; with less financial stress, students perform better academically (Pinto et al. 2001; Ross et al. 1999; St. John 1998). Stories of financial success from individuals to whom students can relate can be a very powerful educational tool.

Investment Education

Content for financial education programming covering the topic of investing should include pragmatic tools for beginning an investment account. Investment education programs often do a great job of covering the basics, such as defining a stock mutual fund or the risk-return relationship. However, program models currently available do not provide the operational information required for students or other audience members to actually begin an investment account. In other words, students often learn they should begin investing for retirement sooner rather than later to benefit from the effect of compounding interest, preferably by investing in a Roth IRA. However, students often leave these seminars or sessions wondering how to actually *start* a Roth IRA. Discount brokerage companies often have special programs for small investors to get started. For example, Charles Schwab currently has a program where account and mutual fund minimums (usually $1,000 and up) are waived if an individual commits to automatically invest $100 or more per month (via withdrawal from a checking or savings account). Schwab offers a suite of exchange-traded funds and no-load mutual funds without transaction cost to populate an investment portfolio either within or outside of an IRA. Other discount brokerages offering similar programs in the past (and thus likely to offer such in the future) include Fidelity, Vanguard, and T. Rowe Price. A best practice for educators may be to bring the actual application paperwork to classes and seminars on investments and go over the forms line by line to make opening these types of important accounts less intimidating and more accessible. Audience members should also be told that each of these companies has toll-free numbers and representatives available to walk individuals through the process of opening an investment account. With less than half of Americans participating in the stock market, educators can make a real difference by helping audience members develop a new positive investing behavior. Simply having an investment account setup will likely encourage further learning about investing.

Tracking Spending

For many collegiate students, going away to college represents the first time in their lives that they have been given a significant level of financial autonomy. This financial decision-making authority often comes with little formal training but substantial socialization from home and peers, both of which can be good and bad influences. The need for formal money management education is a very real necessity for some students. But more generally, all students can benefit from properly tailored exercises that help them think about why they spend money in certain ways and how their best budgeting efforts can be destroyed due to unrecognized consumption and behavioral patterns. Tracking exercises—recording all expenditures for a given period of time—may be one of the singularly best ways for students to identify and alter unconscious spending behaviors that can derail any financial plan. Based on the premise of experiential learning, tracking projects, in combination with financial goal setting, allows students to better understand the construction and purpose of a spending plan; it becomes real to them because it is their own behavior they are trying to improve.

In many situations, the best way for students to learn about their financial priorities and behaviors is to track them for 2–3 months. When doing tracking exercises, every dollar that a student spends should be accounted for in a spending diary, such as a spiral-bound notebook, spreadsheet, or online tool, such as mint.com or ynab.com. At the end of each time period, typically a month, students group their expenditures and total each group. After 1 or 2 months of tracking, students have a very real appreciation for where their money is going and the purpose of those expenditures, and they can identify patterns in their spending behavior. At this point, they are in a good position to develop some financial goals and a spending plan that realistically addresses their own personal spending behaviors.

While some suggest tracking exercises are there merely to help us stick to a spending plan, tracking is much more than that. Many students are simply unaware of how much money they spend overall, let alone on specific budget items (Palmer et al. 2010). When numbers for a spending plan are merely guessed, the budgeting process can feel very pointless and frustrating as performance seldom resembles what was planned, and the end result is often abandonment of the spending plan.

When implementing a tracking exercise over the course of a semester or a quarter, staff should carefully consider how the students will record and report their tracking activities. Participants in tracking exercises have shown a preference for tools or systems that facilitate tracking (Shockey and Seiling 2004; Palmer et al. 2010); however, others have very effectively implemented tracking projects with traditional tools, such as a pencil and notebook (Oaten and Cheng 2007).

Helping students experience the increased financial awareness that tracking provides is a powerful pedagogical tool when teaching students the purpose and power of developing, monitoring, and adjusting spending plans. This increased awareness of spending patterns can be a strong emotional motivator for changing negative spending behaviors. Tracking is also an effective tool in helping students clarify their personal values relating to consumption and money. Students may also begin to recognize social opportunities or settings wherein value-oriented consumption is accepted and more highly regarded.

Tracking, whether manually or through a shared financial account, also provides parents who provide financial support to college students with an opportunity to hold their child financially accountable. Financial accountability provides additional developmental opportunities for students to learn and mature in their money management skills and can lead to improved communication and understanding between students and their financially supportive parents.

Finally, tracking exercises have been shown to provide intrinsic motivation to students to reduce expenditures on alcohol, smoking, and eating out (Oaten and Cheng 2007; Palmer et al. 2010). These ancillary benefits associated with tracking are likely a result of increased self-regulatory strength and stamina (Oaten and Cheng 2007).

UGA Peer Financial Counseling Program

One successful example of a campus-based financial education is the University of Georgia Peer Financial Counseling Program. Although the term counseling is used in the name, the program is predominantly an outreach financial education program. Dr. Brenda Cude collaborated with the university financial aid office and the Georgia Student Finance Commission to implement this program. The program premise is that the best way to reach college students is by having fellow students provide valuable information and experiences that we can relate to and apply in our daily lives. The seven modules in the program were developed to explore critical issues of budgeting, credit use, student loans, and savings and investments. Student speakers present the modules to classes, clubs, residence halls, and other student organizations.

Volunteer Income Tax Assistance and Financial Education

In Bloom's Taxonomy of learning, the highest levels of understanding are evaluating and creating. Often, personal finance curriculum is focused on lower-order learning domains such as understanding and remembering definitions, processes, formulas, and rules. Personal finance seminars and classes may seek to achieve higher-order learning through assignments and how-to projects that seek to apply the memorized material. This can include such things as comparing credit card offers to find the best one for a given situation, comparing mutual funds based on a predetermined set of criteria, planning a budget, comparing price and quality attributes of products to find the best values, or the preparation of taxes and tax planning strategies.

Personal taxation is a basic personal finance topic in the USA as everyone residing in the USA, and every US citizen residing anywhere in the world, is subject to federal income taxation. Memorization of tax laws, such as filing status requirements, dependency exemption eligibility, education credits, and the Earned Income Credit, is important, and the application of each of these specific rules is valuable. However, in order for students to apply the tax laws to their current situation, they must be able to evaluate multiple rules of tax law to determine the correct application.

The need for a more integrated understanding of the tax code is easily illustrated when looking at higher education tax benefits. First, the student must determine whether they are a dependent on someone else's tax return or they are filing for themselves. After this is determined, basic knowledge of what qualifies as a higher education expense must be applied to determine what amount is eligible for higher education tax benefits. However, scholarship awards, distributions from 529 plans, education IRAs, and exempted interest from EE Savings Bonds also affect the amount of expenditures eligible for higher education tax benefits. Also, students filing their own tax return, depending on their status, may claim higher education tax benefits in one of four ways on their tax return. Finally, how the higher education tax benefits are claimed may affect the students' state income tax liability as well. In order to most effectively—and legally—claim the tax benefits of higher education, a student needs to have a deeper understanding of the working parts and how they interact.

How can students gain this deeper understanding? One way in which these higher levels of learning can be reinforced or achieved is through experiential learning. Experiential learning can take many forms, including case studies and service-learning opportunities which take place out of class. For many personal finance topics, real-life assignments and cases tend to immerse the students most deeply into the content—with all of the rich associated context of the question—and produce the deepest learning. Real-life assignments could include the following: going through the process over the telephone of opening a traditional or Roth IRA with a mutual fund company, without committing money to it; selecting the best mutual fund to in which to begin to invest money for a long-term goal; doing research and identifying the "best" credit card available to each student, given their specific circumstances; and having students prepare their own tax return, which is then reviewed by their peers for accuracy. Particularly with tax preparation, students' education can also be richly enhanced by participating in a service-learning project serving both their peers and the local community. The remainder of this section will focus on how service-learning activities can be encouraged and adopted to provide peer-to-peer financial assistance on college campuses while fostering deeper knowledge and understanding of personal finance topics among students. This section will particularly focus on personal finance in relation to income taxes; however, the structure of the peer-to-peer service offering could be duplicated with any number of personal finance topics (e.g., checking and correcting credit reports, student loan planning and management decisions, and campus-based investment clubs).

Many campuses and communities are involved in Volunteer Income Tax Assistance (VITA) programs. At VITA sites, individuals can receive free assistance in preparing and filing their federal and state income tax returns from supervised volunteers who have been certified by the IRS. These VITA sites are staffed by students and community members and may serve focused audiences or the general community. Volunteers can be certified at the basic, intermediate, or advanced levels, thus providing an opportunity for engagement and enhanced learning, regardless of the students' expertise in the tax code. In addition to the certification process, the IRS also provides all VITA sites and VITA volunteers with training, income tax preparation software, and preparation guidance manuals to aid in the accuracy and reliability of the tax returns. Students work best in pairs, and supervisors are always present to assist if the student volunteers have a question (Palmer et al. 2009).

In addition to the tax preparation and filing service, student volunteers routinely invite their friends to get their taxes done. This individualized setting provides additional opportunities for financial aid offices to share specific information with students about a variety of financial aid and personal finance topics. Everyone who works and has had federal income taxes withheld from a paycheck wants to get that money back and is therefore motivated to file a return. Thus, it is not difficult to generate demand for VITA services.

While peers and community members benefit substantially from the free tax preparation and filing services (approximately $150–250 savings when compared to paying a tax professional), students are perhaps the greatest beneficiaries of the service. Students see firsthand the interrelated aspects of personal finance as various financial decisions become manifest on their clients' tax returns. Questions about scholarship income, education credits or deductions, distributions from 529 plans and education IRAs, 1,099 income, tax credits for low-income families and individuals, and so forth force students to reevaluate their basic understanding of tax law as it relates to personal finance and dig a little deeper so that they can help their peers and others answer these questions. Again, the presence of a supervisor is also a powerful learning tool because it provides a safety net for students to explore and experience this new situation, while not losing confidence that they will get stuck with nowhere to turn for help. As students gain this experience, they build confidence to plan their personal finances in such a way as to be ready for tax-filing season. They also gain a deeper understanding of aspects of the tax code that may create extra headaches, as well as rules that could generate extra cash flow for them in later years.

VITA provides a powerful opportunity for students to create not only their tax knowledge, in part by seeing how other areas of personal finance are deeply integrated into the US Tax Code. Finally, students gain confidence in their ability to provide meaningful service to others (Palmer et al. 2010). This confidence will help them professionally and personally as they develop during their collegiate study.

After all, if students who have completed a personal finance class are not even confident enough to accurately complete their own tax returns, it is difficult to say that they have been prepared for the financial realities of our modern lives.

Conclusion

Perhaps, the most important thing to remember is that there is an abundance of resources available to those who want to start a financial education program. All of the universities and program administrators cited in this chapter and throughout the book are eager to share their ideas and resources to help others build financial education programming. Many ways and methods exist, as discussed throughout the chapter, to provide delivery of financial education in interdisciplinary formats and nontraditional classroom settings. The nontraditional delivery formats can allow program directors to effectively target certain subpopulations of students.

Regardless of the delivery format, the programming content should be consistent with the academic level of the students being targeted. Making the programming real to the participants is essential. Experiential learning methods are powerful tools that can help students gain a transformational personal finance experience that will set them up for success for many years to come. Stories of financial success from individuals to whom students can relate can be a very powerful educational tool. In terms of content for online financial management resources, many are available. For example, the NEFE currently offers an online educational component available at no cost to higher education institutions. Many universities may want to first assess the interest in topics and delivery mechanisms on their specific campus as there may be geographical and institutional effects on their specific student population. This type of assessment can also be used as a tool to solicit university administration support for programming efforts of this type.

References

Adams, T., & Moore, M. (2007). High-risk health and credit behavior among 18 to 25 year old college students. *Journal of American College Health, 56*(2), 101–108.

American Council on Education. (2006). *Credit card ownership and behavior among traditional-age undergraduates, 2003-04*. Retrieved October 21, 2011, from http://www.acenet.edu/AM/Template.cfm?Section=CPA.

Angelino, L. M., Williams, F. K., & Natvig, D. (2007). Strategies to engage online students and reduce attrition rates. *The Journal of Educators Online, 4*(2), 1–14.

Braunsberger, K., Lucas, L. A., & Roach, D. (2004). The effectiveness of credit card regulation for vulnerable consumers. *Journal of Services Marketing, 18*(5), 358–370.

Chen, H., & Volpe, R. P. (1998). An analysis of personal financial literacy among college students. *Financial Services Review, 7*(2), 107–128.

Garcia, J. (2008a). *In the red or in the black? Understanding the relationship between household debt and assets*. New York: Demos. Retrieved October 21, 2011, from http://www.demos.org/pubs/redorblack.pdf.

Gartner, K. M., & Schiltz, E. R. (2005). What's your score: Educating college students about credit card debt. *Saint Louis University Public Law Review, 24*(2), 401–432.

Goetz, J., Cude, B., Nielsen, R., Chatterjee, S., & Mimura, Y. (2011a). College-based personal finance education: Student interest in three delivery methods. *Journal of Financial Counseling and Planning, 22*(1), 27–42.

Goetz, J., Durband, D. B., Halley, R., & Davis, K. (2011b). A peer-based financial planning and education service program: An innovative pedagogic approach. *Journal of College Teaching & Learning, 8*(4), 7–14.

Insurance Information Institute. (2011). *Credit scoring.* Retrieved January 16, 2011 from http://www.iii.org/media/hottopics/insurance/creditscoring.

Locke, E., & Latham, G. (1990). *A theory of goal setting & task performance.* Englewood Cliffs, NJ: Prentice Hall.

Lyons, A. C. (2004). A profile of financially at-risk college students. *Journal of Consumer Affairs, 38*(1), 56–80.

Lyons, A. C. (2008). Risky credit card behavior of college students. In J. J. Xiao (Ed.), *Advances in consumer financial behavior research* (pp. 185–207). New York, NY: Springer.

Lyons, A. C., & Hunt, J. L. (2004). The credit practices and financial education needs of community college students. *Financial Counseling and Planning, 14*(1), 63–74.

Mae, S. (2009). *How undergraduate students use credit cards.* Wilkes-Barre, PA: Sallie Mae, Inc.

Nellie Mae Corporation. (1998). *Life after debt: Report of the national student loan survey.* Braintree, MA: Nellie Mae Corporation. Retrieved September 16, 2011, from http://www.nelliemae.com/library/NASLS.pdf.

Oaten, M., & Cheng, K. (2007). Improvements in self-control from financial monitoring. *Journal of Economic Psychology, 28*, 487–501.

Palmer, L., Bliss, D., Goetz, J., & Moorman, D. (2010). Improving financial awareness among college students: Assessment of a financial management project. *College Student Journal, 44*(3), 659–676.

Palmer, L., Goetz, J., & Chatterjee, S. (2009). Service-learning for financial planning students: Making a difference now and for years to come. *Financial Services Review, 18*(2), 157–175.

Pinto, M. B., Parente, D. H., & Palmer, T. S. (2001). College student performance and credit card usage. *Journal of College Student Development, 42*(1), 49.

Ross, S. E., Niebling, B. C., & Heckert, T. M. (1999). Sources of stress among college students. *College Student Journal, 33*, 312–317.

Shockey, S. S., & Seiling, S. B. (2004). Moving into action: Application of the transtheoretical model of behavior change to financial education. *Financial Counseling and Planning, 15*(1), 41–52.

St. John, E. (1998). Loan debt: A new view. *Black Issues in Higher Education, 15*(10), 16–18.

Yilmazer, T., & DeVaney, S. A. (2005). Household debt over the lifecycle. *Financial Services Review, 14*, 285–304.

Chapter 7
Marketing Strategies for Financial Education Programs

Mary M. Bell, Jason McGarraugh, and De'Arno D. De'Armond

Introduction

Marketing, by definition, is a set of complex processes for creating, communicating, and delivering value to customers, and further managing customer expectations and relationships. Whether you represent a for-profit or a nonprofit entity, there is a need for a solid marketing effort (AMA Board 1985). Although you may not need to deploy every marketing theory and concept known to the business world, an arduous task at best, there are still many central marketing theories, concepts, and ideas you may deploy in your efforts to plan, implement, and monitor your program. Marketing efforts center on the exchange of something of value, a tangible product or an intangible service or idea, between two or more parties. Marketing plays an important role in the exchange process by identifying and informing consumers about an organization's services (Bagozzi 1975).

If you are starting a comprehensive campus-based financial education program, the odds are that you won't have a full-time marketing staff. You are fortunate if you have a dedicated marketing budget or any additional paid staff at all. As with any new venture, one person may serve as the CEO, CFO, receptionist, and janitor. Your primary marketing plan responsibility is serving as the *relationship manager*. Relationship

M.M. Bell, Ph.D. candidate (✉)
School of Family Studies and Human Services, Kansas State University,
245 Justin Hall, Manhattan, KS 66506, USA
e-mail: marybell@k-state.edu

J. McGarraugh, M.S.
Neal Financial Group, 1770 St. James Place Suite 360, Houston, TX 77056, USA
e-mail: jason@nealfinancial.com

D.D. De'Armond, Ph.D.
Department of Management, Marketing, and General Business, West Texas A&M University,
Classroom Center 214-C, Canyon, TX 79016, USA
e-mail: ddearmond@mail.wtamu.edu

D.B. Durband and S.L. Britt (eds.), *Student Financial Literacy:*
Campus-Based Program Development, DOI 10.1007/978-1-4614-3505-1_7,
© Springer Science+Business Media New York 2012

marketing involves creating, maintaining, and enhancing long-term relationships with individuals as well as other stakeholders for mutual benefit (Berry 1995). The growth of the program will center on your ability to network and market the program. Therefore, you must put in place a marketing plan that encompasses both vision and reality. This chapter will outline the fundamentals of planning a marketing strategy as well as provide some insight and ideas on how to implement your plan.

Step 1: Define Your Target Population

Start by defining your target population, which should reflect where your program resides. This could be the faculty, staff, and students in your department, or it might be in the student affairs, financial aid, or enrollment management offices. The center of influence method is a sales process in which a salesperson engages with individuals perceived as influential in the buying situation; these individuals are called *centers of influence*.

In the situation given above, these internal contacts have a vested interest in the success of your program. Hold interviews with as many people as you can and retain their information for ongoing marketing of your services. You might even consider conducting a focus group with the target population. The purpose of these interviews is to find centers of influence within your existing network of colleagues and acquaintances. Through these centers of influence, you will find your most accessible target population. To get the highest level of excitement and participation from existing and potential centers of influence, you will have to articulate what they stand to gain. Business leaders and department heads have priorities and goals of their own that they have to meet, and the space on their plate for new opportunities is limited.

Before you meet with anyone face to face, have in your mind an idea you will emphasize as the *return on their investment* in the timeliest manner possible. Investment takes on many different forms, e.g., money return, time return, facilities, and human capital. As you work to develop your ideas about the program, think of how you can explicitly state what those returns are and what they are going to do for those in decision-making roles. In educational frameworks, it might be as simple as stating what students or organizations will learn, how you will assess those learners, and how you will report that knowledge gain. Remember, a curriculum or program without assessment and benchmarking holds little value.

To ensure that your program stands out in the minds of potential partners and champions, you need to think of your concept, idea, or product in a novel way. In your case, you are now a university program sales person. You may not think you even like sales, but you are going to have to sell your concept of a financial planning program to those who are making decisions about program viability. Every concept and/or idea you are trying to pursue has three primary components: (a) feature (physical characteristic), (b) advantage (performance characteristic), and (c) benefit (the ever-so-important "what's in it for me?" characteristic). These three things together make up a unique selling proposition (USP) that will help you stand out from competition and drive home your message. If you keep reiterating the FABs (i.e., feature, advantage, and benefit), your message will be heard in such a way that questions become limited at best.

To deploy the FAB model in your situation, you have to think about it abstractly; you are not selling cars, where you might be able to say, "The car is red, red is fast, red is cool." You have to think in terms of the intangibles of the program, but you can apply the same theory. For example, a feature could be that *students will learn the latest budgeting techniques*. The advantage statement would be that *students will gain insight on how to make every last dollar reach as far as it can*, and the benefit would be that *students will be able to efficiently and effectively utilize their budget to meet their living needs*. This results in a feature that is a characteristic of your program offering, an advantage that is a performance characteristic, and a benefit that is something that showcases what is in it for the student and the decision-makers. For every idea or concept you present, focus on the FABs as you make your proposal to ensure a success marketing strategy.

If you have the means, it will be wise to implement a *client relationship process*, through which you track contact information and communications with both centers of influence and clients. There are many detailed computer programs available that are built specifically to help you systematize your client and prospect communications, such as Salesforce (www.salesforce.com) or E-Z Data (www.ezdata.com). These types of programs typically have a recurring financial cost. If finances are an issue, you can use Microsoft Outlook's contacts, calendars, and task capabilities as an effective replacement. The idea is to track with whom you speak, when you spoke to them, and what you discussed. By obtaining their contact information, you can keep your centers of influence updated on your programs progress. With the high student turnover that exists in academia, it is of the utmost importance to keep accurate records and process descriptions that can be adopted and built upon from year to year.

Step 2: Making a Name for the Program

Branding is the effort an organization makes to keep the perception and recognition of a program positive. The overall perception and accumulated experiences an individual has with your program need to remain as positive as possible. Keeping your program consistent from year to year and keeping your clients and centers of influence updated with current information should be the cornerstone of your marketing plan. There is ample research on successful marketing techniques; one such example is the KISS (keep it simple, silly) model, which basically states that marketing is most effective when it is simple and straightforward (Hoch 2004; Misra 2004). Abstract marketing strategies might be fun to develop, but more simple, yet creative, strategies are likely to yield better results.

You might consider sending a monthly newsletter or e-mail to your contact list. You may even have multiple contact lists: one for previous clients, another for current clients, one for prospective clients, and one for supporters of your program (e.g., university administration and other partners). Marketing directed at clients (past, present, or future) would ideally give a tip on a personal finance topic with a tag line to schedule an appointment to learn more. The letter for non-client supporters should keep readers apprised of the progress and growth of the program as well as contain some success stories from clients or other parts of the program.

Providing financial education in group settings will likely be the natural starting point for your program's outreach. Develop a message and make sure that everyone who communicates your message has an in-depth knowledge of the program's purpose and mission (Burkhart and Reuss 1993). It is vital that you have a mission statement, goals, objectives, and possibly even research interests for the program. These statements should be communicated clearly and directly. Consider posting these statements on the wall of the program's physical facilities as well as on your program website and related social media sites (e.g., Facebook, LinkedIn, university-sponsored website, or blog). All members of your program should be repeating the same message verbatim when asked what it is that they do. Branding is the result of the enduring perception one has after multiple engagements with the program. There are three primary components to consider when making a name for your financial education program: making sure your process is in writing, showing the value of your program, and developing lasting relationships.

Put It in Writing. Develop a written process for servicing centers of influence, clients, and potential clients. By putting a process in writing, you have the ability to train volunteers, staff, students, or others and still keep your message intact. This will simplify your ability to handle volunteer turnover instead of constantly having to retool your message.

Show Value. Show your value through your services. Your best on-campus resource is the student population. If a student has a good experience, they will be an advocate for the program and can become a center of influence with the ability to reach additional clients and opportunities. Students can be your best marketers, both verbally and virtually. They can also be the quickest to destroy your program if the service does not meet their expectations. It will be important to have a concise, consistent motto, phrase, or slogan that can be easily repeated to another student in a few seconds while still conveying the essence of the program's message. For more information on creating slogans on a budget, Steve Cone discusses what has worked in the past, what has failed, and how to be a *wordsmith* of slogans (2008). Oftentimes, creative slogans are rooted in rhetoric that is creatively delivered. It is also important to have an Internet presence, as well as social networking accounts, in order to communicate your message clearly and easily via the Web. Every university, college, or business entity will have different protocols for developing any type of Web or social networking presence. The best place to start inquiring about the protocols would be your department's web designer.

Develop Relationships. Develop a relationship with your campus and local news outlets. Offer to provide them with consistent content for their publications. Consider using press releases for your events. Make financial education program staff available as content experts for interviews with media outlets. You might consider having a webpage dedicated to describing faculty and researchers' work within their fields of expertise and study. You can have their contact information on this page, so the media can contact them directly. More information regarding how to build partnerships for your program is provided in Chap. 8.

Step 3: Getting the Word Out

The next step is putting your marketing plan into action and getting the word out. We will detail the benefits and costs of free vs. paid marketing and then give you some creative marketing ideas that we have found useful for educating the public about a program or service.

Free Versus Paid Marketing

Everyone has a primary constraint: resources! And most of us do not draw from a well of unending resources. Therefore, the first step is to consider all of your resources: monetary, time, quantity of staff, human capital of staff, and the like. Continue brainstorming about the source of your resources, from the obvious to the obscure. Examples may include who your primary centers of influence are, key contacts, and volunteers or staff. Chapter 5 provides a more in-depth discussion of locating resources to support financial education programs. After brainstorming these ideas, begin to prioritize them accordingly. You know which ones are realistic and which ones are not. This will help you as you begin to move into action. The next step is to develop your budget and know the exact amount of money that you have to work with. These steps must be performed before moving forward. Budget development is a function of resources and organizational goals.

There are two main entrepreneurial approaches common in organizations: the percentage approach and the static allotment approach. The percentage approach stipulates that the marketing budget should be a percentage of the overall budget, usually around 9–12%. The advantage of a percentage-of-budget method is that as your program grows and your marketing needs increase, so does your marketing budget. Another approach is the allotment of a static amount of dollars per budget cycle. For example, your program may have limited resources, so you might allocate a flat dollar amount to the marketing budget that would recur each budget cycle.

To begin, you will want to start small, yet think big. You might want to start with a few of the free creative marketing ideas discussed below and then gradually implement more as the service and your resources grow.

Table 7.1 Most effective marketing methods for a financial education program

Type of marketing	Percentage (%)
Word of mouth	87
Mass e-mail announcements	50
Information booth or table	47
Brochures or flyers	47
Campus newspaper advertisement	27
Bulletin board displays	27
Table tents	20
Financial tip of the day/week/month	20
Campus newspaper column	20
Off-campus newspaper column	3
Chalking on campus sidewalks	3

Creative Marketing Ideas

A survey was conducted to learn more about existing financial education programs (see Chap. 2 for details). Respondents were allowed to provide two open-ended responses at the end of the survey. Table 7.1 provides data about which marketing techniques were found to be most effective.

Other means of marketing that were mentioned on the survey were campus radio, Facebook, on-campus events (e.g., wellness fairs, career programs), referrals (e.g., from internal networks, first-year experience classes, finance professionals), partnerships with other offices, money cart (based on the TV game show Cash Cab), and website referrals.

Live Promotions

Live promotions can be very effective and can be efficiently executed by volunteers, students, staff, or others. If you are able to get your volunteers, staff, students, and others excited about the program, then they can be an invaluable (and free) marketing resource. Once the volunteers, staff, students, and others clearly understand and can articulate the vision and mission of the organization, send them to some of the following places with a few fliers or brochures that have more contact information:

• Greek organizations (i.e., sororities and fraternities)
• Service or honorary organizations
• Student nights (back to school or other themes)
• Game day booths
• Classes of professors who will allow a student to make an announcement in class

Written Promotions

Written promotions can be invaluable, but they can also be very expensive. This will require consideration and careful use of the limited resources you will have for the program. Make sure that you get the best bang for your buck.

An idea for a written promotion might include newspaper ads. However, instead of just placing an advertisement, which is often a very expensive endeavor, consider offering to be the content specialist or serve as a resource for the paper. This requires well-developed relationships with your campus and local media. It also requires that you are able to provide them with relevant and accurate information for their stories.

Social media can also be a great resource if it is managed and controlled appropriately. This requires you to deliver timely and relevant content on a regular basis. It can be a great task for a responsible and reliable upperclassman or graduate student. All content should be overseen by the director to make sure that the correct information is getting out to the right population. Some examples of social media use might include Facebook or Twitter updates. The use of social media is simply to enhance existing relationships, but remember that these relationships must already exist (followers or friends) before these updates become valuable.

A tried-and-true method is the use of brochures or fact sheets. In fact, some type of written content in an easy-to-display format is necessary for further explanation of the program and delivery of contact information. These brochures can be set out at various places on campus, such as student financial aid, registrar and cashier offices, student counseling services, student legal services, wellness programs, and the ombudsman's office. You will also want to have a stack of these available for any solicitation sent to the program. This written content can fit on something as small as a business card and should contain the mission of the program and the contact information at a minimum. This should be part of the hook of getting students to come in. Microsoft Word or PowerPoint can be used to create business cards and brochures.

Another idea for written communication is mass e-mails to student groups, such as international student groups, graduate students, and first-year students. You should be able to coordinate this with your student groups on campus, but make sure you provide relevant and useful content. Some universities may require that you purchase the campus Listserv.

School websites can be a great opportunity for getting the word out on a website with high traffic, often for free. Make sure you get approval from the website manager for the content you want to add. Also, you might consider your school's library home page. This page generates much more traffic than you might suspect. Content on these websites should last 1–7 days. Usually, after a full week, the content is stale, and it is time for new news. Finally, another great written resource can be a message board. Message boards can be both physical, such as a board in your student union, and virtual, such as comment boards on news articles. This piece will probably not generate hundreds of referrals just because you posted a comment, but again the point here is to try to reach as many people as possible through multiple avenues.

Other Promotions

Of course, there are numerous ways to share your program. We will give you a few more tips, but just remember: the sky is the limit!

On-campus banks and credit unions can be great opportunities for a referral network. You might find that your on-campus bank or credit union wants a group that would help teach students the basics about money. See if they will offer referrals as well as post marketing materials in their space. A good way to break the ice is to invite the branch manager to view your facilities or be a guest at one of your education seminars. These financial institutions tend to have established networks that can provide cross-promotional opportunities such as career fairs and campus orientations.

The next few ideas might sound a little trite, but you might be amazed at how effective these simple marketing methods might be. Try posting table tents on food court tables. Of course, you will need to check university policy, and it can be an expensive venture, but if your budget allows, place them in the highest traffic areas. Another great traffic location is bathroom stall doors. These one-page solicitations might receive more notice than you imagine! Make sure they are short and sweet as well as catchy. An inexpensive and fun marketing idea is to use sidewalk chalk on high-traffic areas around campus. Just make sure you have permission before writing on the school's property. Again, since we are looking for high-traffic areas, you might consider adding a sign or banner in the student union. For very high-profile and high-traffic areas (e.g., student unions, football stadiums), you will need a banner or sign of some sort to actually attract the attention of those who you are seeking to draw in. This can be as expensive or inexpensive as you make it. (Having an artist in your network to assist with creation of these items is not such a bad idea, either.)

Finally, you might consider having a coupon printed in your campus coupon book or student planners available at the beginning of each school year for students. This can be a great way to remind students about your services and encourage them to come in.

It may be easy to get overwhelmed in this process. Remember, we have all been there: the long, never-ending exhibit halls at conferences. We stop at the booth to chat because they have a cool pen or a neat back scratcher. Other times, we do not even stop at all; we just pick up the item as we rush along. The same thing applies with students. Having more freebies at your table does *not* equal more face time. If you are giving away a free tablet or have the coolest water bottles, you will certainly get plenty of foot traffic, but if your resources are limited, a few nice but inexpensive promotional items and a friendly face behind the table to start a discussion may be enough. Again, keep it simple, silly. Just think to yourself, what would encourage you to stop?

Step 4: Keep Moving Forward

Now, the word is out and your marketing plan is in place. Take a deep breath, but do not think you can stop there. You cannot let your networking opportunities go into remission once you are in the creative marketing stage. After a short time, you will realize that you cannot do this alone (if you have not already!). Therefore, elicit the help of others. Consider asking some of the marketing, communications, or technical writing professors to consider your message as a class project in print or electronic content, graphic design, or videography. It is a great way to expand the project contacts, and you might even get some clients out of the partnerships.

Most students want to be involved. In fact, it is human nature to want to be a part of something bigger than yourself. Therefore, give the volunteers, students, staff, or others a job. Encourage ownership (and thereby responsibility) in the program. Trust them and then hold them accountable just as you would for a term project. Invite and then empower.

When you boil all of this down, you are starting a new business and you need to understand from the beginning what your individual strengths and weaknesses are so you can capitalize on what you do well and outsource what you do not do so well. Without this understanding of yourself, you are placing your success in the hands of Lady Luck. As you continue to educate yourself and expand on your desire to create something great, you might look at the following book recommendations. This short list represents a few of the marketing books that can help get you started.

- *The E Myth Revisited: Why Most Small Businesses Don't Work and What to Do About It* by Michael E. Gerber (1995, New York: HarperCollins). This book walks you through the steps in the life of a business from entrepreneurial infancy through adolescent growing pains to the mature entrepreneurial perspective and shows how to apply the lessons of franchising to any business, whether or not it is a franchise.
- *Identity Branding: Distinct or Extinct* by Robert E. Krumroy (2000, Greensboro, NC: Lifestyles Press). This book is designed to assist the financial professional in creating a distinct and unique local market presence; a perception of superior value that opens a prospect highway to a prospect community that welcomes their presence creates a competitive advantage and solves the issue of "market access."
- *Free Publicity: A TV Reporter Shares the Secrets for Getting Covered on the News* by Jeff Crilley (2002, Dallas: Brown Books Publishing Group). This book will guide you through the secrets to getting media coverage from someone on the inside. You will learn how to get a journalist's attention, when to call and when not to, and what to say and how to say it.

Summary

Building and maintaining a financial counseling program should be looked at as a win-win proposition for all involved. View yourself as a repository of specialized knowledge that everyone needs but that so very few receive or understand. You are creating a conduit of information to help your clients reduce debt, build savings, and manage their lifestyles. Financial problems are often the catalysts to stress that disrupt many aspects of life, such as family and work, and the services you provide can lead to increased fulfillment and productivity for your clients.

Regardless of how your marketing plan materializes, always remember that your main goal is to build strong relationships and create value for your clients and partners. Marketing is a process by which you identify your client, meet the needs of your client, and keep your client. This chapter has covered some of the possible techniques and ideas that have been used to build and promote successful programs. Keep in mind that these ideas were developed over many years and were not all implemented on day 1. The best advice is to choose one or two of the ideas that you are confident you can implement immediately and concentrate on them. When you have successfully turned those ideas into a sustainable process within your program, continue this pattern and you will be surprised how quickly you will achieve your marketing goals.

Finally, as a last piece of advice, in the survey conducted to learn more about existing financial education programs, the editors allowed for a few open-ended responses (Durband and Britt 2011). Other programs offered the following marketing advice for those who are interested in starting a financial education program: "At the college campus level, meet with as many departments as possible to determine needs and promote financial literacy as a resource. Get buy in from staff/faculty to help promote and formalize the program, include a recognizable logo, advertise, use other campus resources to market the program (i.e., department newsletters), and involve community media in marketing the program." We wish you the best of luck as you continue to market and grow your financial education program!

References

AMA Board Approves New Marketing Definition. (1985, March 1). *Marketing News*, p. 1.

Bagozzi, R. P. (1975). Marketing as exchange. *Journal of Marketing, 39*, 32–39.

Berry, L. L. (1995). Relationship marketing of services—growing interest, emerging perspectives. *Journal of the Academy of Marketing Science, 23*(4), 236–245.

Burkhart, P. L., & Reuss, S. (1993). *Successful strategic planning: A guide for nonprofit agencies and organizations*. Newbury Park: Sage Publications.

Cone, S. (2008). *Powerlines: Words that sell brands, grip fans, and sometimes change history*. City: Bloomberg Press.

Durband, D. B., & Britt, S. L. (2011). *Perspectives on university financial education programs: Research survey highlights*. Unpublished raw data.

Hoch, S. (2004). *Wharton on making decisions*. New York: Wiley.

Misra, R. B. (2004). Global IT outsourcing: Metrics for success of all parties. *Journal of Information Technology Cases and Applications, 6*(3), 21.

Chapter 8
Financial Education Program Partnerships

Sonya L. Britt and Joseph Goetz

Introduction

According to Merriam-Webster, a *partnership* is defined as (a) "the state of being a partner," (b) "a legal relation existing between two or more persons contractually associated as joint principals in a business," or (c) "a relationship resembling a legal partnership and usually involving close cooperation between parties having specified and joint rights and responsibilities." As evidenced by this definition, partnerships should be taken seriously and involve agreement from all parties involved in the partnership. Countless sources have documented the benefit of merging knowledge from multiple sources for the benefit of helping clients, students, or the society as a whole. For instance, the Centre for the Advancement of Interprofessional Education in the United Kingdom brings the corporate world and academic world together to improve the quality of care for individuals, families, and communities (see http://www.caipe.org.uk/). The Financial Therapy Association based in the United States brings together multiple fields of study (e.g., financial planning, marriage and family therapy, psychology, social work) and multiple professions (e.g., corporate and private practice and academia) to stimulate and disseminate clinical, experimental, and survey research on financial therapy. Hundreds, if not thousands, of other organizations are developing collaborative partnerships to help them achieve their goals. The purpose of this chapter is to explain the myriad benefits of partnerships, offer

S.L. Britt, Ph.D. (✉)
Institute of Personal Financial Planning, School of Family Studies
and Human Services, Kansas State University,
317 Justin Hall, Manhattan, KS 66506, USA
e-mail: sbritt@k-state.edu

J. Goetz, Ph.D.
Department of Housing and Consumer Economics, University of Georgia,
205 Dawson Hall, Athens, GA 30602, USA
e-mail: goetz@uga.edu

D.B. Durband and S.L. Britt (eds.), *Student Financial Literacy:*
Campus-Based Program Development, DOI 10.1007/978-1-4614-3505-1_8,
© Springer Science+Business Media New York 2012

ways to locate partners for campus-based financial education programs, and present how to develop, maintain, and terminate partnerships.

Benefits of Partnerships

University Benefits

An obvious benefit to universities for creating partnerships to promote financial literacy is a reduced dropout rate among their students. Research substantiates that the sharing of financial information often translates into the reduction of current financial problems and the prevention of future concerns; with less financial stress, students are found to perform better academically (Pinto et al. 2001; Ross et al. 1999).

High graduation rates and students graduating on time are high priorities for most colleges and universities, but students are increasingly dropping out or delaying graduation due to financial reasons. One study found that about 20% of student loan borrowers drop out of college (Gladieux and Perna 2005). Students often drop out of college to work additional hours to manage their debt payments. Alternatively, students will stay in school and work additional hours, which often means enrolling in a reduced academic hours and consequently delaying graduation—another major concern among college and university administrators.

As students are borrowing at an increasing rate to finance their education (The Project on Student Debt 2011) and the financial world becomes increasingly complex, the authors of this chapter contend that universities have a responsibility to ensure students graduate with at least a minimal level of financial knowledge. Research has illustrated that certain students are more financially vulnerable than others, including women and minorities, low-income students, and first-generation students (Lyons 2004). Universities can particularly benefit from targeting these student groups and others with financial education programming. Students who graduate from their college or university with less debt and the knowledge needed to be financially successful are more likely to reach their goals and also contribute to the alma mater.

Many colleges and universities, particularly land-grant universities, share in a tripartite mission of instruction, research, and outreach. The outreach component typically refers to knowledge and service that benefits the greater community. Engaging students in service not only appears to reduce student attrition rates and encourage students to apply the skills they learn in the classroom (Whitt et al. 2008), but it is also an effective strategy to improve relations between an academic institution and a local community. Thus, universities can benefit in terms of improved public relations by partnering with a community agency to provide financial education for students (even employees), especially during times of economic stress. Specific examples of these types of partnerships are provided later in this chapter.

Student Benefits

Students as recipients and providers of financial education services have a remarkable number of benefits. First, students as recipients of financial education services have the possibility of increasing student retention as discussed in section "University Benefits." Not previously mentioned is the impact students can have as providers of financial education services.

According to individuals engaged in multidisciplinary partnerships in institutions of higher education, focusing on student learning is a critical component of any partnership on college campuses. A student-to-student, or peer-to-peer, model for delivering financial education may be optimal on a college campus. One study of students in peer-to-peer helping roles across campuses found that more than 75% of all higher education institutions use some model of peer education in the delivery of student services (Carns et al. 1993). Consistent with social learning theory, students (rather than professionals) presenting financial education may improve the likelihood that a target audience of students would be more receptive to the content and messages delivered (Fabiano 1994; Sloane and Zimmer 1993). The positive outcomes associated with peer-based counseling and education in high schools and colleges are well established (see Cox 1999; D'Andrea and Salovey 1996; Ender and Newton 2000; Nichols and Lumley 1999; Parkin and McKeganey 2000). For these reasons, students receiving financial education or counseling from other students may be an ideal strategy for many campuses, particularly those institutions that have academic degree programs in financial planning, wherein there is a natural market for recruiting peer financial educators. Programs such as the Peer Financial Counseling Program at the University of Georgia, which has a degree program in financial planning, have found substantial success recruiting students from diverse backgrounds (such as financial planning, marriage and family therapy, psychology, economics, accounting, and agriculture finance) and training them to present financial education seminars. Once students are selected and trained as peer educators, they share countless teachable moments with their peers as those students navigate their financial lives. Furthermore, peer educators can serve as activists on campus, such as lobbying for a university course in personal finance or for a student fee to support the establishment of a financial education program or counseling center on campus. Based on experiential learning theory (Kolb 1984), a peer-based model creates an enhanced learning and developmental experience for the student educators. Students providing financial education services may develop many of the skills that will be needed after entering the workforce, such as skills in presentation development, interpersonal and group communication, and public speaking, which will serve to ease their transition into the professional world (Goetz et al. 2005, 2011a). Past research establishes that students who engage in peer education training and become peer educators develop a heightened sense of leadership and increased knowledge of the associated peer education topic (e.g., Badura et al. 2000; Klein et al. 1994). Many students who volunteer or participate as part of a course in a financial education program may be considering or preparing for careers in financial education or financial services. These students can often apply hours of service toward the experience requirements for nationally recognized certifications in financial services such as the Certified Financial Planner™ (CFP®), Accredited Financial Counselor (AFC), or Certified Retirement Counselor (CRC®) professional designations (Goetz et al. 2011b). Students providing financial education either one-on-one or via group presentations who are not interested in financial careers still receive the opportunity to develop communication and presentation skills, which are transferable to most other careers.

Partnering with an academic program or department to recruit students into a financial education or counseling program can be very effective. Consistent with the effects of service-learning (i.e., teaching that emphasizes civic responsibility), students participating as financial educators helping other students or those in the greater community often develop a stronger sense of ethics and intention to be active in future community service and pro bono work (Jacoby 2003; Palmer et al. 2009). Through a service-learning model, students providing financial education services as a component of a university course requirement may become more engaged in the learning process and learn more effectively by addressing a community need. Past empirical research has established service-learning as a highly effective pedagogical technique, specifically in developing students' abilities in leadership, teamwork, and cultural sensitivity, as well as the sense of social responsibility and ethics previously mentioned (Batchelder and Root 1994; National Service-Learning Clearinghouse 2011).

Community Benefits

To maximize the positive impact of financial education programs, you may want to consider partners in your surrounding community. A large-scale partnership between Arizona State University and the City of Phoenix offers much to be learned about partnerships. The City of Phoenix reportedly spent over $200 million to build a downtown campus of Arizona State University. According to Debra Friedman, university vice president, dean, and professor at Arizona State University, "one of the things that makes this particular partnership noteworthy is that it stands as an example of purposeful planning" (Friedman 2009). The idea of developing such a partnership began in 1985 and came to fruition 21 years later in 2006. The partnership yields benefits to both the city and the university. According to Friedman, the partnership works because (a) it allows students to learn where they work, (b) positive relationships have been built based on mutual respect and self-interest where each party receives benefits, and (c) the university is outward looking with an action-oriented research and service agenda, which allows for more community involvement.

While it is unlikely that a financial education program would reach the depth of the partnership described between a major university and a large metropolitan city, much can be learned from their partnership. First of all, "collaborations have to be able to develop, change, and grow with new circumstances and changing conditions. These depend upon personal relationships of a particular kind: an academic expert with a practitioner expert" (Friedman 2009). Further, if possible, it is best if a financial education program were located within a center or institute vs. a school or department because, as Friedman noted, centers and institutes have more focused missions, especially in regard to producing research with practical implications. Centers and institutes also offer direct services to community members (including students) more often than schools and departments. A smaller example of a community partnership is training students at your university to provide financial education programming to the larger community through a community organization, such as a church, homeless shelter, or public library. Other examples of possible community partnerships are described in the sections that follow.

In summary, creating a partnership between students and the university to provide financial education programming is a highly effective strategy to bring financial education to the campus and local communities. Colleges and universities partnering with enrolled students to provide financial education on campus yields many benefits, which are nonreplicable through the use of other partners.

Locating Partners

In an environment focused on furthering the education of youth, it is important to consider the knowledge and expertise that can be offered within the university and greater community. Your expertise should be focused on financial education of college students. Other professionals have different specialties that allow you to spend more time doing what you do best and taking advantage of other's specialties to assist you in your mission. As noted by McCartney (2009):

> Co-professional work often involves professionals who have nominally equal status that neither is the boss of the other in formal employment terms and each has their own area of knowledge and expertise to share. Working together with equals should be a key feature in co-professional work, although in practice some may prove to be more equal than others (p. 26).

A critical element of McCarney's statement is the importance of forming equal partnerships. Just as with other types of relationships (e.g., a marriage), all partners must have an equal balance of benefits and costs to remain in the relationship. If costs exceed the benefits, the partnership will most definitely fail. McCarney explained that equal partnerships can occur in a multidisciplinary environment (two professionals working separately), co-teaching (two professionals working together), or consultation (one professional providing contracted services for another) environment.

Before beginning your search for new partners, you should complete a needs analysis to determine the types of support you require. Once you determine what your needs are, you should first consider searching internally for assistance. What can your larger affiliation (e.g., academic unit, student affairs unit) provide in terms of expertise, resources, and networking? If they are unable to meet some or all of your needs, you can look to other departments within your college or university. After exploring internal options, there are options to consider within your larger community or city.

As legislative support continues to decrease for many universities, there is an increased focus on extramural funding. There are a number of foundations and organizations that support efforts to increase financial literacy. The National Endowment for Financial Education (NEFE), Financial Industry Regulatory Authority (FINRA), United States Department of Agriculture (USDA), and Certified Financial Planner Board of Standards, Inc. (CFP Board), to name a few, have all provided financial support to universities for teaching, research, and service related to financial education. Grant funding can help cover university operating costs, retain faculty through salary supplements, hire full- or part-time staff, fund graduate assistantships, and provide the resources needed to increase the financial well-being of students and community members. NEFE already partners with numerous colleges and universities to provide online financial education to college students (see www.cashcourse.org).

Table 8.1 provides a summary of potential internal and external partners, including the benefits associated with a symbiotic relationship between these partners and your financial education program. This list is not exhaustive but should be viewed as a starting ground for being creative in identifying potential partners. Applied examples of how similar partnerships have come to fruition are provided in the two sections that follow.

Campus Partners

One program director said the best advice for someone wanting to start a financial education program is to utilize the connections on campus. There are several potential partners who likely have just as much to gain from a new partnership as does the financial education program. If interested in setting up a financial counseling and education clinic that will provide students (and perhaps faculty and staff or community members) one-on-one services, it is recommended that you review other similar programs implemented at other schools across the country. However, already established counseling centers, family therapy clinics, or psychology clinics on your own campus also provide excellent models from which to identify and develop the necessary operations and processes, particularly those that may be specifically required by your institution. A campus psychology or family therapy clinic may be open to partnering beyond sharing their processes; they may be willing to share space and infrastructure as well. This is the case at the University of Georgia, where what used to be a marriage and family therapy clinic for the past 20 years has evolved into a multidisciplinary clinic providing financial education and counseling services, nutrition education, and legal problem solving, home environment and design services, and family therapy services (see www.aspireclinic.org). Students

Table 8.1 Partnership opportunities

Potential partner	Internal or external	What they may be able to provide	What you can provide
Academic program	Internal	Student counselors, faculty advisors, physical space, operational supplies, training	Internship opportunity for students, specialized programming for specific classes
Banks	External	Physical space, operational supplies, training	Specialized programming for bank customers
Certified Financial Planner Board of Standards	External	Grants, training materials	Research on student behavior (as providers and receivers of financial education services)
Cooperative Extension	Internal or external	Physical space, operational supplies, training, access to community members	Trained students ready for employment
Counseling centers	Internal or external	Student counselors, faculty advisors, physical space, operational supplies, training, client referral	Specialized programming for clients and providers of counseling centers
Financial aid office	Internal	Physical space, operational supplies, training, client referrals	Trained students ready for employment
Financial Industry Regulatory Authority	External	Grants, training materials	Research on student behavior
Habitat for Humanity	External	Client referrals, training	Trained students ready for employment
Internal Revenue Service	External	Ability to participate in Volunteer Income Tax Assistance program	Volunteers for income tax assistance program
National Endowment for Financial Education	External	Grants, access to CashCourse educational program	Research on student behavior
National Foundation for Credit Counseling	External	Student counselors, faculty advisors, physical space, operational supplies, training	Trained students ready for employment

(continued)

Table 8.1 (continued)

Potential partner	Internal or external	What they may be able to provide	What you can provide
Nonprofit local agencies	External	Client referrals, training	Trained students ready for employment
Student affairs	Internal	Physical space, operational supplies, training, client referrals	Specialized programming for clients
Student housing	Internal	Physical space, training, client referrals	Specialized programming for clients
Student legal services	Internal	Physical space, training, client referrals	Specialized programming for clients
United States Department of Agriculture	External	Grants, training materials	Research on student behavior

from each respective discipline (i.e., family therapy, financial planning, dietetics, and law) have become increasingly aware of a more holistic approach in working with their clients as cross referrals are now commonplace in the clinic. This is an example of where a new financial counseling and education program was able to leverage the infrastructure and expertise associated with an already established clinic by creating a partnership with another academic program. The complementary nature of the services also supported demand for the financial education and counseling services.

In light of the advice of current partnership users, you must know your context (Whitt et al. 2008). For financial education programs, that means identifying who else on your campus is involved in financial transactions involving students. The obvious partner is the office of financial aid or business office. When students receive their financial aid funding, they may realize they do not have enough money to meet their living expenses. Making a referral to the financial education program can get the student back on track with their budget. The office of admissions (undergraduate and graduate levels) is likely to see a number of requests for information on how to pay for school. Housing and transportation are the two largest components of an individual or household's budget. Therefore, a partnership with residence life and Greek life on money management workshops geared toward housing expenses is a great one to develop. Resident assistants or community advisors within the residence halls are often the first to recognize that a student is in distress, and this may include financial trouble. Housing officials would benefit from having a place to send students for help and the financial education program benefits from the connection to students in need.

A large number of colleges and universities have well-established campus-based psychology or family therapy clinics. It is common for individuals and couples seeing a therapist or counselor to also be experiencing some form of financial stress (Aniol and Synder 1997; Miller et al. 2003). As such, these clinics present a natural partnership opportunity either through a referral mechanism or service-integration model. For example, at the University of Georgia and at Kansas State University, the financial planning programs and family therapy programs have partnered in a clinic to provide both therapy services and financial counseling services. In fact, student therapists and student financial counselors will often work together to assist clients experiencing both financial and relational distress, which often go hand in hand. Alternatively, a financial education program could partner with clinics to provide financial education for their staff, thereby indirectly serving their clients. At the very least, clinicians should be equipped to identify financial vulnerabilities of their clients and know how to make an appropriate referral to another campus office or financial professional.

Along these same lines, partnering with a family therapy training program is a great opportunity to offer a financially focused premarital counseling group. If your institution does not have a family therapy training program, local therapists may be interested in partnering with your financial education program. A financially focused premarital counseling group offered by the authors had a greater response than any other group offered. Traditional premarital counseling tends not to spend a great

Table 8.2 Sample financially focused premarital counseling outline

Topic	Activities
Family of origin	Sign consents and discuss expectations
	Introduction of group members
	Draw earliest memories of money and discuss with partner
	Draw a genogram of each partner's family and indicate any significant money memories associated with family members
Expectations	Discuss general expectations of future spouse
	Complete a goal-setting worksheet
	Complete a draft budget
	Complete a budget commitment contract
Lifestyle	Discuss repayment of existing and future debt
	Talk about general life stages and what to expect (e.g., stress!)
	View each partner's credit report
Communication and conflict resolution	Discuss conflict resolution strategies
	Complete a money personality quiz
	Have partners practice solving an ongoing or anticipated conflict
Planning for the future	Discuss financial ramifications of common goals (e.g., buying a home, having children)
	Calculate the costs of such goals
Questions and answers	Complete a financial feelings assessment
	Discuss love languages

deal of time on financial issues despite the known correlation between relationship satisfaction and financial satisfaction (Britt et al. 2008). The group conducted by the authors discussed the topic of money in each of the six group sessions in addition to a traditional topic included in premarital counseling groups. An abbreviated outline of the group is shown in Table 8.2. Other programming opportunities are provided in Chap. 6.

In the unfortunate event that students become involved in a legal situation, the student legal services or judicial affairs office may be a good referral source. It may be the case that your institution already offers financial education outreach for non-students through a certification program or national association affiliation. Search your institution's website for "financial education," "financial literacy," "financial outreach," or "financial center" to determine if these potential partners exist for you.

Another successful partnership developed by the authors of this chapter is between a campus-based financial education program and a substance abuse recovery program. The financial education program provided biweekly financial seminars for the substance recovery program, and the substance recovery program provided financial support for the financial groups as well as referrals for individual financial education appointments.

Finally, if your school is a land-grant university, you are probably already familiar with Cooperative Extension. Each state has a Cooperative Extension program operated by the USDA through the state's land-grant university. The goal of Cooperative Extension is to provide free education to the public (particularly in rural areas) on topics such as agriculture, food safety, nutrition, and financial matters. To locate the nearest Cooperative Extension agency to you, please visit www.csrees. usda.gov and click on the extension link. Extension specialists make great guest speakers for your staff or as a special programming event for students.

Community Partners

Local nonprofit agencies are often interested in partnering with university programs due to appreciation for motivated student personnel to work with their clientele and, in some cases, their limited resources. The majority of financial education programs surveyed for this book appear to be operating in a similar fashion to a nonprofit credit counseling agency (see www.nfcc.org to locate a nonprofit counseling agency in your area). A few of the financial education programs surveyed for this book utilize National Foundation for Credit Counseling (NFCC) member agencies as guest speakers, trainers, and counselors. Partnering with a NFCC member agency creates a natural avenue for those recipients of financial education who may require additional one-on-one assistance or a debt management plan. Other possible community partners include homeless shelters or programs designed to work with families that are in imminent danger of homelessness. Although foreclosure and housing counseling may move beyond the scope of some campus-based financial education programs, the individuals being served by these organizations also need assistance learning the basics about credit and debt, as well as budgeting and dealing with creditors.

Habitat for Humanity is a national nonprofit Christian housing ministry whose mission is to provide safe, affordable housing for low-income families. Houses are sold to partner families at no profit and financed with affordable, no-interest loans. Unacceptable credit is a deterrent for many families. Many times the local affiliates are able to work with the families to improve their credit scores so that they do qualify. Financial counseling and education is an ongoing process with each family to ensure that they begin to build wealth. A memorandum of understanding (MOU) can be created with a local Habitat affiliate as a cross-referral mechanism to your financial education program.

Many communities have domestic violence shelters. One common component found within the cycle of violence is economic dependence. For this reason, nonprofit organizations serving survivors of domestic violence may be an ideal partner for a university financial education program. Whether it is through one-on-one financial counseling or education workshops, female survivors of domestic violence, who have often been disempowered through a cycle of violence, can come to feel financially empowered through the acquisition of financial knowledge. As one example, the UGA Family Financial Planning program has a partnership with a local organization working to end domestic violence and support survivors of domestic violence called Project Safe (www.project-safe.org). Students enroll in a practicum course in financial planning wherein they provide financial education to small groups who are participating in the Project Safe program, which is then followed by one-on-one financial counseling for individuals who desire additional assistance. Students participating in this partnership complete sensitivity and operations training provided by Project Safe personnel; supervisory responsibilities are shared by Project Safe and UGA faculty. Within the current partnership, one-on-one financial counseling for the Project Safe client is voluntary; however, social agencies are often willing to make financial education a required component within their broader program eligibility criteria. In terms of participants' motivation levels and reaching those in need, there are obvious costs and benefits associated with mandatory vs. voluntary participation.

The financial marketplace is becoming increasingly abstruse, and individuals are being forced to assume more financial responsibility. However, almost all low-income households and many middle-income families lack access to professional financial planners who adhere to a fiduciary standard (i.e., legally required to do what is in the best interest of the client). At the same time, many individuals lack even a remedial understanding of important personal finance topics such as income tax planning, employee benefits planning, investing, and retirement planning. Partnering with the Internal Revenue Service (IRS) to implement a Volunteer Income Tax Assistance (VITA) program on campus or in the community (with another community partner) can provide an opportunity for both students and community members to improve their financial knowledge and well-being. The VITA program provides free tax filing assistance to low- and moderate-income individuals. Financial education can also be provided during (or immediately before or after) the tax form preparation process. Students as a partner in this program can benefit from this service-learning experience (see Palmer et al. 2009). The UGA Family Financial Planning Program partners with the IRS and the Georgia United Credit Union to bring free tax filing assistance and financial education to the local community. Both the credit union and university provide financial and supervisory support for the program. The IRS provides a testing and certification process for the students. Partnering with a credit union allows for greater accessibility for members of the community who are unbanked to create an account and to save a portion of their tax refund.

Developing and Maintaining Your Partnership

Now that you have identified your needs and potential partners, it is time to strategically form your partnership with a formal contract that addresses expectations, authority and decision-making, and management duties of partners. In a study of partnerships between academic and student affairs programs, a group of researchers identified seven principles of good practice for creating and sustaining effective partnerships (Whitt et al. 2008). Each of the following principles is discussed in detail below along with examples of how you can apply their principles in a financial education program:

1. Develop partnerships that reflect and advance the institution's mission.
2. Partnerships should provide the opportunity for students to learn in both formal and informal environments.
3. Effective partnerships build and nurture relationships with partners.
4. Partners must recognize, understand, and attend to institutional culture.
5. Make certain your values match that of your partners.
6. Use resources creatively and effectively.
7. Demand and cultivate shared leadership between partners.

The first principle is to develop partnerships that reflect and advance the institution's mission, which is self-explanatory. Second, partnerships should provide the opportunity for students to learn in both formal and informal environments. A financial education program is an ideal way for students to learn about money management practices in a classroom setting and follow up with more individualized attention to their personal financial situation from a financial educator. An even more profitable learning situation is when students studying personal finance or a closely related major can apply their skills in an internship-like environment by educating other students on positive money management practices. One financial education program director surveyed for this book mentioned the use of a student advisory board to involve students who may not have the content skills to help facilitate the program but who want other students to know about the services offered by the financial education program. The student advisory board meets every 2 weeks to discuss marketing strategies and outreach opportunities that would be engaging to students (e.g., hosting educational events in a game show setting where prizes are awarded for correctly answering financial questions). A student advisory board would also be helpful for schools who do not have the capacity or expertise to offer financial education programs, but that want to help other students know about virtual financial education resources.

The third principle of effective partnerships is to build and nurture relationships with partners. Making note cards with staff photos on the cover is a fun and easy way to send thank you or general notes of appreciation to partners. A more time-intensive way to build and nurture relationships is to prepare a quarterly e-mail or newsletter with program updates. Partners love hearing about the progress that happens with the help of their resources. Hosting an annual luncheon for all of the financial education program's partners is a more expensive yet highly notable way to thank partners for their work. Such an event may be used to generate additional donations from partners through a silent auction or free-will donations.

Fourth, partners must recognize, understand, and attend to institutional culture. For example, if the culture of the institution is heavily focused on alumni support, then partnerships should work together to highlight how the financial education program can help students develop a gift plan no matter how small the gift. Alumni associations may even be a potential partner for financial education programs to explore because of the potential for expert assistance from recent alumni and financial support.

It is traditional financial planning practice to ask clients to assess their values and make sure that their goals reflect their values. This is the fifth principle for effective partnerships recommended by Whitt et al. (2008). It is difficult (if not impossible) to build a partnership based on incongruent value systems.

In a budget-constrained environment, it is important to use resources creatively and effectively, which is principle six. Sharing office space with another program may not be a hindrance but actually a good referral source by the increased traffic to your office. Generally, you can post information on your website at low or no cost. With students' accessibility to mobile devices, putting information on the web may be a much more effective way of getting financial education out to the masses vs. printed brochures.

Finally, the seventh and final principle for creating and sustaining effective partnerships according to Whitt et al. (2008) is to demand and cultivate shared leadership between partners. This principle is discussed in greater detail in the following section under authority and management duties.

Additional words of advice from individuals engaged in academic and student affairs partnerships are to (a) know your context, (b) focus on student learning, (c) take advantage of opportunities, (d) engage in assessment, and (e) expect partnerships to be a lot of work (Whitt et al. 2008). An effective partnership will have a shared vision and purpose with clear and realistic objectives (Percy-Smith 2005). To share your vision, purpose, and objectives with potential partners requires that your organization first understands these concepts. Have a meeting with the leaders of your program and at your institution to identify short-term and long-term goals of the program. This will help ensure a clear and cohesive view from within before adding additional views. Some programs have developed advisory boards to aid in communication of the program goals, which has proven effective. It is important to clearly communicate expectations regarding data collection and outcome assessment. In most cases, it makes sense that both partners will be conducting some form of assessment, but a coordination of assessment efforts between partners can increase the efficiency of this process. In certain instances, it may make sense to partner with a specialist in program evaluation available through the university. Implementing best practices in program assessment can become invaluable later in terms of program justification and funding opportunities.

One of the disadvantages of having students directly involved in the management and delivery of financial education programming is that the turnover rate is high! However, that is the ultimate goal of universities, so a plan must be in place to help with the continuous transition of new members of the program. An advisory board made up of students, faculty, staff, and administration can aid in the transference of knowledge to new students. A student mentoring program can also be helpful in establishing a strong continuity of programming, whereby more advanced students are assigned as personal mentors to students just beginning as a financial educator.

Managing Expectations

A key aspect to keep in mind is that "no lasting partnership springs forth fully formed" (Friedman 2009). To help with possible events that may occur during a partnership, is important to have clearly defined expectations. You could think of entering a partnership as being very similar to signing a contract. As with other contracts, it is important to clearly define the consideration of all parties involved, the time frame of product or service delivery, the responsibilities of each party, and the compensation of parties.

A contract is not legally binding unless there is an offer and acceptance between two parties to engage in activity for a legal purpose as well as consideration by competent parties. Consideration implies that each party receives something of value from entering the contract. Financial education programs are able to provide referrals to other qualified professionals and/or free or low-cost educational sessions or workshops, or they could be a free source of marketing promotion for partners. Financial education programs can ask partners to help with any need, such as financial resources, equipment, supplies, space, participant and educator incentives, marketing, referrals, etc.

For financial education programs, it is recommended to maintain operations based on the academic year, semester, or quarters. It is dangerous to establish a partnership with an internal or external partner and find out later that the partnership is not working and have no way to dissolve the relationship. Some partners may want to be your exclusive partner, so having a shorter time frame with possibilities of a renewal contract is helpful. For example, if your school has two on-campus financial institutions, they may not want to partner with you at the same time since they likely view one another as competitors. If one financial institution wants to form a partnership where they provide free T-shirts to workshop participants, without a defined time limit of how many workshops they are supporting, you may discover that the other is willing to provide free T-shirts *and* candy to workshop participants. Being able to accept the second institution's offer is certainly advantageous, even if you must wait until the following academic year.

There are a countless number of ways a partner can support a financial education program. The only stipulation is that the partner agrees to the responsibilities the financial education program asks. Problems may arise when partners do not follow through on their responsibilities. Including a clause in your partnership agreement about the consequences of not meeting expectations is vital. You may need to terminate activities that were generating a benefit to the partner. Additional information on terminating a partnership is included in a later section of this chapter.

It is not uncommon for financial education programs to operate from a pro bono standpoint. The staff members will probably receive compensation, but the individuals providing services may be volunteers. Hence, financial compensation of partners is not necessary for many programs. Compensation may be received in other forms, such as referrals to the partner for additional services or free marketing for the partner.

Your college or university may have legal requirements on what you can and cannot include in a partnership agreement or MOU (check with the legal services program at your institution). If you are allowed freedom to develop your own partnership agreement, you may consider some of the following points from Nolo's (2011) *Creating a Partnership Agreement* guide for businesses, namely, authority and decision-making, management duties, admitting new partners, and resolving disputes. Since your program is likely to be a nonprofit organization, which may or may not receive payment for services, not all of Nolo's items for inclusion in a partnership agreement are relevant.

Authority and Decision-Making

It is up to the financial education program to determine how equal they want the
partnership to be and what they want to allow partners to do. For instance, do they
receive naming rights within in your program? How much decision-making power
do your partners receive? Are partners allowed to vote on matters related to the
program? Do they get to decide on the content of education sessions? There are no
right or wrong answers, yet each of these items should be addressed in a written
agreement.

Management Duties

Will partners be allowed to supervise you or some of your staff? Will partners manage financial aspects of your program? Will partners provide individual or group
educational services? Percy-Smith (2005) has offered additional guidelines on the
forms a partnership can take ranging from complete and total integration where
partners form a united organization to more of a formal referral program between
the partners with several levels of involvement in between. Neither of the extremes
is the ideal partnership arrangement; instead, finding a middle ground of integration
of partners into management decisions would be preferred.

Nurturing Partnerships

Rewarding partners is always a good idea. A handmade certificate can convey a
huge amount of appreciation when presented well. Asking your partners to also
evaluate the effectiveness and value of the financial education program will help
you grow as a program.

Terminating Your Partnership

The MOU should indicate how long the partnership will last. Annual updates to
MOUs aid in refreshing partners' and new staff members' knowledge of the expectations of both parties. The MOU should clearly state that the partnership is only to
exist for predefined period of time (ideally an academic year). When that that time is
up, both parties are expecting to part ways; if, however, the partnership is going well,
a partnership can easily be continued in most instances given that the infrastructure
and processes have already been developed. The idea here is to begin with the end in
mind or to insert definitive progress points and criteria that must be met for the partnership to continue. In the event partnership disputes arise, it is preferred that resolu-
tion is achieved between the partners. Nevertheless, in situations where partners are

This memorandum of understanding is entered into by and between the agencies shown below:

I. Agencies:
Financial Education Program
Contact Information

Partnering Agency
Contact Information

II. Statement of Services to be Performed:
The parties hereto, agree by the execution of the Memorandum of Understanding to participate in an interagency collaborative effort to provide financial planning education for clients at the Partnering Agency.

III. Obligations of the Financial Education Program:
The Financial Education Program agrees to:
a. Provide four 15-30 minute marketing presentations to clients in a group setting at the Partnering Agency.
b. Educate the Partnering Agency's clients about the Financial Education program.
c. Collaborate with the Partnering Agency's staff to coordinate client care, when appropriate.

IV. Obligations of the Partnering Agency:
The Partnering Agency agrees to:
a. Identify and refer patients to the Financial Education Program who are in need of financial planning services.
b. Collaborate with the Financial Planning Program to coordinate client care, when appropriate.

V. Terms of Agreement:
This agreement is to begin [insert date] and shall terminate [insert date]. The presentation dates will be determined upon the signed completion of this agreement.

The Undersigned Agencies do hereby certify that (a) the services specified above are necessary and essential for activities that are properly within the statutory functions and programs of the effected agencies and (b) the proposed arrangements serve the interest of efficient and economical administration.

Financial Education Program:

_____   _____
Director's Signature   Date

Partnering Agency:

_____   _____
Director's Signature   Date

Fig. 8.1 Sample memorandum of understanding

unable to resolve an issue, you may want to write into your MOU that disputes will be handled through your institutions' mediation or arbitration services.

Sample Memorandum of Understanding

A sample MOU, which covers the expectations of partnerships, is shown in Fig. 8.1. This MOU can be altered to fit your program's needs for developing a new partnership or making a current partnership more formal.

Summary

You now have the knowledge necessary to develop profitable partnerships for your financial education program. It is up to you to apply your new knowledge! The fact that you are reading this chapter says you recognize the importance of doing your research and proceeding with due diligence before beginning a new partnership. The value of this background work cannot be overstated. The authors encourage you to first examine already established partnerships that are similar in nature and explore the possible relationships with all potential partners before making a commitment to move forward. The right partnership is truly a symbiotic relationship that has a synergistic effect on all partners' goal attainment.

References

Aniol, J. C., & Synder, D. K. (1997). Differential assessment of financial and relationship distress: Implications for couples therapy. *Journal of Marital and Family Therapy, 23*(3), 347–352.

Badura, A. S., Millard, M., Peluso, E. A., & Ortman, N. (2000). Effects of peer education training on peer educators: Leadership, self-esteem, health knowledge, and health behaviors. *Journal of College Student Development, 41*, 471–478.

Batchelder, T., & Root, S. (1994). Effects of an undergraduate program to integrate academic learning and service: Cognitive, prosocial cognitive, and identity outcomes. *Journal of Adolescence, 17*(4), 341–355.

Britt, S., Grable, J. E., Nelson Goff, B. S., & White, M. (2008). The influence of perceived spending behaviors on relationship satisfaction. *Financial Counseling and Planning, 19*(1), 31–43.

Carns, A. W., Carns, M. R., & Wright, J. (1993). Students as paraprofessionals in four-year colleges and universities: Current practice compared to prior practice. *Journal of College Student Development, 34*, 358–363.

Cox, J. R. (1999). *A guide to peer counseling.* Lanham, MD: Rowman & Littlefield.

D'Andrea, V. J., & Salovey, P. (Eds.). (1996). *Peer counseling: Skills, ethics, and perspectives* (2nd ed.). Palo Alto, CA: Science & Behavior Books.

Ender, S. C., & Newton, F. C. (2000). *Students helping students: A guide for peer educators on college campuses.* New York: John Wiley & Sons.

Fabiano, P. M. (1994). From personal health into community action: Another step forward in peer health education. *Journal of American College Health, 43*, 115–121.

Friedman, D. (2009). An extraordinary partnership between Arizona State University and the City of Phoenix. *Journal of Higher Education Outreach and Engagement, 13*(3), 89–100.

Gladieux, L., & Perna, L. (2005). *Borrowers who drop out: A neglected aspect of the college student loan trend.* San Jose, CA: The National Center for Public Policy and Higher Education.

Goetz, J., Durband, D. B., Halley, R., & Davis, K. (2011a). A peer-based financial planning and education service program: An innovative pedagogic approach. *Journal of College Teaching & Learning, 8*(4), 7–14.

Goetz, J., Tombs, J. W., & Hampton, V. (2005). Easing college students' transition into the financial planning profession. *Financial Services Review, 14*(3), 231–251.

Goetz, J., Zhu, D., Hampton, V., Chatterjee, S., & Salter, J. (2011b). Integration of professional certification examinations with the financial planning curriculum: Increasing efficiency, motivation, and professional success. *American Journal of Business Education, 4*(3), 35–46.

Jacoby, B. (2003). *Building partnerships for service-learning.* San Francisco: Jossey-Bass.

Klein, N. A., Sondag, K. A., & Drolet, J. C. (1994). Understanding volunteer peer health educators' motivations: Applying social learning theory. *Journal of American College Health, 43*(3), 126–130.

Kolb, D. A. (1984). *Experiential learning: Experiences as a source of learning and development.* Englewood Cliffs, NJ: Prentice-Hall.

Lyons, A. C. (2004). A profile of financially at-risk college students. *Journal of Consumer Affairs, 38*(1), 56–80.

McCartney, C. E. (2009). Joining up working: Terms, types and tensions. In J. Forbes & C. Watson (Eds.), *Service integration in schools.* Rotterdam, Netherlands: Sense Publishers.

Miller, R. B., Yorgason, J. B., Sandberg, J. G., & White, M. B. (2003). Problems that couples bring to therapy: A view across the family life cycle. *American Journal of Family Therapy, 31*(5), 395.

National Service-Learning Clearinghouse. (2011). *Impacts/outcomes.* Retrieved October 23, 2011, from http://www.servicelearning.org/topic/theory-practice/impacts.

Nichols, L., & Lumley, L. (1999). Involving students in the development of a peer education program for college women. *Journal of College Student Development, 40,* 422–427.

Nolo. (2011). *Creating a partnership agreement.* Retrieved October 23, 2011, from http://www.nolo.com/legal-encyclopedia/creating-partnership-agreement-29906.html.

Palmer, L., Goetz, J., & Chatterjee, S. (2009). Service-learning for financial planning students: Making a difference now and for years to come. *Financial Services Review, 18*(2), 157–175.

Parkin, S., & McKeganey, N. (2000). The rise and rise of peer education approaches. *Drugs: Education, Prevention and Policy, 7*(3), 293–310.

Percy-Smith, J. (2005). *What works in strategic partnerships for children?* Barnardos: Barkingside.

Pinto, M. B., Parente, D. H., & Palmer, T. S. (2001). College student performance and credit card usage. *Journal of College Student Development, 42*(1), 49.

Ross, S. E., Niebling, B. C., & Heckert, T. M. (1999). Sources of stress among college students. *College Student Journal, 33,* 312–317.

Sloane, B. C., & Zimmer, C. G. (1993). The power of peer health education. *Journal of American College Health, 41,* 241–245.

The Project on Student Debt. (2011). *Quick facts about student debt.* Retrieved October 23, 2011, from http://projectonstudentdebt.org/files/File/Debt_Facts_and_Sources.pdf.

Whitt, E. J., Nesheim, B. E., Guentzel, M. J., Kellogg, A. H., McDonald, W. M., & Wells, C. A. (2008). "Principles of good practice" for academic and student affairs partnerships. *Journal of College Student Development, 49*(3), 235–249.

Chapter 9
Assessing Financial Literacy

Sandra J. Huston

Introduction

Providing education is an efficient method of helping students improve their stock of knowledge and skill. Just as a person can amass financial assets for future use, people can accumulate knowledge and skills to draw upon when making decisions and/or performing various tasks. While the former is called financial capital, the latter is referred to as human capital. Education is the business of enhancing human capital; financial education is the process of augmenting human capital specific to personal finance. Financial education programs are designed to enhance a person's knowledge and skills regarding personal finance. This particular stock of human capital specific to personal finance is described by the term financial literacy. Financial literacy has been defined as measuring how well an individual can understand and use personal finance-related information (Huston 2010). The primary goal of financial education is to increase financial literacy.

How do you know if students are benefiting from financial education? The answer requires an assessment of financial literacy. Ideally, a financial literacy assessment (FLA) would take place before and after the administration of a financial education program to gauge improvement in human capital specific to personal finance. While there are certainly a multitude of educational approaches available for enhancing financial literacy (some are discussed in other chapters of this book), the human capital improvement we are trying to measure is less variable in nature (see Fox et al. 2005; Lyons et al. 2006). Collecting data regarding FLA from multiple individuals can provide research opportunities within a financial education program; these will be discussed in a subsequent chapter of this book as well.

S.J. Huston, Ph.D. (✉)
Department of Personal Financial Planning, Texas Tech University,
15th Street & Akron, Room 262, Box 41210, Lubbock, TX 79409, USA
e-mail: sandra.huston@ttu.edu

D.B. Durband and S.L. Britt (eds.), *Student Financial Literacy:*
Campus-Based Program Development, DOI 10.1007/978-1-4614-3505-1_9,
© Springer Science+Business Media New York 2012

This chapter focuses on the usefulness of assessing financial literacy along with the various elements to be considered in the measure, including the context, concept, content, instrument creation, and implementation. The chapter is organized into five main sections:

1. Why assess financial literacy?
2. What to include in a financial literacy assessment?
3. How to develop a financial literacy assessment?
4. Existing measures of financial literacy
5. How to use a financial literacy assessment?

Why Assess Financial Literacy?

There are three main constituencies that can benefit from FLA within a financial education program: students, financial educators, and program administrators. FLA is a valuable tool for gauging program impact for these three audiences and provides opportunities for reporting outcomes, identifying needs, adjusting course materials, evaluating teaching methods, conducting research, and providing funding leverage.

Students invest resources (time and/or money) into education activities to enhance human capital stocks with the goals of increasing their productivity across all areas of their lives. Investing in financial education provides the opportunity to increase financial literacy to reduce the likelihood of making costly financial mistakes. Increased financial literacy may also be associated with increasing the likelihood of improved financial well-being. Providing students with feedback on their level of financial literacy can help them understand where they need improvement and how they compare to others. Delivering a financial education program would ideally include providing the student with an indication of their potential return on investing in this activity. Useful feedback provides both an absolute and relative indication of human capital quality. For example, if a student is assessed prior to and after taking a financial education class, he or she will be able to determine how much their own stock of human capital specific to personal finance has improved. Giving the student some context (either in relation to others or a standard threshold) will allow the student to evaluate his or her financial literacy level and to determine if additional enhancement is required.

Financial educators can use FLAs to evaluate certain educational materials and exercises, as well as the efficacy of different teaching methods. These assessments can be used by program administrators as part of a comprehensive program evaluation process to help identify specific educational needs, assist in evaluating educators and program offerings, provide collaboration opportunities for research, provide evidence to justify program creation or continuation, and support fund-raising activities.

What to Include in a Financial Literacy Assessment?

To answer this question, there are a number of elements that must be considered, including program goals and the three "C's," namely, assessment context, concept, and content. Before developing an assessment strategy, you must be very clear about identifying the specific nature of what you are trying to measure, what types of knowledge and skills are important to assess, and what topics should be included. Using program goals as a filter will help you be specific and thoughtful in addressing these issues.

First and foremost, the assessment goals must be clearly established. These will stem from the goals of your program. If you are providing a financial education program that includes all of the basic content areas of personal finance, then your assessment should also include these content areas. What if you offer a class that specifically focuses on credit management, for example? Should you design an assessment instrument that evaluates this specific content only? It depends. It depends on the goals of the program. If the goal of the financial education program is to increase financial literacy levels, a comprehensive FLA may be used or several instruments may be developed that, in combination, represent the knowledge and skill specific to personal finance. There are advantages and disadvantages to each approach.

Using one assessment tool is simple and cost-effective, allows you to determine the educational impact (assuming pre- and post-administration) in relation to all areas of personal finance, and provides consistency and comparability among all program offerings, educators, and students. On the other hand, using a universal comprehensive assessment instrument may not allow for in-depth analysis and may present some confusion for participants completing the assessment for interventions that focus on specific content (such as a credit management class). Developing several assessments also has advantages in terms of providing superior opportunities for more specific content and concept analyses as well as identification of program needs. However, several assessments do not allow for direct comparison, provide additional logistical challenges, and can be more costly in terms of administration and analysis. The type of assessment chosen will ideally support program evaluation.

Once you have aligned assessment objectives with program goals, assessment context, concept, and content need to be considered. Figure 9.1 provides an overview of the relation between financial education, financial literacy, personal finance behavior, and financial well-being. Financial education is designed to directly impact a person's human capital specifically related to personal finance and indirectly is hypothesized to affect financial behavior and well-being. When evaluating the impact of financial education, the more closely the assessment is linked to measuring change in human capital, the better. Assessments that focus on change in behavior and/or well-being are prone to measurement error from other influences that are either exogenous (e.g., family, friends, culture, religion) or endogenous (e.g., time preference, behavioral biases) (Hung et al. 2009).

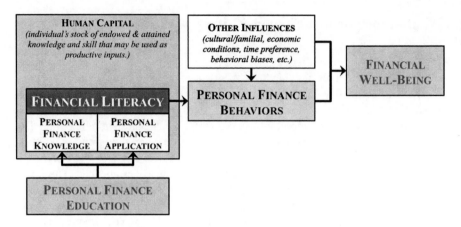

Fig. 9.1 The human capital context of financial literacy

An optimal FLA will include both knowledge and skill (application) components. Many equate financial knowledge with financial literacy. However, to get an accurate assessment of financial literacy, it is imperative to recognize and assess the financial skill, including the ability and confidence to apply financial knowledge, in addition to assessing one's level of financial knowledge.

While it is important to understand that financial literacy involves different types of human capital (specifically knowledge and skill), it is equally important to understand the breadth of personal finance content that is involved within the construct. If you are attempting to assess an overall measure of financial literacy, comprehensive content is required. According to Huston (2010), there are three main content areas within financial literacy: (a) personal finance fundamentals, (b) resource intertemporality, and (c) capital protection.

Personal finance fundamentals include the basic types of knowledge and skills that are required to understand and navigate the financial marketplace. This type of content includes the time value of money, purchasing power/inflation, the relation between life and financial goals, and the human-to-financial-capital tradeoff over the life cycle, personal financial statements and ratios, and tax basics.

Resource intertemporality refers to the transfer of financial resources between time periods and includes both borrowing and investing. Borrowing is when an individual brings future resources into the present to fund current consumption through the use of credit or loan products (e.g., credit cards, consumer loans, or mortgages). Content related to borrowing can include elements specific to borrowing products (e.g., loan/credit sources, APR, finance charges, loan terms, credit scores) as well as aspects related to the types of expenditures borrowing is most appropriate for (e.g., education, homes, vehicles). Investing is when an individual saves current financial resources to use for future consumption through the use of investment products (e.g., certificates of deposit, stocks, bonds, mutual funds).

Capital protection refers to preserving the value of capital assets through a risk management plan, including insurance (e.g., property, health, disability income, life). These capital assets can be financial (e.g., cash and investment assets), durable assets (e.g., vehicle, home), or human (i.e., the income-generating human capital assets an individual possesses). People can do many things to protect or enhance their human capital, for example, eat a balanced diet, exercise regularly, avoid risky behavior, invest in learning skills, or acquiring knowledge that is more valued in the labor market. Other examples of human capital protection include purchasing insurance to protect against disability (when you are unable to trade your human capital for labor income) or premature death (when you have dependents that rely on your human capital). Other methods of preserving wealth include tax planning (within the context of retirement and/or estate planning); protecting against identity theft, longevity risk, and long-term health-care costs; and establishing an emergency fund to provide a cushion in the event of the unexpected.

Financial literacy is essentially considered to be the basic human capital, including both knowledge and skill, related to personal finance that is required to competently navigate the financial marketplace and avoid costly financial mistakes. In a comprehensive sense, this personal finance content includes basic concepts, circumstances surrounding the transfer of resources between the present and future, and strategies that provide protection against loss of financial, durable goods, and human capital.

How to Develop a Financial Literacy Assessment?

Once you have aligned the objective of your assessment with the goals of your program and determined what specific human capital improvements you are intending to measure (both in terms of concept and content), you are ready to create the specific instrument you will use to assess financial literacy. There are several elements to consider when creating an instrument to measure financial literacy, including format, number and type of individual items, data collection and analysis method, and interpretation of results. To help illustrate these elements, an example of a FLA process follows, and then each element is discussed in general and in relation to the example provided.

The Financial Literacy Assessment Project: An Example

For illustration purposes, the *FLA* project at Texas Tech University will be used to provide an example of a FLA instrument development process. Between 2007 and 2010, a research team at Texas Tech University developed and tested an instrument designed to assess adult financial literacy levels as part of a telephone survey design. The project was divided into eight phases primarily based on Tuckman's (1965) stages. The team project development process is summarized in Table 9.1.

Table 9.1 Summary of the *Financial Literacy Assessment* project at Texas Tech University

Timeline	Stage	Activities
Summer/Fall 2007	Form	Forming ideas, building a team, and establishing a plan of action (POA)
		Form team (originally 4 faculty, 4 students) and objectives/ goals
		Consult existing literature (measures and concepts)
		Establish scope (originally 8 topic areas, CFP Board)
Spring 2008	Storm	Developing conceptual framework (CF) and scope
		Struggling with concepts and framework—paucity in prior literature
		Brainstorming—2 dimensions, 4 elements, over 9 topic areas in personal financial planning (PFP)—topics selected based on what was typical in personal finance textbooks, create scoring grid
		Web survey to test 89 potential items (2 months, $N=509$)
Summer 2008	Transform	Analyzing item data to create instrument to measure financial literacy
		Team transformation (4 faculty, 2 students), CF transformation (from 2 to 3 dimensions—i.e., incorporate sophistication)
		Refinement of scoring grid, match with instrument
		Pretest original instrument (1 month, $N=36$)
		Data collection using CATI at Earl Survey Research Lab on TTU campus
Fall 2008	Norm	Using pretest sample results to standardize and finalize instrument
		Survey in field for 2 months, $N=502$
		Data preparation
Spring 2009	Conform	Reviewing by internal (team) and external (expert panel) groups for critique and validation
		Data analysis, seek funder for subsequent revised survey
		Recruit and convene expert review panel for external review process
		Expert panel review (3 month process), $N=8$
Summer 2009	Reform	Making adjustments/improvements to instrument based on review
		Analyze review feedback—implement changes
		Secure funder, prepare revised instrument, and survey items
Fall 2009	Perform	Administering and monitoring data collection with revised instrument
		Survey in field for 3 months, $N=1,037$, collected using CATI at ESRL@TTU
Spring 2010	Inform	Analyzing results from revised survey, disseminate findings
		Publish and promote survey results
		Explore creation of web version to incorporate instrument and scoring grid results (for use with clients/students/research participants)
		Investigate national-level data collection opportunities

In the initial (first four) stages of development, a plan of action was devised, a working conceptual framework and content parameters were established, potential instrument items were tested, a survey was constructed and pretested, and data were collected and analyzed. During the first stage, a team was formed to establish the specific scope and objectives of the assessment. For this particular project, the goal was to develop a general instrument to measure financial literacy among an adult population. This required the measure to be comprehensive and include items that represented the breadth of personal finance human capital. During the second stage of development, the specific human capital dimensions to be measured were identified. In the original model, two dimensions were identified and revised during the later stages of the project. From an initial pool of 89 instrument items, 26 were selected for the original instrument during the third stage of development. A scoring grid was then devised to help interpret the data generated from administering the instrument items. In the fourth stage of development, the original survey was administered; data were collected and subsequently prepared for analysis.

The remaining stages of the development process were devoted to reliability and validity testing and instrument improvement. This included an extensive project review by internal team members as well as an external review process. In the fourth stage of development, data were analyzed, a panel of expert reviewers was identified, an evaluation packet was created, and during the fifth project phase, the project was sent out for external review as well as an internal evaluation of the project to date. The external review panel was comprised of eight members, including five experts in the area of FLA, as well as financial planning practitioners and personal finance educators. During the sixth stage, the research team analyzed the results from the review and made adjustments to the instrument. The final instrument, incorporating three conceptual dimensions and comprised of 20 items covering four content areas (basics, borrowing, building, and protection), was tested during the seventh phase of the project. During the final project phase, the results were analyzed, and the revised instrument was found to be valid and reliable.

The construct of financial literacy used in the revised, and final instrument is comprised of two main elements (knowledge and application) and four main content areas (basic personal finance concepts, borrowing, building, and protection of income and assets) (Huston 2010). Figure 9.2 presents the two main elements: knowledge (understanding attained through education and/or experience) and application (appropriate use of knowledge). Application is measured by the ability to objectively demonstrate appropriate use of knowledge and by the confidence to use one's knowledge. The convergence of knowledge and application form a third dimension (sophistication), which is also captured in the conceptual model, the assessment instrument, and the scoring grid developed to aid with instrument interpretation.

The FLA instrument reflects the conceptual model in that it contains 20 items covering the four content areas within the human capital dimensions of knowledge and application regarding personal finance. The instrument contains two knowledge questions, two ability questions, and one confidence question for each of the four personal finance content areas. Basic personal finance concepts include elements

Model of Financial Literacy

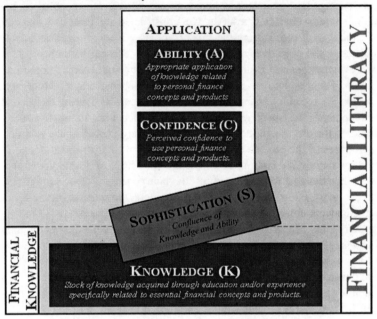

Fig. 9.2 Conceptual model of financial literacy

such as time value of money, purchasing power, and personal finance accounting. Intertemporal transfers of resources include both borrowing (bringing future resources into the present for consumption through the use of revolving credit and installment loans) and building assets (saving present resources for future consumption through the use of saving accounts, stocks, bonds, or mutual funds). Protecting resources (income generation, assets, or both) includes the use of insurance products, tax and estate planning, or other risk management techniques.

FLA items contribute to the financial literacy score as demonstrated in Fig. 9.3. Knowledge items contribute up to 40% (8 points), and ability items contribute up to 40% of the total score with 20% (4 points) from confidence items and 20% (4 points) from application items. The remaining 20% (4 points) of the score is calculated through concordance of the eight knowledge-application pairings, and the result represents financial sophistication. This dimension captures how well the knowledge and application of knowledge match up within each content area (i.e., 2 pairs per content area).

A financial literacy scoring grid (see Fig. 9.4) is constructed to help interpret the financial literacy score. The target zone (being financially competent) represents high scores on all of the dimensions: knowledge, ability, and sophistication. The danger zone represents either low scores on all of the dimensions (financial unawareness) or low scores on at least two of the three dimensions. Financial overconfidence represents those with high ability, but low knowledge and sophistication, while

| Personal Finance Area | KNOWLEDGE (K) | APPLICATION | | SOPHISTICATION (S) |
		Ability (A)	Confidence (C)	
BASICS (BA)	BA-K1 BA-K2	BA-A1 BA-A2	BA-C1	BA-S1 BA-S2
BORROW (BO)	BO-K3 BO-K4	BO-A3 BO-A4	BO-C2	BO-S3 BO-S4
BUILD (BU)	BU-K5 BU-K6	BU-A6 BU-A7	BU-C3	BU-S5 BU-S6
PROTECT (PR)	PR-K7 PR-K8	PR-A8 PR-K8	BR-C4	PR-S7 PR-S8
FINANCIAL LITERACY SCORE	40%	40%		20%

Fig. 9.3   Financial literacy assessment instrument

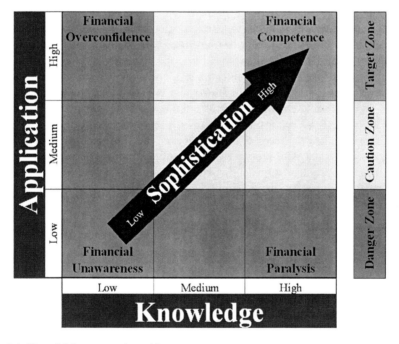

Fig. 9.4   Financial literacy scoring grid

financial paralysis occurs when individuals have high knowledge, but low ability and sophistication. The caution zone represents a variety of scores in between the target and danger zones.

The financial literacy scoring grid helps to interpret results from the raw scores generated from the FLA instrument. An individual, or financial educator, can readily assess where a potential lack of human capital may exist. A low score may be the result of either low stocks of all human capital elements (i.e., financial unawareness), low levels of knowledge (financial overconfidence), or low levels of skill (financial paralysis).

Creating Your Own Assessment Instrument: Considerations

The administration method and assessment format, length, item structure, and interpretation are important elements to be considered. Using program goals to influence the evaluation process will help determine the specific human capital dimensions and content of the FLA to be developed, as will identifying the target audience. It is optimal to include knowledge and skill within the assessment tool. As seen in the FLA project example, knowledge and the ability to apply knowledge can be ascertained using objective items, while a person's confidence in using knowledge is more subjective in nature. The target audience for the FLA project was the American adult population.

The administration method and assessment format are key components that influence many other assessment instrument considerations. First, you need to be establish whether the administration will be done in-person or remotely. If face-to-face, the format options for administration are a survey (completed on-site), an interview, or an observation. If the instrument will be administered remotely, the format choices are telephone survey or interview, a mail survey, or a computer-based survey. Off-site evaluation is more costly and has the risk of lower response rates, but may allow the assessor to have a better gauge of retained human capital. It may be consistent with program goals to use a combination of administration methods and instrument formats. For example, you may decide to administer the assessment instrument online as part of the registration process to obtain a baseline assessment and then administer it again after the intervention to evaluate program impact. In the FLA project example, a telephone survey using computer-assisted telephone interview (CATI) software was used to obtain baseline data.

The assessment tool comprises the length (number of items) and is another important element. The objective is to include enough items to assess the human capital components and content areas under consideration without making the instrument too long and taxing for the respondents. Huston (2010) has recommended that at least three to five items per content factor be included in the assessment instrument. To develop a comprehensive FLA, which includes the four main content areas, it would require an instrument ranging from 12 to 20 individual items. In the FLA project example, the instrument consisted of 20 items. The entire survey, which included the assessment plus an additional 20 demographic and behavioral items, took an average of 10 minutes to complete via telephone.

In terms of item structure, subjective information from respondents may be gleaned using summative scales, probing statements, or both. The subjective questions within the FLA project instrument were measured using Likert-type scale items ranging from 0 (no confidence) to 10 (a great deal of confidence). A qualitative method of collecting more subjective-type responses is to use open-ended questioning. While probing statements provide more opportunity for the respondent to elaborate, analyzing the responses across participants becomes more complex. The structure for objective items may be implemented using a range of options from bivariate (i.e., true or false) to an open-ended response design. True or false items present the least challenge, while the open-ended response arrangement presents the greatest burden of recall for the respondent. The objective questions within the FLA project used a middle-range multiple choice structure with three options, in addition to an "I don't know" alternative if the respondent was unable to provide a response. Including an "I don't know" response provides an additional method of assessing respondent confidence regarding knowledge level or ability to apply knowledge, depending on the specific nature of the question.

Another factor to consider when creating an assessment instrument is to establish how the results will be interpreted. Any data generated by administering the assessment requires some type of analysis. It is optimal to consider this as the assessment instrument is being developed. There are many options which are dependent upon the administration method and assessment structure and the specific types of items used. As an example, in the FLA project, a scoring grid was devised to aid with instrument interpretation. In addition to obtaining an overall total, scores for each of the concept dimensions were individually calculated and plotted on the grid to determine the specific nature of the respondent's financial literacy in comparison to his or her financial literacy level. A similar approach could be adopted to analyze content areas within the financial literacy rather than human capital dimensions modeled in Fig. 9.4. This type of interpretation approach allows for more in-depth analyses regarding particular concept and/or content deficiencies. Whatever interpretation method is devised, it is important to have a process in place to provide explanation of data collected. This determination has implications for how the FLA may be used.

Existing Measures of Financial Literacy

Before beginning the process of developing your own FLA or using the FLA described above, you may want to consider two other more well-known FLAs. Each assessment tool offers a unique perspective into financial literacy. It is the role of your financial education program staff members to determine which assessment is the preferred method of assessing financial literacy.

The Jump$tart Coalition's Personal Financial Survey

The Jump$tart Coalition for Personal Financial Literacy was formed in 1995, and in 1997 Lewis Mandell developed a Personal Financial Survey (Jump$tart Survey) that was administered to high school seniors in US public schools. To date, the Personal Financial Survey has been administered to high school seniors six times: in 1997, 2000, 2002, 2004, 2006, and 2008. In 2008, a version of the survey was administered to full-time college students for the first time.

The Jump$tart Survey consists of 49 questions, 31 items to measure financial literacy in addition to 18 classification questions that captures demographic and other descriptive information. The Personal Financial Literacy Survey is available at the Jump$tart coalition's web site (see http://www.jumpstart.org/survey.html). Detailed information about the survey is available in Dr. Mandell's (2009) book, *The Financial Literacy of Young American Adults*, which is available online at http://www.jumpstart.org/assets/files/2008SurveyBook.pdf.

Within the Personal Financial Literacy Survey, financial literacy is assessed through 31 multiple choice questions in the areas of income, money management, saving and investing, and spending and credit. The income category of the instrument consists of seven questions (23% of instrument items). Three questions highlight the importance of education, skill, and location in relation to income generation; one question tests the understanding of income sources, and the remaining three questions are devoted to taxes and income. The money management category consists of five items (16% of instrument items). Two questions are about financial goals and plans, and the remaining three questions focus on insurance. The savings and investment portion of the financial literacy instrument consists of eight items (26% of instrument items). One question is devoted to budgeting for savings, one question focuses on saving and investing strategy, two questions deal with the impact of taxes and inflation on saving and investment decisions, and the remaining four items test knowledge regarding risk, return, and liquidity. The final content category, spending and debt, contains the greatest proportion of instrument items (11, or 35% of all items). Spending now vs. later, consumer rights, and credit over-extension are each represented by one item. Credit history and transaction instruments are each represented by two questions, and the remaining four items focus on the cost of credit.

In 2005, Lucey found that while the surveys had some degree of overall reliability, there was less support for validity in terms of construct, congruency, and prediction. Although this instrument has been widely used among the high school population, it is has not been clearly established that this 31-item instrument provides a valid measure of financial literacy. The Jump$tart instrument is not based on any systematic conceptualization of financial literacy, is focused on knowledge only, and appears to lack validity in terms of capturing the human capital specific to personal finance.

American Life Panel and Financial Literacy Assessment

The American Life Panel (ALP) is an Internet panel of adult respondents (aged 18 and over). Each month, approximately 500 households are surveyed, 300 using a

Fig. 9.5 Hung et al.'s (2009) conceptual model of financial literacy

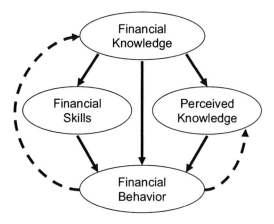

random-digit-dial (RDD) sample, and 200 are re-interviewed from the RDD sample surveyed from 6 months prior. Between 2006 and 2009, ALP administered four different survey waves (by different researchers) designed to assess financial literacy. Waves 5, 12, and 64 are more knowledge oriented, while Wave 11 is more action oriented.

In their paper *Defining and Measuring Financial Literacy*, Hung et al. (2009) provide a conceptual model of financial literacy (see Fig. 9.5).

Wave 5 (*N* = 1,151) incorporated a 13-item instrument designed by Annamaria Lusardi and Olivia Mitchell. The wave 5 instrument contains five basic personal finance questions along with eight more advanced investment items. The Wave 12 financial literacy module was designed by Miles Kimball and Robert Willis and consists of 70 Likert-style, 12-point items to determine confidence in financial knowledge pertaining to portfolio diversification, time value of money, annuities, and financial institutions. Waves 64 and 11 were developed by Angela Hung, Andrew Parker, and Joanne Yoong. Wave 64 consists of 23 items and incorporates three dimensions of financial literacy—basic (using the five questions from wave 5), investing (using the eight wave 5 question plus six additional items on financial investment products and markets), and life insurance (using four items on life insurance and annuity products). The financial knowledge waves (5, 12, and 64) assess financial literacy by calculating a percentage score. Wave 11 uses an investment experiment approach involving portfolio fund allocation, where financial literacy was equated with choosing a portfolio with the lowest fee funds.

Hung et al. (2009) determine that these four measures hold up in terms of reliability and appear to be consistent, suggesting they are measuring a similar underlying concept. Some indirect evidence such as correlation with behavioral outcome and related demographics (such as education) is provided to address construct validity; however, no direct measures (such as expert consensus) were used for verification.

Comparison to the Instrument Developed by the Financial Literacy Assessment Project

The FLA instrument developed by the Financial Literacy Assessment Project team at Texas Tech University has similarities and differences in comparison to both the Jump$tart Personal Financial Survey and the four financial literacy waves within the ALP.

All surveys discussed were targeted to an American audience. The Jump$tart instrument was originally designed for high school seniors (and more recently applied to full-time college students), while all of the ALP waves were administered to an adult population, aged 18 and older. The FLA instrument was specifically designed to be administered to an adult (18 and over) audience.

The Jump$tart instrument does not appear to be based on a systematic conceptualization of financial literacy, and all items are focused on assessing financial knowledge. The designers of Wave 64 within the ALP survey do provide a conceptual framework that differentiates financial knowledge from application (skill and confidence or perceived knowledge)—similar to the FLA instrument—but also incorporates financial behavior (unlike the FLA instrument). However, the majority of the ALP financial literacy waves focus primarily on measuring knowledge (with the exception of Wave 11, which measures application of knowledge). The FLA 20-item instrument includes items designed to measure knowledge (8 items) and application through the ability to apply knowledge (8 items) and confidence to apply knowledge (4 items). In addition, the FLA instrument attempts to gain objective insight into financial sophistication by assessing how well a respondent's knowledge corresponds to their application of that knowledge.

In terms of content, all of the instruments have identified some degree of content differentiation. ALP Wave 64 identifies three content dimensions (basic, investing, and life insurance), with the majority of questions devoted to investing (61%, i.e., 14 out of 23 items). The Jump$tart survey has four content categories (income, money management, saving and investing, and spending and debt). While the Jump$tart survey has the greatest proportion of questions devoted to spending and debt (35%), none of the four waves within the ALP include the borrowing aspect of personal finance. The FLA instrument identifies four content areas (basic, borrowing, building, and protection) and devotes equal weighting among the four content areas (i.e., 25%, or 5 questions for each content area).

With regard to scoring, all of the knowledge-based surveys (Jump$tart, ALP waves 5, 12, and 64) determine financial literacy through the calculation of a percentage score (either total or domain specific), with a higher score indicating greater financial literacy. In the FLA instrument, a specific scoring system was devised to ensure that a respondent has an adequate score across all construct dimensions (i.e., knowledge and application) to be considered financially literate. Differentiation by construct dimension as well as content categorization provides increased opportunity to analyze financial literacy deficits and devise appropriate intervention strategies.

All of the surveys are able to provide evidence to suggest at least a sufficient degree of reliability. However, instrument validation is not as apparent, especially for the Jump$tart instrument. Although the ALP Wave 64 instrument provides some indirect evidence of validity in terms of construct content (even though an arguably important content area, borrowing, is absent), the FLA instrument is the only one that has documented an external review process for validation by consensus among a panel of experts.

How to Use a Financial Literacy Assessment?

As suggested by Lyons et al. (2006), program evaluation (which includes FLA) should not be an afterthought and requires purposeful and strategic planning. Careful consideration and development of the FLA tool can assist in program evaluation and documentation of impact. Data collection is costly, both in terms of time and money, so you want to make certain that it is done in an appropriate and helpful way and that there is a defined plan for using the data to garner the greatest benefits possible.

It is important to ensure that the FLA tool used is in close alignment with the human capital components the financial education program is designed to influence. Assessment tools that include behavioral and/or well-being measures are further removed from capturing the effects of education compared to instruments that incorporate human capital—knowledge and skill—elements. It may be desirable to collect behavioral indicators as part of the larger program evaluation process, but relying on such indicators to demonstrate education impact is not recommended.

Equally important to developing an appropriate assessment tool is advanced planning regarding the interpretation of collected data. Ideally, the outcome from this advanced planning will provide practical and useable feedback that will benefit both financial educators and program administrators. High-quality assessment data can provide numerous advantages for both constituent groups.

Financial educators can use assessment results to evaluate student progress. It is optimal to collect pre- and post-intervention assessments to adequately gauge students' human capital production. Feedback can be directly provided to the students in both absolute and relative terms. For example, suppose a student begins a financial education class with a low level of financial literacy (as evidenced by a pre-intervention assessment) and after the class is assessed at a higher level of financial literacy, but still does not meet the threshold to be considered financially literate. We have determined in an absolute sense that the financial education class appears to have aided the student in developing increased human capital related to personal finance; however, in a relative sense, this student needs to continue producing personal finance human capital in order to be considered financially literate.

Financial educators can also use assessment data as a diagnostic tool to indentify and pinpoint individual student problem areas (either human capital dimensions or personal finance content areas) that require further enhancement. Pre-intervention assessment results can alert a financial educator to specific student and/or group needs, and post-intervention assessment results can be helpful in evaluating particular teaching methods or curriculum content. As data are collected and analyzed over time, results can be used to create and share best practices with colleagues and administrators.

In terms of growing or modifying specific courses within a program, potential areas for curriculum adjustments or new course needs can be identified by aggregating assessment results from groups of students representing the target population. Program administrators can use assessment data to evaluate and identify areas for current course improvements—including insight into teaching and curriculum effectiveness within and among various courses within the program.

Program administrators can use assessment data as a component of demonstrating overall program impact, especially when the pre- and post-intervention assessment protocol is adopted. The ability to demonstrate program impact is becoming increasingly important in providing justification for program existence, especially within organizations and institutions with stressed or shrinking budgets. Programs that can unambiguously demonstrate impact and value have superior leverage opportunities with regard to awards from grants and contract providers.

Finally, some funding agencies provide opportunities for combination program and research grants (e.g., FINRA Investor Education Foundation and the National Endowment for Financial Education [NEFE]). To fully use data collected, program administrators can team up with financial literacy and/or financial education researchers to apply for these grants that will contribute to research and provide a valuable avenue for securing program funding.

References

Fox, J., Bartholomae, S., & Lee, J. (2005). Building the case for financial education. *Journal of Consumer Affairs, 39*(Summer), 195–214.

Hung, A. A., Parker, A. M., & Yoong, J. K. (2009). *Defining and measuring financial literacy* (RAND Working Paper Series WR-708). Retrieved April 1, 2011, from http://ssrn.com/abstract=1498674.

Huston, S. J. (2010). Measuring financial literacy. *Journal of Consumer Affairs, 44*(Summer), 296–316.

Lucey, T. (2005). Assessing the reliability and validity of the Jump$tart survey of financial literacy. *Journal of Family and Economic Issues, 26*(2), 283–294.

Lyons, A. C., Palmer, L., Jayaratne, K. S. U., & Scherpf, E. (2006). Are we making the grade? A national overview of financial education and program evaluation. *Journal of Consumer Affairs, 40*(2), 208–235.

Mandell, L. (2009). *The financial literacy of young American adults: Results of the 2008 National Jump$tart Coalition Survey of high school seniors and college students.* Washington, DC: Jumpstart Coalition, Retrieved April 1, 2011, from http://www.jumpstart.org/assets/files/2008SurveyBook.pdf.

Tuckman, B. W. (1965). Developmental sequence in small groups. *Psychological Bulletin, 63*(6), 384–399.

Chapter 10
Financial Education Research Opportunities

So-hyun Joo and Swarn Chatterjee

Introduction

The rising debt levels across college campuses (Norvilitis et al. 2003) provide an opportunity and need for greater research of financial management practices and credit behavior of college students. More research is necessary to inform college administrators, parents, and public policy makers about the various determinants of financial management practices and debt management behavior of college students as well as to provide information on the various ways in which financial literacy and education can play a role in mitigating the problem of increasing debt levels in the college student community. Interestingly, one study noted that while a significant portion of college students were found to be charging tuition fees to their credit cards (The Educational Resources Institute [TERI] 1998), another study found that the students with credit card debt largely underestimated the length of time it would take to pay off the debt in its entirety (Somers and Cofer 1997). Clearly, it is problematic if students are heavily relying on credit cards for college expenses without a plan to pay off their debt. This problem is further complicated by the fact that students also tend to overestimate their income-earning potential and their ability to pay off outstanding debt upon graduation (Eskilson and Wiley 1999). Previous studies suggest that this problem can be solved by increasing financial literacy and by developing financial management skills among college students and others (Lusardi 2008; Norvilitis and Santa Maria 2002). Nevertheless, further research is necessary for developing an efficient and effective model of delivery for financial education

S. Joo, Ph.D. (✉)
Department of Consumer Studies, Ewha Womans University, 11-1 Daehyun-Dong,
Seodaemun-Gu, Seoul 120-750, South Korea
e-mail: sohyunjoo@ewha.ac.kr

S. Chatterjee, Ph.D.
Department of Housing and Consumer Economics, The University of Georgia,
205 Dawson Hall, Athens, GA 30602, USA
e-mail: swarn@uga.edu

D.B. Durband and S.L. Britt (eds.), *Student Financial Literacy:
Campus-Based Program Development*, DOI 10.1007/978-1-4614-3505-1_10,
© Springer Science+Business Media New York 2012

and for designing financial education programs that can be used for improving financial management behavior of college students.

Among the more common formats for campus financial education programs are peer financial planning and counseling programs, informational handouts, video and audio presentations, presentation material and instructor's manuals, student workbooks, and games and role-playing activities. However, there has been very little research done to evaluate the outcomes of different programming efforts. There is research, though limited, on high school financial education programs that shows that students who participate in the program have an increase in their savings over a 3-month period (Boyce and Danes 1998). The current situation on college campuses calls for a broader array of similar research activities at 2- and 4-year colleges that can inform the interested stakeholder regarding whether and which type of campus financial education programs can reduce the mismanagement of revolving credit by college students and help in improving their financial management practices. According to Danes et al. (1999), the usefulness of evaluation within an educational program can be summarized with three key aspects: (1) evaluation is useful to judge the merit or worth of a program, (2) it is useful to improve a program, and (3) it is useful to generate knowledge about what is needed. In this regard, conducting research with financial education program in colleges and universities will produce various potential outcomes.

In this chapter, we summarize the findings of previous research carried out in the areas of financial literacy, student financial practices, and credit behavior, and we discuss the practical implications of the research. We also discuss the opportunities for future research for financial education programs.

Financial Literacy Research

The Meaning of Financial Literacy

Financial literacy has been defined as a comprehensive term, which includes knowledge, skills, and resources (Mason and Wilson 2000). Probably one of the most comprehensive definitions of financial literacy is the one from Vitt et al. (2000). They defined financial literacy as:

> The ability to read, analyze, manage, and communicate about the personal financial conditions that affect material well-being. It includes the ability to discern financial choices, discuss money and financial issues without (or despite) discomfort, plan for the future, and respond competently to life events that affect every day financial decisions, including events in the general economy. (p. xii)

As illustrated in the above definition, financial literacy does not simply mean the ability to comprehend personal financial terms and issues. It includes the ability to analyze, manage, and communicate to make everyday personal financial decisions. Consider the definition of financial literacy by Mason and Wilson (2000) who defined financial literacy as a "meaning-making process" in which individuals use their knowledge, skills, and resources to make sound financial decisions that produce optimal outcomes. Later, Cude et al. (2006) reported that one common theme of financial literacy definitions was the behavioral component. For example, Cude and her associates cited Hogarth's (2002) definition of financial literacy to show the significance of behavioral components of financial literacy. According to Hogarth (2002), financially literate individuals are knowledgeable and understand financial terms and can use the knowledge and understanding to display desirable financial practices. To address the behavioral components, Johnson and Sherraden (2007) suggested an alternative concept for financial literacy—financial capability. They argued that "individuals need to develop financial knowledge and skills but also gain access to financial policies, instruments, and services." Specifically, Johnson and Sherraden addressed the significance of "financial experiences" in financial literacy concepts. Lusardi (2008) distinguished these as basic financial numeracy and advanced financial literacy. The basic financial numeracy is the level of understanding basic financial math, such as interest rates and inflation (cognitive knowledge) while advanced financial literacy includes decision-making choices in the financial marketplace, such as risk diversification between company stock and mutual funds (behavioral aspects).

Financial literacy is a key determinant of financial well-being for consumers (Joo 2008). As Alan Greenspan, the former chairperson of the US Federal Reserve Board, argued at the turn of the millennium, obtaining and mastering basic financial skills is the "primary means for creating new economic and financial opportunity for everyone" (Greenspan 2003). However, various reports show that financial literacy levels for the general public are low. Lusardi (2006) summarized survey results for adolescents, adults, workers, and older respondents, and nearly all of the surveys showed undesirable and somewhat disappointing results. Many people living in the United States do not have a working knowledge of interest rates, prices of bonds, or risk characteristics of investment instruments, such as mutual funds and stocks. For the average college student body, the level of financial literacy is not adequate. The 1998 survey by Chen and Volpe showed an average college student financial literacy score of 53%, a survey with African American college students reported financial literacy scores of 30% on average (Murphy 2005), and a recent Jump$tart survey of college students' financial literacy reported an average score of 62% (Mandell 2008).

Those who develop college financial education programs should be equipped with a clear understanding of financial literacy concepts. As shown in the previous literature review, the behavioral aspects of financial literacy are very significant; therefore, when developing financial education programs for college students, program coordinators should carefully consider including features that improve students' problem-solving and decision-making abilities in real-world financial situations.

Measuring Financial Literacy

Due to behavioral aspects of the financial literacy concept, measuring financial literacy is not an easy task. Much of the research to date has used combinations of questions measuring (a) levels of understanding of fundamental concepts such as interest rates and basic financial numeracy and (b) degrees of informed decision making with real-life financial planning choices, such as cash management, credit management, and retirement planning.

Financial literacy measurement often uses multiple choice (often including true or false) questions in the subject areas of cash management, credit management, retirement planning, investment, insurance, and general economic understanding. One of the specific financial literacy measurements is worth noting in this section. The Jump$tart Coalition for Personal Financial Literacy started a financial literacy survey for US students in 1997 and has conducted biennial surveys between 2000 and 2008. The Jump$tart financial literacy questions were developed by Dr. Lewis Mandell and include 31 multiple choice financial literacy questions covering the topics of income, money management, saving and investing, and spending and credit. According to the Jump$tart Coalition, the financial literacy questions were developed as age- and life-cycle-appropriate *case studies* to make them relevant to the students (Jump$tart n.d.). As such, the Jump$tart questionnaire tried to measure functional decision-making aspects of financial literacy. Other measurements exist and are discussed in Chap. 9.

Financial Literacy and Related Factors

There are a number of factors associated with the way in which individuals, particularly college students, obtain, learn, and retain knowledge that have an impact on financial literacy. Research on topics specifically and generally related to financial literacy and knowledge has identified demographic and socioeconomic factors, psychographic and attitudinal factors, and background and situational factors that have an influence on the level of financial literacy exhibited by individuals.

Demographic and Socioeconomic Factors

Lyons et al. (2007) used two different regressions (ordinary least squares [OLS] and quantile) to identify specific subgroups and their characteristics in regard to financial literacy to provide implications for targeted financial education for the general public. From their OLS regression, they found that those who had lower levels of education and income, those who were older, or those who identified Hispanic were less knowledgeable than others from a general public sample. From their quantile regression analyses, they were able to find the different effects of each demographic characteristic on financial literacy (in this case, a credit knowledge score) levels. For example, Lyons and her associates found that the effects of education are more salient for those who had lower credit knowledge scores. Edmiston and Gillett-Fisher (2006) and Kotlikoff and Bernheim (2001) also found education and income to be positively related with financial knowledge.

Regarding gender difference in financial literacy and knowledge of young men and women, Chen and Volpe (1998) reported that male students had higher levels of financial literacy than female students from their multi-university survey of more than 900 students in various states in the USA. Later, in 2002, Chen and Volpe tried to explain the possible reasons of gender differences in financial literacy by examining individual students' interests in personal financial issues and sources of education. They premised that education and experiences can have a significant impact on the financial literacy of college students, and they investigated students' experiences and interests in knowledge attainment in various subject areas during their college education. According to Chen and Volpe, female college students generally have lower levels of willingness to learn about personal financial topics than male college students. For example, more male students believed that personal finance is important and ranked personal finance as an important subject than did female students. In addition, the male students had higher levels of perceived financial knowledge than female students.

There is a large amount of literature on gender differences between the ways men and women handle personal finances. For instance, Edwards et al. (2007) reported gender differences in financial communication; specifically, female college students were more open with their parents about financial matters than their male counterparts. When considering the finding that females are generally less risk tolerant than males (Harris et al. 2006) and have lower lifetime earnings than males, the gender gap in financial literacy should be examined and evaluated more closely.

College campus financial education programs may need to include gender-specific content. For example, programs for female students may need additional curricula for improving cognitive financial understanding, such as financial numeracy and financial math, and programs for male students may need a focus on for financial communication.

Psychographic and Attitudinal Factors

Research on personality traits and financial literacy and behavior typically employs one of two methodologies. Some researchers have used personality traits as independent variables, whereas others have attempted to explain personality traits with financial variables (e.g., financial literacy, beliefs, satisfaction, and behaviors). Grable and Joo (2001) replicated an earlier study by Hira and Mugenda (1999) and found a significant relationship between and among financial beliefs, financial satisfaction, behavior, and self-worth (i.e., self-esteem) by reporting positive associations between financial satisfaction, self-esteem, and financial attitudes. Those who had positive and desirable attitudes toward themselves were more satisfied with their financial situations, and positive attitudes toward personal finances tended to improve the levels of financial satisfaction. Therefore, financial education programs should include evaluations of financial attitudes of students and should work toward promoting positive and desirable self and personal finance attitude formation.

Roberts and Jones (2001) examined college students' compulsive buying behaviors, money attitudes, and credit card usage. One of the key findings from their study was that attitudes toward money, especially in the power and prestige domains, were a driving force of compulsive buying. Those who considered money as a symbol of power and prestige tended to exhibit their comparative social power with what they purchased.

Perry and Morris (2005) found that general financial management behaviors, such as budgeting, saving, and controlling spending, can be influenced by a person's level of personal control (i.e., locus of control), financial knowledge, and income. One noteworthy finding from the Perry and Morris study was the identification of both direct and indirect impacts of perception of personal control on financial behavior. They noted that locus of control influences financial behavior not only directly but also indirectly by mediating financial knowledge. Perry and Morris said that:

> Individuals may not take full advantage of their knowledge or financial resources unless they feel that they control their own financial destiny. Although knowledge and income are important, those who believe that financial outcomes are due to luck or chance, i.e., externals, will be less likely to take steps to manage their finances. (p. 301)

This important finding suggests that personality traits and attitudes likely interact with financial knowledge. The direction and strength of the interaction could be either positive or negative in relation to financial behavior. If accurate, a finding that suggests an interaction between personality traits and financial knowledge (i.e., financial literacy) may lead toward promoting desirable financial behaviors.

Finally, Norvilitis et al. (2006) examined and tested associations between and among various personality traits (e.g., materialism, compulsive buying, sensation seeking) and problematic financial behaviors such as consumer debt. They argued that the associations between certain personality traits and consumer debt are unclear. Their research attempts were unsuccessful in finding significant effects of personality traits (e.g., sensation seeking, materialism, attitudes toward debt) on college students' credit card debt.

Background and Situational Factors

Especially for college students, background characteristics such as parents' financial literacy, interaction with parents, and socialization factors can influence financial literacy. In a study of nearly 2,000 college students from Louisiana and Georgia, Cude et al. (2006) noted the significance of family members in shaping college students' financial literacy. College students selected parents as one of the most significant financial information sources, and those students who had parents who were married showed higher levels of financial literacy. Cude et al. also reported that college students mentioned that they receive various financial messages from their parents and tried to meet their parents' expectations in terms of good financial practices; however, inconsistent behaviors of students' parents (e.g., parents told them to be financially responsible but covered their bad financial behaviors) negatively influenced students' financial literacy.

Research shows that students from states with mandated financial literacy programs have higher levels of financial literacy (Gutter and Copur 2011; Tennyson and Nguyen 2001). The impact of the financial education on financial literacy has been widely reported. For example, Danes et al. (1999) showed that a carefully developed financial education program by the National Endowment for Financial Education (NEFE) had significant positive influence on financial literacy. In their study with mandated financial literacy programs on high school students' financial literacy, Tennyson and Nguyen found that the effectiveness of mandated education is statistically significant for programs that require teaching of personal financial concepts within specific courses only. The simple requirement of having a financial-planning curriculum did not influence students' financial literacy, but specific requirements that guarantee students receive specialized financial education positively influenced financial literacy for high school students. Gutter also found a significant impact of mandated education on students' financial knowledge and behavior. He surveyed more than 15,000 college students in 2008 and explored the impact of high school financial education policy in different states in the USA. Gutter's research showed that education had a clear impact on improving students' financial literacy. Similar results were also noted for the general public. For example, Bernheim et al. (2001) reported evidence of the long-term effects of high school financial education on wealth in later life.

Student Financial Practice Research

Money Management Practices and Related Factors

Henry et al. (2001) found that more than half of the college students in their study did not practice budgeting. Joo et al. (2003) found that approximately half of college students paid off their credit card bills in full while the remainder revolved their balances. Joo et al. further found that approximately 40% of the students in their study did not know the interest rates charged on their credit cards.

Mandell (1998) found that students who had an affluent upbringing appeared to be more sheltered by their parents from the financial realities of life and had lower financial knowledge than those who came from lower-income families. Conversely, Tennyson and Nguyen (2001) found that students coming from more prosperous families had significantly greater socialization with respect to information on savings and investments, and were more likely to have higher financial literacy scores. It is also not clear whether the choice of a major in college has an effect on the financial literacy of college students. Whereas Chen and Volpe (1998, 2002) found that business majors had significantly more financial knowledge than nonbusiness majors, Joo et al. (2003) showed that a college major was not a significant factor in the credit card attitudes of students. Similarly, studies by Norvilitis and Santa Maria (2002) and Murphy (2005) did not show a college major to be a significant predictor of financial literacy or credit behavior among college students.

Many of the previous studies have found that women scored lower in measures of financial knowledge than men (Chen and Volpe 1998; Jones 2005; Lusardi and Mitchell 2006; Borden et al. 2008). Hogarth and Hilgert (2002) found that when compared with other age groups, the 18–24 age group had significantly lower financial knowledge than the other groups. In Joo et al. (2003), no significant gender difference was found in the attitude toward credit among college students. Bell et al. (2001) did not indicate any significant gender difference in the perception of debt and borrowing. Therefore, there is no clear consensus as yet with regards to whether there exists gender differences in the credit attitudes of individuals.

Credit Behavior Research

Credit Behavior in General

The rising debt burdens of college students continue to be an issue of concern across college campuses. The trend of rapidly rising costs of attending college along with declining financial aid packages have forced many college students to finance their education by taking out expensive loans at higher interest rates (College Board 2010; Lyons 2008). One example of this higher interest borrowing is credit card debt. Recent studies on the use of credit cards to pay for college costs show that approximately a quarter of the students charge their tuition to a credit card, and nearly 70% use credit cards to pay for other school-related expenses (Nellie Mae 2005). Additionally, Lyons (2008) found that approximately half of the students who receive financial aid also resort to credit cards to pay for expenses that are not covered with financial aid. A Nellie Mae (2002) study found that the likelihood of having a credit card and the risk of carrying a credit card balance increased with the students' grade level in college. Approximately half of the freshmen students had one or more credit cards, and the percentage of students with credit cards increased to 96% for seniors. Previous studies have shown that most students use their credit cards responsibly (Joo et al. 2003; Lawrence et al. 2003; Lyons 2004, 2008; Nellie Mae 2005). Lyons (2008) found that students who were financially independent of their parents had higher student loans and had other types of borrowing, such as mortgage, personal, and car loans, and were more likely to have higher credit card balances. Similarly, Draut and Silva (2004) found that students coming from lower-income families were more likely to have a credit card debt of $7,000 or more than students coming from higher-income families. Further, Lyons (2008) found that students who carried more credit card debt were more likely to have obtained their first credit card either prior to or in their first year of attending college. Interestingly, under the newly passed Credit Card Accountability, Responsibility, and Disclosure (CARD) Act of 2009, students under 21 will either need a cosigner or will have to provide evidence of their ability to repay debt in order to open a credit card account (S. 414, 2009). There will be a research need in the near future to study the effectiveness of this policy in mitigating the credit card debt of college students.

Studies by Adams and Moore (2007) and Nelson et al. (2008) have found that risky credit card behavior, such as carrying credit card balances of $1,000 or more, was associated with other injurious practices such as substance abuse, unhealthy dietary practices, unsafe sex, and aggressive driving. Previous studies of college students have found that carrying higher levels of credit card debt was also associated with compulsive buying behavior (Roberts and Tanner 2000), poorer academic achievement (Lyons 2008; Pinto et al. 2001), financial stress (Grable and Joo 2006), and suicide (Manning 2000; Norvilitis and Santa Maria 2002; Oleson 2001). According to Lyons (2008), the risky credit card behavior among college students included reaching the cards' credit limits and nonpayment of full credit card balances. The study suggests that students with lower-grade-point averages and minority students were more vulnerable to engage in risky credit card behavior. Lawrence et al. (2003) did not show race and ethnicity to be significant predictors of higher credit card debt among college students. Conversely, responsible credit behavior has been found to be positively associated with academic success, better physical health, and mental health (Shim et al. 2009; Xiao et al. 2009).

Gender and Credit Card Use

Many of the previous studies have found differences in the credit card behavior of male and female college students (Jamba-Joyner et al. 2000; Micomonaco 2003; Lawrence et al. 2003). However, there have been other studies in the past that have not found any significant gender difference in the borrowing decisions of students (Bell et al. 2001). Extant research has, however, shown that females are more likely to carry balances for longer time periods than males (Jamba-Joyner et al. 2000). Previous studies have also found that female students were more likely to have a credit card than their male counterparts (Lawrence et al. 2003). Other studies have found that female students carried more credit cards and had higher levels of school and credit card debt than male students (Micomonaco 2003).

Spending Habits and Credit Card Use

Hayhoe et al. (2000) found that college students who liked shopping with a credit card were more likely to borrow on their cards. They also found that there were significant gender differences in both the credit behavior and financial management practices of college students. The authors found that while the female students used their credit cards to spend on clothing, the male students used their credit cards to spend on eating at restaurants, electronics, and entertainment. Another interesting finding of this study was that the female students were more likely to practice budgeting, balance their checkbooks, plan their spending, and save regularly. Other studies have found that female students carried more credit cards and had higher levels of school and credit card debt than male students (Micomonaco 2003). The Micomonaco study also found that female students were more likely to access credit card cash advances than male college students. In a recent study on the spending habits of college students, Norum (2008) found that compulsive spending behaviors of students were positively associated with credit card usage. Adams and Moore (2007) found that excessive credit card usage among students is positively associated with risky health behavior, and the authors proposed further research on the implementation of intermediation strategies in line with those that have been used to reduce risky health behaviors among college students. Palmer et al. (2001) showed in their study that those students whose parents are involved in their credit borrowing decisions are less likely to carry credit card balances than students with no parental involvement.

Money Attitudes and Credit Behavior

A scale for the measurement of money attitudes was developed by Hayhoe et al. (1999). The scale measured money attitudes based on the responses to questions about behavior, knowledge, and feelings associated with credit cards and revolving debt. The Hayhoe et al. study found that there was a significant difference in the money attitude scores of students who had credit cards and those who did not. They also found that there was a significant difference in the money attitudes of students with three credit cards or less and students with four or more credit cards. In other previous studies related to money attitudes and credit card behavior of college students, the authors have found that affective credit attitude scores related to happiness drawn from carrying a credit card have been linked to higher outstanding credit card debt among college students (Hayhoe et al. 2000). Similarly, Joo et al. (2003) found that there was a positive correlation between credit card ownership, card use, and credit attitude. Chien and DeVaney (2001) found a positive association between attitudes towards credit and the likelihood of carrying a credit card balance. Yang et al. (2005) examined credit card attitudes among college students in the UK and the USA and concluded that affective and behavioral attitude scores were strongly associated with the number of credit cards owned by college students. Interestingly, in a study based on a survey of college students, Robb and Sharpe (2009) found that higher levels of financial knowledge were positively associated with the carrying of credit card balances among college students.

Future Research Opportunities

This chapter provided an overview of the previous research related to campus financial education programs. It specifically focused on the need for financial literacy research within the college student community and for research on the financial management practices and credit behavior of college students. There is a need for more in-depth and comprehensive research related to the financial literacy and credit behavior of college students. One such example is examining the relationship between financial literacy and its consequences. For the adult population, financial literacy has been reported to influence retirement planning (Lusardi and Beeler 2007; Lusardi and Mitchell 2007), debt problems (Lusardi and Tufano 2009; Stango and Zinman 2007), stock market participation (Van Rooij et al. 2007), and overall financial well-being (Joo 2008). Research identifying possible outcomes of financial literacy or illiteracy of college students will produce practical guidelines for curriculum development. There have been hypothetical assumptions of the possible relationship between financial literacy and academic performances in college students, and this can be one of the research topics to be studied by financial education programs in colleges and universities.

In terms of financial management and credit behaviors, one of the weaknesses of previous research stems from the data-gathering methods used. Most of the previous research used survey methods to gauge college students' financial management and credit behaviors in order to identify related factors of such behaviors. As such, psychological factors and background reasons of college students' financial management and credit behaviors have been identified superficially. In-depth interviews or focus groups may be useful to examine the psychological reasoning of certain financial behaviors of college students.

To determine the effectiveness and efficacy of financial educational programs, measuring the effects of the educational program with sound methodological research design is necessary. For example, longitudinal panel data could be gathered to assess the long-term effects of financial education. An experimental study could be utilized to identify possible outcomes of the educational program. In addition, programs of various forms (e.g., in-class lecture, one-on-one counseling, presentations, and utilizing instant reaction devices such as smart phones) of financial education could be compared in terms of their impact on financial literacy.

With the rapid changes in society in terms of sciences and technology, research reflecting these technological advances is necessary. One of the most desired forms of financial information sources for college students is multimedia (Cude et al. 2006). According to Cude et al., college students prefer immediate feedback on their personal financial issues, and they are very interested in receiving information from the university. Universities need to provide information through the most widely used information outlets by college students. Smart phones and social network systems and other forms of new media are more and more common, and research is required to examine the various outcomes (positive or negative) of such outlets in terms of improving financial literacy and desirable financial behaviors. Research endeavors in connecting financial literacy with other more concrete and functional terms such as financial capability and financial wellness are also recommended. With a clear concept of proposed outcomes, such as financial capability and financial wellness, it will be much easier to evaluate the effectiveness of financial education programs in colleges and universities.

Providing financial education program brings automatic and instant opportunities for various researchers in financial planning topics. Well-designed research agendas with clear objectives will produce beneficial outcomes for university personnel, student leaders, and research scholars who are interested in developing or improving campus-based financial education programs. Program directors without formal research training may need to collaborate with financial planning or consumer-economics-based academic programs to work on research initiatives. Working with graduate students who are required to write research papers could provide opportunities to develop research agenda.

In addition to the existing and emerging research opportunities discussed in this chapter, other possibilities that new program directors of campus-based financial education programs can pursue include collaboration with institutions that engage in research and conduct surveys on experiences of college students. The Higher Education Research Institute (HERI), which is based at UCLA, is an example of an institution that provides such opportunities. HERI is home to the Cooperative Institutional Research Program (CIRP), which conducts surveys on the experiences of freshman, first-year, and senior-year college students. In the recent past, researchers from some campus-based financial education programs have collaborated with HERI to conduct surveys on financial experiences of senior-year college students (College Student Survey Highlight Report 2003). More recently, another survey on the financial debt of college students was included in the 2008 version of the College Senior Survey (Liu et al. 2009). Program directors can avail themselves of similar opportunities to collect baseline information for incoming freshman students and then longitudinally track the factors that may affect respondents' financial decisions, attitudes, and experiences with managing credit as they progress through college. Another possibility is to explore the different delivery mechanisms of financial education that college students would prefer. Recent studies (Goetz et al. 2011) have found that a student's major in school was associated with his or her preference for receiving financial education; however, more research is necessary in this area to determine which method of delivery for financial education is most effective among college students.

References

Adams, T., & Moore, M. (2007). High-risk health and credit behavior among 18- to 25-year-old college students. *Journal of American College Health, 56*(2), 101–108.

Bell, S., Grayson, J. P., & Stowe, S. (2001). Student attitudes toward debt—A study of Atkinson faculty of liberal and professional studies, York University and Ryerson University. *Journal of Student Financial Aid, 31*(3), 7–20.

Bernheim, B. D., Garrett, D. M., & Maki, D. M. (2001). Education and saving: The long-term effects of high school financial curriculum mandates. *Journal of Public Economics, 80*, 435–465.

Borden, L., Lee, S., Serido, J., & Collins, D. (2008). Changing college students' financial knowledge, attitudes and behavior through seminar participation. *Journal of Family and Economic Issues, 29*(1), 23–40.

Boyce, L., & Danes, S. M. (1998). *Evaluation of the NEFE high school financial planning program*. Englewood, CO: National Endowment for Financial Education.

Chen, H., & Volpe, R. P. (1998). An analysis of personal financial literacy among college students. *Financial Services Review, 7*(2), 107–128.

Chen, H., & Volpe, R. P. (2002). Gender differences in personal financial literacy among college students. *Financial Services Review, 7*(2), 289–307.

Chien, Y., & DeVaney, S. A. (2001). The effects of credit attitude and socioeconomic factors on credit card and installment debt. *Journal of Consumer Affairs, 35*, 162–179.

College Board. (2010). *Trends in college pricing*. Retrieved July 1, 2011, from http://trends.collegeboard.org/downloads/College_Pricing_2010.pdf.

College Student Survey Highlight Report. (2003). *2003 College student survey*. Retrieved July 1, 2011, from http://www.depts.ttu.edu/pasa/files/03CSSHighlights.pdf.

Credit Card Accountability, Responsibility and Disclosure (CARD) Act of 2009, S. 414, 111th Congress, Xth Sess. (2009).

Cude, B. J., Lawrence, F. C., Lyons, A. C., Metzger, K., LeJeunne, E., Marks, L., et al. (2006). College students and financial literacy: What they know and what we need to learn. *Eastern Family Economics and Resource Management Association 2006 Conference Proceedings*, 102–109.

Danes, S. M., Huddleston-Casas, C., & Boyce, L. (1999). Financial planning curriculum for teens: Impact evaluation. *Financial Counseling and Planning, 10*(1), 25–37.

Draut, T., & Silva, J. (2004) *Generation broke: Growth of debt among young Americans*. New York: Demos. Retrieved July 1, 2011, from http://www.demos-usa.org/pubs/Generation_Broke.pdf.

Edmiston, K. D., & Gillett-Fisher, M. C. (2006). Financial education at the workplace: Evidence from a survey of Federal Reserve Bank employees. *Federal Reserve Bank of Kansas City Community Affairs Working Paper 06-02*.

Edwards, R., Allen, M. W., & Hayhoe, C. R. (2007). Financial attitudes and family communication about students' finances: The role of sex differences. *Communication Reports, 20*(2), 90–100.

Eskilson, A., & Wiley, M. G. (1999). Solving for the X: Aspirations and expectations of college students. *Journal of Youth and Adolescence, 28*, 51–70.

Goetz, J., Cude, B., Nielsen, R. B., Chatterjee, S., & Mimura, Y. (2011). College-based personal finance education: Student interest in three delivery methods. *Journal of Financial Counseling and Planning, 22*(1), 27–42.

Grable, J., & Joo, S. H. (2001). A subsequent study of the relationships between and among self-worth and financial beliefs, behavior, and satisfaction. *Journal of Family and Consumer Sciences, 93*(5), 25–30.

Grable, J. E., & Joo, S. (2006). Student racial differences in credit card debt and financial behaviors and stress. *College Student Journal, 40*, 400–408.

Greenspan, A. (2003). *Remarks by Chairman Alan Greenspan at the 33 rd annual legislative conference of the congressional black caucus*, Washington, DC, September 26, 2003. Retrieved July 21, 2011, from http://www.federalreserve.gov/boarddocs/speeches/2003/20030926/default.htm.

Gutter, M., & Copur, Z. (2011). Financial behaviors and financial well-being of college students: Evidence from a national survey. *Journal of Family and Economic Issues, 32*(4), 699–714. doi:10.1007/s10834-011-9255-2.

Harris, C. R., Jenkins, M., & Glaser, D. (2006). Gender differences in risk assessment: Why do women take fewer risks than men? *Judgment and Decision Making, 1*(1), 48–63.

Hayhoe, C. R., Leach, L., & Turner, P. R. (1999). Discriminating the number of credit cards held by college students using credit and money attitudes. *Journal of Economic Psychology, 20*, 643–656.

Hayhoe, C. R., Leach, L., & Turner, P. R. (2000). Differences in spending habits and credit use of college students. *Journal of Consumer Affairs, 34*, 113–133.

Henry, R. A., Weber, J. G., & Yarbrough, D. (2001). Money management practices of college students. *College Student Journal, 35*, 244–249.

Hira, T. K., & Mugenda, O. M. (1999). The relationships between and among self-worth and financial beliefs, behavior, and satisfaction. *Journal of Family and Consumer Sciences, 91*(4), 76–82.

Hogarth, J. (2002). Financial literacy and family and consumer sciences. *Journal of Family and Consumer Sciences, 94*, 14–28.

Hogarth, J. M., & Hilgert, M. A. (2002). Financial knowledge, experience and learning preferences: Preliminary results from a new survey on financial literacy. *Consumer Interests Annual, 48*(1). Retrieved June 22, 2011, from http://www.consumerinterests.org/files/public/FinancialLiteracy-02.pdf.

Jamba-Joyner, L. A., Howard-Hamilton, M., & Mamarchev, H. (2000). College students and credit cards: Cause for concern? *Journal of Student Financial Aid, 30*(3), 17–26.

Johnson, E., & Sherraden, M. S. (2007). From financial literacy to financial capability among youth. *Journal of Sociology and Social Welfare, 34*(3), 119–146.

Jones, J. E. (2005). College students' knowledge and use of credit. *Journal of Financial Counseling and Planning, 16*(2), 9–16.

Joo, S. (2008). Personal financial wellness. In J. J. Xiao (Ed.), *Handbook of consumer finance research* (pp. 21–34). New York: Springer.

Joo, S. H., Grable, J. E., & Bagwell, D. C. (2003). Credit card attitudes and behaviors of college students. *College Student Journal, 37*, 405–415.

Kotlikoff, L. J., & Bernheim, B. D. (2001). Household financial planning and financial literacy. In L. J. Kotlikoff (Ed.), *Essays on saving, bequests, altruism, and life-cycle planning* (pp. 427–478). Cambridge, MA: MIT Press.

Lawrence, F. C., Christofferson, R. C., Nester, S. E., Moser, E. B., Tucker, J. A., & Lyons, A. C. (2003). *Credit card usage of college students: Evidence from Louisiana State University*. University of Illinois at Urbana-Champaign, Research Information Sheet #107.

Liu, A., Ruiz, S., DeAngelo, L., & Pryor, J. (2009). *Findings from the 2008 administration of the College Senior Survey (CSS): National aggregates*. Los Angeles: Higher Education Research Institute, UCLA.

Lusardi, A. (2006). *Financial literacy and financial education: Review and policy implications* (Policy Brief 2006-PB-11). Bloomington, IN: Networks Financial Institute, Indiana State University.

Lusardi, A. (2008). *Financial literacy: An essential tool for informed consumer choice?* (NBER Working Paper No. 14084). Cambridge, MA. Retrieved June 19, 2011, from http://www.nber.org/papers/w14084.

Lusardi, A., & Beeler, J. (2007). Saving between cohorts: The role of planning. In B. Madrian, O. Mitchell, & B. Soldo (Eds.), *Redefining retirement. How will boomers fare?* (pp. 271–295). Oxford, England: Oxford University Press.

Lusardi, A., & Mitchell, O. S. (2006). *Financial literacy and planning: Implications for retirement wellbeing* (NBER Working Paper No. 17078). Cambridge, MA. Retrieved June 22, 2011, from http://www.dartmouth.edu/~alusardi/Papers/FinancialLiteracy.pdf.

Lusardi, A., & Mitchell, O. S. (2007). Baby boomer retirement security: The roles of planning, financial literacy, and housing wealth. *Journal of Monetary Economics, 54*, 205–224.

Lusardi, A., & Tufano, P. (2009). *Debt literacy, financial experiences, and overindebtedness* (NBER Working Paper No. 14808). Cambridge, MA. Retrieved June 23, 2011, from http://www.nber.org/papers/w14808.

Lyons, A. C. (2004). A profile of financially at-risk college students. *Journal of Consumer Affairs, 38*(1), 56–80.

Lyons, A. C. (2008). Risky credit card behavior of college students. In J. J. Xiao (Ed.), *Handbook of consumer finance research* (pp. 185–208). New York: Springer.

Lyons, A. C., Rachlis, M., & Scherpf, E. (2007). What's in a score? Differences in consumers' credit knowledge using OLS and quantile regressions. *Journal of Consumer Affairs, 41*, 223–249.

Mandell, L. (1998). *Our vulnerable youth: The financial literacy of American 12th graders*. Washington, DC: Jump$tart Coalition for Personal Financial Literacy.

Mandell, L. (2008). *The financial literacy of young American adults*. Washington, DC: The Jump$tart Coalition for Financial Literacy.

Manning, R. (2000). *Credit card nation*. New York, NY: Basic Books.

Mason, C., & Wilson, R. (2000). *Conceptualizing financial literacy* (Research Series Paper 2000:7). London: Business School, Laughborough University.

Micomonaco, J. P. (2003). *Borrowing against the future: Practices, attitudes, and knowledge of financial management among college students.* Master's thesis, Virginia Tech, Virginia.

Murphy, A. J. (2005). Money, money, money: An exploratory study on the financial literacy of black college students. *College Student Journal, 39*(3), 478–488.

Nellie Mae. (2002). *Undergraduate students and credit cards: An analysis of usage rates and trends.* Retrieved June 22, 2011, from http://www.nelliemae.com/library/research.html.

Nellie Mae. (2005). *Undergraduate students and credit cards in 2004: An analysis of usage rates and trends.* Retrieved June 20, 2011, from http://www.nelliemae.com/library/research_12.html.

Nelson, M. C., Lust, K., Story, M., & Ehlinger, E. (2008). Credit card debts, stress and key health risk behaviors among college students. *American Journal of Health Promotion, 22*(6), 400–412.

Norum, P. S. (2008). The role of time preference and credit card usage in compulsive buying behavior. *International Journal of Consumer Studies, 32,* 269–275.

Norvilitis, J., Merwin, M. M., Osberg, T. M., Roehling, P. V., Young, P., & Kamas, M. M. (2006). Personality factors, money attitudes, *financial knowledge*, and credit-card debt in college students. *Journal of Applied Social Psychology, 36,* 1395–1413.

Norvilitis, J. M., & Santa Maria, P. (2002). Credit card debt on college campuses: Causes, consequences, and solutions. *College Student Journal, 36,* 357–364.

Norvilitis, J. M., Szablicki, P. B., & Wilson, S. D. (2003). Factors influencing levels of credit card debt in college students. *Journal of Applied Social Psychology, 33,* 935–947.

Oleson, M. (2001). Student credit card debt in the 21st century: Options for financial aid administrators. *NASFAA Journal of Student Financial Aid, 31*(3), 35–44.

Palmer, T. S., Pinto, M. B., & Parente, D. H. (2001). College students' credit card debt and role of parental involvement: Implications for public policy. *Journal of Public Policy & Marketing, 20*(1), 105–113.

Perry, V. G., & Morris, M. D. (2005). Who is in control? The role of self-perception, knowledge, and income in explaining consumer financial behavior. *Journal of Consumer Affairs, 39,* 299–313.

Pinto, M. B., Parente, D. H., & Palmer, T. S. (2001). College student performance and credit card usage. *Journal of College Student Development, 42*(1), 49–58.

Robb, C. A., & Sharpe, D. L. (2009). Effective personal *financial knowledge* on college students' credit card behavior. *Journal of Financial Counseling and Planning, 20*(1), 25–43.

Roberts, J. A., & Jones, E. (2001). Money attitudes, credit card use, and compulsive buying among American college students. *Journal of Consumer Affairs, 35,* 213–240.

Roberts, J. A., & Tanner, J. F. (2000). Compulsive buying and risky behavior among adolescents. *Psychological Reports, 86*(3), 763–770.

Shim, S., Xiao, J., Barber, B., & Lyons, A. C. (2009). Pathways to life success: A conceptual model of financial well-being for young adults. *Journal of Applied Developmental Psychology, 30*(6), 708–723.

Somers, P., & Cofer, J. (1997). Sing the student loan blues: Multiple voices, multiple approaches? In *Proceedings from a national symposium: Student loan debt: Problems and prospects* (pp. 97–128). Washington, DC: The Institute for Higher Education Policy.

Stango, V., & Zinman, J. (2007). *Fuzzy math, disclosure regulation and credit market outcomes.* Retrieved June 20, 2011, from http://www.dartmouth.edu/~jzinman/Papers/Stango&Zinman_Bias&CreditDisclosure_nov07.pdf.

Tennyson, S., & Nguyen, C. (2001). State curriculum mandates and student knowledge of personal finance. *Journal of Consumer Affairs, 35*(2), 241–262.

The Educational Resources Institute [TERI]. (1998). *Credit risk or credit worthy? College students and credit cards.* Boston, MA: The Educational Resources Institute.

Van Rooij, M., Lusardi, A., & Alessie, R. (2007). *Financial literacy and stock market participation* (NBER Working Paper No. 13565). Cambridge, MA. Retrieved June 20, 2011, from http://www.nber.org/papers/w13565.

Vitt, L. A., Anderson, C., Kent, J., Lyter, D. M., Siegenthaler, J. K., & Ward, J. (2000). *Personal finance and the rush to competence: Personal financial literacy in the U.S.* Middleberg: The Fannie Mae Foundation.

Xiao, J. J., Tang, C., & Shim, S. (2009). Acting for happiness: Financial behavior and life satisfaction of college students. *Social Indicators Research, 92*(1), 53–68.

Yang, B., James, S., & Lester, D. (2005). Reliability and validity of a short credit card attitude scale in British and American subjects. *International Journal of Consumer Studies, 29*(1), 41–46.

Chapter 11
Evaluating Financial Education Programs

Jonathan J. Fox, Suzanne Bartholomae, and Kate S. Trombitas

Introduction

Universities have a long history of significant investment in the financial education of their students. Be it through the financial aid, student loan, student wellness, or student affairs offices, the hope is that counseling and instruction in personal finance is a worthwhile investment of scarce university resources. While the costs of such counseling and education are real and easy for schools to determine, the benefits are less immediate and tangible. These benefits will only be made clear through careful assessment of the impact and efficacy of campus financial education programs. This chapter explores the recent history of financial education program evaluation and its documented impact on college and university campuses. Our overall assessment of the existing and rapidly growing literature is that the benefits of financial education and counseling remain unclear, and thus, we propose an ideal, more comprehensive, and rigorous structure for evaluation for new and existing college financial education programs. Through a methodical approach to evaluation, the benefits of financial education will be made clear and the costs will be potentially justified.

At this point, some of the best evidence of the impact of campus financial counseling and education comes from anecdotal evidence. The power of these stories cannot be underestimated. These stories are commonly cited as the main evidence of

J.J. Fox, Ph.D. (✉)
Department of Consumer Science, The Ohio State University,
206 Campbell Hall, Columbus, OH 43210, USA
e-mail: jfox@ehe.osu.edu

S. Bartholomae, Ph.D.
Department of Human Development and Family Science, The Ohio State University,
135 Campbell Hall, Columbus, OH 43210, USA
e-mail: bartholomae.1@osu.edu

K.S. Trombitas, M.A.
Financial Education, NSLP, 5695 Foster Avenue, Worthington, OH 43085, USA
e-mail: KateT@nslp.org

D.B. Durband and S.L. Britt (eds.), *Student Financial Literacy:*   141
Campus-Based Program Development, DOI 10.1007/978-1-4614-3505-1_11,
© Springer Science+Business Media New York 2012

both the need for financial education and ultimate program impact. Evidence-of-impact anecdotes, such as the following, are consistently shared by almost all providers of financial education on campuses:

- Mary was a struggling student in 2009 when she found her way to a money management office on campus. She shared with the financial educator about her difficult childhood, her emancipation from her parents at a young age, and her desire to stay in school despite the lack of financial or family support that many of her peers enjoyed. Together, Mary and the financial educator drafted a plan to get Mary to graduation.
- John stumbled upon his school's financial education center by accident in 2011 while headed to the recreation center for a workout. Earlier in the day, he had all but decided to drop out of college because the stress related to student loan debt was beginning to be too much for him to manage. As a first-generation college student navigating college finances largely on his own, John did not understand the difference between grant money and loan dollars and learned in a financial education session that his indebtedness was actually only a third of what he had estimated.
- During her first term on campus, Candace attended a free financial education workshop and learned about credit scores and the importance of monitoring her credit history. After returning to her dorm room, Candace pulled her credit report and discovered a mortgage loan in her name that did not belong to her: she had been a victim of identity theft.

Following their financial education sessions and workshops at their respective campuses, Mary, John, and Candace were provided with follow-up surveys to evaluate their progress and assess their overall satisfaction. Through these follow-up evaluations, campus staff learned that Mary had graduated, John had decided to stay in school, and Candace had found out that a family member had stolen her identity and she, Candace, was taking legal action to rectify her situation. All credited the school's financial education programs with helping them succeed.

All campuses providing financial education have students with similar stories, and capturing and sharing these stories can be thought of as the essence of effective program evaluation. These stories can then be used to share the impact and efficacy of programs with stakeholders and administrators, make the case for an increase in resources dedicated to financial education on campus, suggest changes for existing programming, identify gaps in services and programs, and shed light on trends affecting our students.

In this chapter, we draw from phone interviews conducted with financial education practitioners at institutions throughout the country. The goal was to learn more about existing practices for assessing financial education efforts on campus. While there are plenty of success stories like those of Mary, John, and Candace, key players in most institutions did not feel they were effectively evaluating their programs. Budget and time constraints were the most common reasons cited for inadequate evaluation practices, followed by a general lack of assessment expertise among program staff. Overall, almost every campus contacted felt they could be doing more to capture the stories and measurable impact of their programs.

In this chapter, we propose a comprehensive framework for financial education evaluation that can be adopted by college and university personnel. We highlight challenges facing providers of financial education programs wishing to evaluate the effectiveness of their programming. We advocate for an established evaluation framework to guide stakeholders in financial education programs. Without question, the costs of deliberate program evaluation methods can be prohibitive for some education providers. However, the adoption of a more consistent and comprehensive evaluation framework will better capitalize on economies of scope. Widespread adoption of a more consistent approach to program evaluation will facilitate program comparison and aid in identification of best practices in financial education that take place on campuses and in university-sponsored programs.

Financial Education Program Evaluation

Based on phone interviews with campus student affairs administrators, we have learned of all types of financial education programs on campus, from for-credit courses and one-time workshops to one-on-one personalized sessions and online tutorials. Despite the delivery method, one thing was clear when it came to evaluation: satisfaction surveys, or immediate program responses, were the norm and very little happened beyond internal reporting. Among 30 campus financial education programs, 70% currently collect evaluation data of immediate impact such as participant satisfaction and change in attitudes, knowledge, or skills (Durband and Britt 2011). Similarly, immediate program responses indicating participant satisfaction levels and self-reported increases in knowledge were part of 80 of the 90 financial education programs offered to a range of audiences (Vitt et al. 2000). Satisfaction surveys provide a look at a student's overall happiness with the financial education program, behavior intention, and willingness to recommend the service to a friend, but they do little to demonstrate program impact on intended outcomes, such as reduced stress or refined plans for debt repayment. These satisfaction surveys can also deliver data concerning usage numbers and demographics of participants. While gathering these immediate benefit data may be an accessible starting point for a financial education program, evidence of long-term benefit is still needed (Braunstein and Welch 2002).

Evaluation data for program improvement (participant rating of instructors, educational materials, and overall program) were collected by six of ten schools. Intermediate data (e.g., tracking the potential change of financial practices and behaviors (33%)) and long-term impact data (23%) collection occurs with less frequency (Durband and Britt 2011). When asked to rate the quality of their current financial literacy programs, most financial aid professionals ($n=96$) reported the program quality as good (45%), followed by very good (22%), fair (20%), excellent (9%), and poor (4%) (Student Lending Analytics 2010).

Delivery Needs Analysis

The impact of financial education on student changes in knowledge, attitudes, and behavior has not been fully vetted in the empirical literature; however, a growing body of work by universities, academicians, and organizations has established the need for increased financial literacy. There is convincing evidence of low financial literacy levels among college students, as well as the need, demand, interest, and preference for university-sponsored financial education. For example, HigherOne (2011) administered a nine-question financial knowledge quiz to 5,488 college students and found seven in ten students received a failing score and less than 30% answered six or more questions correctly. Almost half of the students reported that the financial literacy programs provided by their schools could greatly improve.

Moving beyond financial literacy levels, other studies have conducted needs assessments to identify college student interest in financial education programs— from financial topics students would be interested in learning about, how they would like the information delivered, to the level of interest in financial services on campus. A needs assessment conducted in 2005 at the University of Hawaii–Manoa guided the subsequent development and delivery of a financial education program in 2006 (Masuo et al. 2007). Students ($n=411$) rated their interest in 20 financial topics and rank-ordered the presentation and delivery of financial information. Faculty and staff ($n=21$, 47% response rate) teaching and counseling in personal finance fields completed the same survey. Between students and staff, there were significant differences for nine of the 20 financial topics. College students identified investing for the future, getting ahead financially after graduation, avoiding credit problems, and budgeting as the top four topics of interest, while faculty and staff identified budgeting, avoiding credit problems, making the most of student loans, and avoiding identity theft, scams, and frauds as their top four topics. Students focused on the future whereas faculty and staff focused on avoidance and immediate problems. There were no significant differences in the comparison of preferred methods of receiving financial information between students and faculty and staff. Students preferred information as part of a financial aid interview, a special event with food, and an extra credit class and through a Web site or at new student orientation (Masuo et al. 2007).

Targeting higher education administrators at a southwestern public university, Vienne and Slate (2009) interviewed ten students about the need to develop a center with financial education and counseling programs sponsored by the university. Volunteers were first-year students from a survey class. Students reiterated three themes during the focus group interviews: help with personal budgeting, financial education to achieve independence, and help to obtain personal responsibility of spending habits.

Needs assessments have explored student interest in campus-based financial counseling centers. Online responses from 509 undergraduates at the University of Georgia, solicited via e-mail through the Office of Student Financial Aid, identified student interest in receiving financial education by way of three modes of delivery.

A reason noted by the researchers for exploring student delivery preferences is that each method required varying degrees of institutional commitment. The study found the greatest proportion of students preferred to learn via online resources (80%), followed by learning at a workshop (43%), or counseling center (26%). The authors recommended that colleges and universities deliver all three types of financial education to achieve the greatest impact (Goetz et al. 2011). Jariah et al. (2004) administered a survey to every tenth student picking up their student loan at a public university in Malaysia ($n = 1,500$). From this sample of students, 90% reported wanting to learn financial management; about three quarters were interested in learning about the topic of savings and investing, followed by budgeting. Roughly 80% of students desired financial counseling as a campus service. In a survey conducted among faculty, staff, and students at the Ohio State University, Doll (2001) found that most students would use a student-staffed financial counseling center, while only a small portion of the faculty would use such an on-campus resource. Similar to Masuo et al. (2007), the Ohio State study showed the strongest student demand for forward-looking information on investing, housing, and even retirement.

Using an online survey, the University of Illinois' Office of Student Financial Aid collected financial information in 2001 from 835 randomly selected undergraduate, graduate, and professional students (Lyons 2004). The study profiled students at risk for credit card mismanagement (e.g., balance exceeding $1,000, payment delinquency, maxed credit limit, or revolving balance) and identified the need for campus financial services and education. Students were asked to identify from which on-campus format they would prefer to receive financial information. Students more likely to be at risk of credit card mismanagement preferred the online delivery of financial information over in-person counseling services, seminars, and workshops. Information about money management and credit card debt in the form of handouts or pamphlets was also preferred by this group. Compared to students not at risk of financial mismanagement, at-risk students were more likely to use a financial service offered by the university and were more likely to prefer information on money management rather than credit card debt (Lyons 2004).

Nellie Mae (2007) studied credit card behavior and credit education preferences of 210 graduate students, a subsample from a larger credit bureau analysis of 1,149 graduate students. Four in ten students expressed the desire for financial management information as college freshmen and 54% would have liked it throughout their time as undergraduates. The mode of delivery for financial education in order of most preferred was one-on-one counseling, formal classroom instruction, and finally, informal group setting. Only somewhat preferred were online tutorials and workbooks, and the least-preferred methods were posted tips on campus, parents, and e-mail. College student preference for one type of delivery does not stand out, nor does the effectiveness of the type of program delivered.

College students from public and private universities and colleges ($n = 63$) across Minnesota participated in focus groups to explore the potential of using podcasts to provide financial education (Hendrickson et al. 2010). Themes that emerged include the importance of making financial information accessible to students as they need it and individual or small group involvement to allow personalized learning opportunities. Podcasts should be structured to include an overview of the financial topic; the information should cover a range of basic to complex information and be "clear, concise, and well organized and provide topics that are real-life, relevant to student concerns" (para 12). Students wanted podcasts to include professional, reliable, unbiased sources and additional contact information. Formats for delivering financial information that were of interest to students included podcasts and written materials.

Financial Literacy Needs Analysis

Evidence has been collected linking the financial literacy of college students and various financial behaviors and outcomes. One of the earliest and most often cited works is a study of financial literacy levels and financial decision making by Chen and Volpe (2002). They studied 924 students from 13 public and private universities. The authors highlighted the need for personal finance education among college students based on the failing median score of 56% on a 36-question general financial knowledge test. Students' poor knowledge of personal financial management led to incorrect and potentially expensive mistakes in the areas of general knowledge, savings and borrowing, and investments. Perhaps the most significant contribution of the Chen and Volpe (2002) study was the finding that financial decisions were highly influenced by financial knowledge. Approximately 89% of students with higher levels of financial literacy made good spending decisions in a hypothetical situation, whereas only 68% of students with lower levels of financial knowledge made the correct choices. Male students and students with more work experience had higher scores. African American students had the lowest financial literacy scores across several financial topics (Chen and Volpe 2002). Students in the Chen and Volpe study did best on questions where they have some experience (e.g., auto insurance and apartment leases) and poorest on questions where they had the least experience (e.g., taxes, life insurance, and investing), and these findings suggest that "financial experience could increase financial literacy, and studies that find an effect of financial literacy on financial behavior should test for reverse causality" (Amromin et al. 2009, p. 5).

The student affairs office of six public and five private Malaysian universities provided a random selection of 350 students for Sabri and MacDonald (2010) to study financial literacy. With a 65% response rate and 2,519 reporting, the study linked financial literacy (25 questions) to savings behavior (three items) and financial problems (10 questions) and hoped to link the evidence to strategies for financial education on campus. College students with greater financial literacy, who had consumer experiences early in their childhood, demonstrated more conservative spending patterns, and female students were more likely to engage in positive savings behavior.

Peng et al. (2007) studied the long-term impact of taking a personal finance class in high school, college, or both on the investment knowledge and savings behavior among 1,039 university alumni. Participating in a personal finance class in college appeared more effective in terms of enhancing one's investment knowledge than taking the class in high school, yet the personal finance education impact on savings behavior seemed to be lacking. Peng et al. argue that critical financial outcomes (namely credit card use and paying bills) are more apparent in the lives of college students than high school students, leading to stronger links between classroom information and personal financial practices.

Moving Beyond Basic Needs Assessments

Tightening budgets at colleges and universities heightens the need for evidence-based justification for offering costly financial counseling and education. Needs assessment provides an important foundation; however, the evaluation component of specific programming can provide data that demonstrates whether an educational initiative makes a difference. Rigorous evaluation is mostly absent in the financial education program evaluation literature. Studies of financial education lack randomized research designs, systematic study, replication, generalizability, and agreement on outcomes. Fortunately, published evidence on different financial education initiatives has increased over the past several years. Here we bring together financial literacy and education studies from academic journals, working papers, and conference proceedings.

As seen throughout this book, financial education can be delivered in a variety of methods, whether it is a semester-length course, a seminar or workshop, or counseling sessions. According to Mandell's (2008) study, previous financial education in either high school or college does not seem to make a difference in financial literacy scores, whether it is semester-length money management or personal finance course in high school or college. Mandell's national study of college students found the mean college score for all students is 61.9%, 59.3% for those who had a semester-length course in money management or personal finance in high school, and 60.1% for those who had a similar course in college. Better-than-average financial literacy scores were achieved by those who had a high school or college course in economics. Far better scores were obtained by those who had a college course in finance or accounting, and the best scores were obtained by those college students who played a stock market game in high school (Mandell 2008). Most college-level personal finance courses meet a programmatic need of a curriculum (e.g., financial planning majors) and not specific student outcomes associated with financial behavior. Moreover, self-selection seems a key issue in explaining the lack of difference between those in personal finance classes in either high school or college.

Like Mandell's (2008) study, previous coursework in personal finance (designated as economics or business courses) in either high school or college did not predict better scores on the Jump$tart financial literacy survey among students (*n* = 192) at Saint Anselm College (Lalonde and Schmidt 2011). At Texas A&M University–Commerce, previous financial education in a high school economics or financial planning course made no difference in test scores among the 407 freshmen surveyed (Avard et al. 2005). Students ($n=49$) enrolled in a managerial finance and portfolio management course showed marginal to no improvement on the Jump$tart posttest administered at the end of the semester (Seyedian and Yi 2011).

The effectiveness of a 10-week elective (1.5 credits) personal finance course designed for health professionals was studied (Chui 2009). In 2006 and 2007, 143 students completed the Jump$tart survey pre- and posttest. The average baseline score (pretest) was 60% and significant improvement was achieved in the end-of-course posttest score of 90%. Course evaluations were also used as an outcome measure; the course was consistently highly rated. The author noted the limitation of using the Jump$tart survey, as it was designed for high school students (Chui 2009). The influence of other factors, such as financial experience, was not considered with respect to the knowledge score. This course offering was developed after pharmacy graduate students expressed interest in the option of a personal finance course. The course, designed to be individualized, personalized, and highly interactive, was delivered to second-year students enrolled in a 3-year doctor of pharmacy program (Chui 2009). With mixed evidence, college administrators do not have sound evidence to endorse a for-credit, semester-length course.

The efficacy of delivering financial information in college workshops is also inconsistent. Bowen and Jones (2006) used a pretest–posttest design to determine the efficacy of an educational intervention regarding credit card and money attitudes among freshmen and sophomores. Based on a two-session intervention, there was a significant improvement in overall credit card knowledge score, and a majority of students changed, or planned to change, their credit card practices in a positive manner. At the University of Virginia (2007), undergraduate Pell Grant recipients were randomly invited to attend a financial management education workshop ($n=73$); another group did not receive the invitation to training ($n=72$). Both groups were administered a pretest (11 knowledge questions) in 2006 and a posttest in 2007. The Office of Student Financial Services administered the surveys and workshops. Both groups improved their overall test scores, although both groups received failing marks of 45% or lower on both pre- and posttests. There was no significant difference in the level of knowledge between the treatment and control group. However, it was noted that despite the failing financial knowledge scores, the students reported they were practicing responsible money management. The knowledge scores were not associated with ownership of a savings account, maintenance of a budget, overspending, misusing their credit card, or requesting a credit report. The experiment was somewhat limited due to low attendance at the workshops, with only 19 students attending at least one workshop; however, the study's use of a control and treatment group is a highly desirable and, hopefully, soon to be widely replicated methodological approach.

The use of peer educators in financial education is becoming more common on campuses, yet the educational value of this format is still unknown. Members of an accounting and finance honor society, Beta Alpha Psi (BAΨ), engaged in a financial literacy service-learning project directed at first- and second-year undergraduates at Louisiana State University (DeLaune et al. 2011). The BAΨ members followed the national initiative *Financial Literacy of College Students* designated by the BAΨ Board of Directors for the 2007–2008 academic year. The group developed and presented three skits on credit, spending, and retirement, reaching 490 undergraduate business students. The three topics were presented in 90 minutes and attendees completed 12 financial knowledge questions pre- and post-presentation. The post-presentation survey asked three questions related to the effectiveness of the presentation. Approximately 42% of attendees reported improvement in their financial knowledge. It was reported that some of the audience members planned some behavioral change (e.g., ordering free credit report)—a precise accounting was not shared. Another component of evaluation was the reflection of the student presenters' experience and the technical, interpersonal, and communication skills developed from participating in the project. The article stated that the student members had "extremely positive" responses to their involvement in the service-learning project.

Nationally, the student group placed first in the *Best Practices* category while competing against other BAΨ student groups. The first-place recognition was couched as an outcome on the effectiveness and quality of the service-learning project. This is an example of a student organization presenting the technical content of personal finance to peers. Lacking in the evaluation was some measure of the effectiveness of peer delivery; the relevance and effectiveness of the topics, format, and visual aids (YouTube videos); and long-term measures of effectiveness such as whether students retained the financial information and whether the knowledge changed their financial behavior (DeLaune et al. 2011).

University of Arizona students ($n=93$) participated in a 90-minute seminar covering credit cards and other financial topics that was delivered by students serving with Credit Wise Cats (an initiative of Students in Free Enterprise) (Borden et al. 2008). Based on the pre- and posttest surveys, the study showed an immediate result in increased financial knowledge (seven items) and intent to change behavior (increasing savings, investing, and other sound financial practices, as well as reducing ineffective financial behaviors) following the peer-led seminar. Financial knowledge did not predict effective financial behaviors (seven items reflecting sound financial practices) or risky financial behaviors (four items reflecting unsound financial practices). Lower financial knowledge did predict an attitude toward credit that was more avoidant. Whether peer-led financial education actually influenced a change in behavior or sustained change in financial knowledge is unknown without follow-up research. The authors advocate for financial education with a shorter format, such as seminars or workshops, over a longer-term course largely due to the already crowded academic schedule of undergraduates. However, the study does not test length of delivery. The publication did not share information on the selection process of students, number of students who attended the seminar, frequency of seminar offering, or response rates.

Upper-level accounting majors delivered two 90-minute mandatory financial literacy workshops for freshmen enrolled in an introduction to business course at a small midwestern university (Rosacker et al. 2009). There was a significant increase in financial literacy scores (13 items focusing on debt and financial management) among students completing both pre- and posttests ($n=41$ in 2007 and $n=60$ in

2008). Examining the individual test items, the authors asserted that some topics are not effectively delivered in this mode of financial literacy workshop (e.g., spending instruments, credit card finance charges, safe saving, paycheck deductions, retirement income, business taxes, growth vehicles, and income sources) while some topics are (e.g., finance charges, comparative earnings, savings programs, credit card theft, and income tax). Their study did not compare modes of delivery; rather, only one type was analyzed.

Ideally, peer-delivered education programs should also measure the change in financial literacy, knowledge, and behavior of the student instructors. An opportunity was missed in these studies of student-led education. Similarly, over a 10-week period, small teams of college students from North Carolina A&T State University served as instructors of the Stock Market Game to students enrolled in alternative high schools (referred to as middle colleges). High school students were administered a pre- and posttest to assess learning, but no metrics were used with the college students.

The value of integrating financial concepts into existing college curriculum was demonstrated in a study by Zhu (2011). To address concern about waning student interest and learning, an Old Dominion University instructor of software engineering redesigned his object-oriented programming course by integrating savings, debt management, and investment topics into the hands-on exercise and programming examples (Zhu 2011). Student interest and learning outcomes improved; the course GPA increased from 2.48 to 3.42 between Spring 2008 and 2009. A survey of 24 students in the redesigned course showed that students experience a positive effect of using financial concepts on learning programming (71% of students agreed that they found that the mortgage calculator application helped them learn programming and debt management) and a positive effect of learning programming and financial information together (79% agreed that "computer tools can help me to make better financial decisions" and "I am interested in learning to write programs that help me to manage and reduce debts," and 67% agreed that "computer tools can help me to reduce my expenses"). Financial knowledge was not tested in the course evaluation (Zhu 2011). As mentioned, the literature on college students and financial literacy and education has increased over the past few years; however, efforts and issues related to program evaluation mirror those at the national level. In 2009, RAND assessed the quality of evaluation efforts of 56 federal financial and economic literacy education programs. The report found:

> More than half of all programs, and almost all agencies, reported ongoing or planned evaluation activities. However, the wide range of metrics and methods made it difficult to systematically establish effectiveness or to compare results across programs and agencies. For example, many programs reported significant efforts to measure program outputs, including the use of participant questionnaires and, in a small number of cases, testing. For a smaller number of programs, impact evaluations were reported with the goal of understanding the effects of the program on participants. However, relatively few evaluations actually reported systematically implementing pre- and post-designs or a control group, which indicates that actual program effects could not be clearly identified. While some variation in evaluation is consistent with the wide variation in the types of reported program offerings, as well as agency goals and structure, the data also suggest that insufficient technical and financial resources and failure to plan strategically may act as constraints (Hung et al. 2009, p. viii).

Clearly, the challenge of quantifying and sharing the measured impact of financial education is not constrained to college campuses. However, college and university administrators have a unique opportunity to contribute significantly to the growing academic literature by reporting on methodologically sound evaluations of financial literacy programs. In the academic setting, we benefit from easy and continual access to the treated (educated) population. It is also relatively easy to draw a reasonable control (non-educated) group. Further, it is feasible to follow both treatment and control groups through their financial lives when done in conjunction with alumni associations. With this distinct advantage in mind, we next present an ideal methodological approach to evaluation for adoption by university and college program administrators. The hope is that through consistent approaches to evaluation, the links between education treatment, knowledge, and behavior changes can be made more clear and useful for fellow financial educators.

A Framework for Guiding the Evaluation Process

As evidenced by our review, there is room for growth in the quantity and quality of program evaluation conducted on financial education delivered to college students. Efforts in designing and delivering financial education programs in universities often take place without considering whether such efforts are effective and without integrating the evaluation component as part of design and delivery. Meaningful program evaluation is an essential and integrated element of successful programs. In this section, we will discuss a framework for conducting a sophisticated evaluation of your program grounded in theory and relying on previous research and free resources. However, we also recognize that program assessment can be a daunting and time-consuming process, so we will begin with an outline of accessible program evaluation techniques and tips for leveraging campus resources as you work toward more rigorous methods.

Basic data is critical to have when reporting on your program to administration and can be easily collected. This data, such as number of students served and demographics of students served, can easily be gathered through surveys offered before or after a treatment. Another option available at most campuses is a card reader that collects this data from student identification cards when swiped. Often, these card readers can be set up in offices or at events for little or no charge, and data is collected electronically and sent directly to your e-mail inbox.

One step beyond tracking program audiences is evaluating whether the participants felt satisfied with their experience. This measure does *not* look at the effectiveness of the treatment on knowledge, skills, confidence, or abilities but does provide a gauge of how successful the student felt the service was and if the student is willing to refer a friend. These data can be used to suggest changes to service offerings and make the case for new resources to support existing services.

Finally, qualitative data can be reasonably collected through posttreatment surveys and can provide a powerful narrative about your program or service. Again, this data does not measure the success of the treatment; rather, it provides a frank assessment of the offering through the students' own words. This type of data, while not especially scientific, can often be the most convincing of all when working with administration or when creating marketing materials.

As previously referenced, conducting a financial education program on a college campus comes with the perk of operating in an arena full of assessment professionals and subject matter experts who are willing and able to assist with your program evaluation. This expertise may take the form of helpful faculty from various campus departments, graduate students looking for theses or dissertation topics, or instructors who have an experiential learning component in their classroom or campus research centers. Leveraging this expertise, along with the framework described in the coming pages, leads to a well-designed evaluation that will "document individual program implementation and effectiveness, but also address collectively and cumulatively which programs work for whom, how, when, where, and why" (Weiss 1988, p. 4). With a more systematic, consistent, and collaborative approach to financial program evaluation on campuses, stronger evidence of any link between financial education and targeted outcomes may emerge.

Most programs appear to be making some effort toward evaluation, yet with little commonalities in the approach taken. Limited and inconsistent measurement inhibits our ability to understand how outcomes and effects are achieved by programs (Weiss 1988). Some programs conduct informal evaluations (e.g., phone calls or self-evaluations) with students or instructors providing information. Other program evaluations involve more formal measurement methods, such as surveys (Hopley 2003). Measurement of program success is also inconsistent. The measurement of financial literacy among college students alone lacked agreement in the content, topics, and competencies. Outcome measures will vary significantly by the program goals, audience, and delivery method; thus, consistently defined measures present some difficulties.

A critical feature of any useful evaluation or approach to measurement is reliability and validity. A measure is valid when it measures what it is intended to measure. There are several types of validity, but content and construct validity are particularly important when constructing an evaluation measure. Content validity shows that items measure all dimensions of a construct. Construct validity is determined by the degree to which the items measure what is intended to be assessed. The Jump$tart financial literacy survey, though criticized for its psychometric rigor, is the closest to a standardized measure that exists and has frequently been administered to college student populations. The content validity of the Jump$tart survey was determined by educators and experts in personal finance who judged how well it represented financial literacy (Lucey 2005). Reliability measures the consistency and stability of an instrument. For example, the Jump$tart survey is a reliable instrument if a student receives relatively the same score on multiple administrations of the financial literacy test when factors remain the same.

In a broad assessment of current financial education evaluation efforts, Lyons et al. (2006) outline the practical challenges and significant costs of assessing programs. Using focus group findings from 60 financial professionals and educators, Lyons et al. describe evaluation practices as secondary to program delivery, often being underfunded and delegated to educators with no evaluation expertise or experience. Moreover, evaluation efforts were not found to be driven by learning outcomes, and much debate remains on critical measures of program success. Most appropriately, Lyons et al. conclude that a thorough evaluation is neither possible nor recommended for all program providers. Evaluation funding and expertise is in short supply in most programming efforts. Targeted evaluation efforts to show program impact for selected programs, along with the establishment of national outcome and evaluation guidelines, were advocated.

Program evaluations generally fall into one of two categories, a process, or formative, evaluation and an impact, or summative, evaluation (Scriven 1981). A formative evaluation collects information that provides feedback for educators and program organizers to make improvements in the program itself. For example, over three semester offerings, Stolle and Dumpe (2009) developed, delivered, and refined *Me and My Money*, a personal financial literacy course at Kent State University offered as an elective for nonbusiness majors. Summative evaluation collects information on whether the program is making a difference in previously identified and desired outcome measures (Scriven 1981). Summative evaluation information deals more with the issue at hand—whether or not financial education impacts financial behavior—as well as gathering evidence of program satisfaction, increased knowledge levels, or increased levels of confidence.

Given the wide range of impact evidence gathered from existing financial education programs, it is not surprising that no single evaluation framework appears to be guiding financial educators. An overarching framework for the evaluation of financial education programs would provide a guide or road map for collecting information about program development, delivery, effectiveness, and accountability. Widespread adoption of key elements in a common framework will not only make program evaluation less daunting for financial educators (by providing a guide and frame of reference) but also contribute to consistency in data collection and clarity in program comparison.

Several program evaluation frameworks exist, and there is significant overlap among these frameworks. At the most general level, evaluation boils down to managing: (a) the engagement of the stakeholders, (b) program focus, (c) data collection, (d) data analysis and interpretation, and (e) the use of the results (University of Wisconsin Extension 2011). In other words, good evaluation is all about conducting and following sound research practices. Engagement of funders, university officials, students, program organizers, and instructors throughout the process gives evaluation the appropriate level of emphasis throughout the program life cycle. All too often, evaluation is described by program officials as an afterthought, but it is the only means of demonstrating program impact. Beginning with determining the focus of the program, a full-team approach will better define the *logic* behind the program. Often, a *logic model* is used at this stage of the evaluation where desired program outputs or impacts are traced backward through outputs (activities and participation), which result from program inputs (invested resources). Such impact-focused planning for programs can provide a solid footing for evaluation as desired impacts can be established early and measured throughout the process. For example, if university and program administrators agree that the desired impact of the program is to reduce stress levels attributable to student loan indebtedness, then not only do evaluators know they need to work on a valid and reliable measure of debt stress, but they also know they need to select activities (e.g., classes, workshops, counseling) and participants (e.g., students, parents, faculty) to best link to this focused outcome. Finally, these activities need to be delivered with the best possible management of limited resources, the inputs in the logic model.

The logic model approach is driven by the identification and selection of key outcomes (Julian et al. 1995). Program planners and university officials will benefit from an investment of time and energy in the careful selection of desired impacts of a financial education program. It is tempting to overreach in this stage of program and evaluation planning as all student affairs staff want successful programs with far-reaching impact; unfortunately, such comprehensive programs are near impossible to prove effective. A helpful tool to moderate the tendency to overreach in outcome selection is the transtheoretical stages of change model (Prochaska and DiClemente 1983). When applied to personal finances, the stages of change approach can help break down longer-term outcomes, like reduced levels of indebtedness, to a more immediate acknowledgment of an indebtedness problem.

The transtheoretical model outlines behavior change as a series of steps including (a) precontemplation (not even thinking about changing), (b) contemplation (acknowledging the need for change), (c) preparation (planning a course of action), (d) action (overt change in behavior), and (e) maintenance (working to prevent relapse and becoming free from the temptation of old behavior). With each stage being identified as a known and critical step along a route to behavior modification, evaluators can set movement from one stage to the next as a desired program outcome. In the consumer debt example, instead of complete elimination of all credit card debt, simple acknowledgment of a problem with credit card debt (movement from precontemplation to contemplation) could be the identified goal of the program. Such a goal would be much easier for student affairs staff to measure and show impact in a short time frame.

When desired outcomes are reasonable, attainable, known, and agreed upon by university stakeholders, the planning for data collection and analysis can begin. Again, universities and colleges hold a distinct advantage over other providers of financial education in this data collection and analysis portion of the evaluation. Universities house all the necessary expertise in measurement, survey design, and analysis. Student affairs professionals can easily partner with counterparts in academic departments (e.g., economics, sociology, statistics, psychology, student and public affairs, public health) on what has become a cutting-edge research topic. Finally, colleges and universities are filled with talented and motivated authors. Using and sharing the results of program evaluations in peer-reviewed publications will go a long way toward clearing the existing ambiguities in the effectiveness of financial education programs.

In conducting these evaluations of campus financial counseling and education programs, Jacobs' (1988) five-tiered approach to evaluation can be used as a basic guide. The advantage of this framework is that it encourages evaluation to occur in each stage of programming, from conception to implementation to conclusion and follow-up. An additional benefit underlying this framework is the assumptions that evaluation (a) should be collected and analyzed in a systematic manner, (b) is an essential component to every program, (c) serves several functions, (d) has many audiences, and (e) should not detract from delivering a program (Weiss 1988). Finally, the five-tiered approach is comprehensive in scope; it entails both formative and summative evaluation. Knox (2002) advocates that when planning and coordinating the impact evaluation process, the impact evaluation should be part of information drawn from a process that is both formative and summative. Thus, we not only determine what is having the desired impact on campuses, we also learn how to conduct the financial education better next time.

The elements of a comprehensive program evaluation, as outlined by Jacobs (1988), can be summarized in five key steps: (a) preimplementation, (b) accountability, (c) program clarification, (d) progress toward objectives, and (e) program impact. The components of the model build upon one another, with each level requiring "greater efforts at data collection and tabulation, increased precision in program definition, and a greater commitment to the evaluation process" (Jacobs 1988, p. 50). Program evaluators using this five-tiered approach can engage in several levels at once, and while it is stepwise, previous levels may need to be revisited (Jacobs 1988). Immediately evident is the fact that evaluation is a graduated process, where identification of program impact comes only in the final stages of an involved, often costly, and comprehensive process. University administrators need to be fully committed to the process in advance, and expectations need to be managed in a way to allow the process to take full course. Without an understanding and commitment to the full evaluation process, university administrators expecting clear results at the program impact level will be disappointed. The table outlines key stages and links each stage to applications in financial education.

In Jacobs' (1988) terminology, the preimplementation tier of an evaluation occurs during the initial organizational stages of a program and is more commonly known as needs assessment. Needs assessment allows those planning financial education programs to determine the targeted goals and plan an effective program. Vitt et al. (2000) report that only 22% of the 90 financial education programs reviewed conducted any formal needs assessment. In many instances, Vitt et al. found program organizers to have assumed the need for financial education so great that no further evidence was required. Testing financial literacy levels among college students, and identifying any deficiencies, is an ideal approach to needs assessment for pure financial education. Among students, the need for improved financial literacy is linked to financial education's assumed potential to demonstrate higher retention and graduation rates, lower loan default rates and debt levels, reduced risky credit card payment behavior, lower financial stress, and other positive outcomes that may be the result of sound financial management and high financial literacy levels. The financial literacy research provided by the Jump$tart Coalition establishes and identifies a national need for college student financial education (Mandell 2008). On the institutional level, linking their institutional persistence data and student inventory data with data about student financial stress and concerns, Saint Catherine University was able to obtain grant funding to support their current and future efforts of their *Money Doesn't Grow on Trees* program (Richter Norgel et al. 2009). Showing that students who are financially *fit* perform better in school is an ideal justification for the need for financial education on campus and thus a good example of work done in the preimplementation stage of evaluation.

The second stage, or "accountability tier," of the evaluation consists of collecting information on the education and services provided, the cost of the program, and basic program participant information (Jacobs 1988). The goal of this stage of the process is to document who has been reached by a program and in what way. Accountability is also important in determining whether the population in need of financial education has been served. It is also important to provide program data to funders, participants, and the university community, with a larger goal of using amassed program utilization data to draw broader attention to the issue of financial literacy (Jacobs 1988). Frequently, accountability in financial education programs is measured by collecting information during registration, an exit survey, or some other indication of participation. A prime example of the impact of accountability data is Consumer Federation of America's America Saves program in Cleveland. In a press release based on a program survey, an estimated 10,000 Cleveland residents were persuaded to save more, and 1,500 savers were officially enrolled for accounts, counseling, and workshops (Cleveland Saves 2002). Based on these results, America Saves programs are now offered on college campuses. Such significant and compelling figures can immediately signal positive community impact and begin building the case for the continuation and growth of the program.

The third tier, program clarification, is used to assess an ongoing program's strengths and weaknesses and to reassess program goals and objectives (Jacobs 1988). Relative to other phases, program clarification contains more formative information for program organizers and university officials. In this stage of program evaluation, program planners review the mission, goals, objectives, and strategies being used in an overall effort to improve the financial education provided. After reviewing data from the preimplementation stage, university administrators and program organizers determine if the intended students are being served and whether the definition of the target student needs to be broadened or narrowed. Additionally, information drawn from observations by program staff and students is utilized to improve the program during this stage of evaluation (Jacobs 1988). For classroom-delivered material, information used for program clarification is commonly derived from an exit survey of teacher ratings, overall satisfaction with the class, and increases in knowledge. In early stages of a financial education or counseling program, open-ended comments of participants often guide program changes. A more rigorous method of providing evidence for program clarification would be through the use of a pre- and posttest, then linking high-impact levels to best program practices. The National Endowment for Financial Education's evaluation of the High School Financial Planning Program® effectively uses this pre- and posttest approach to measure increases in financial knowledge, confidence, or intended improvements in financial behavior following the delivery of financial education (Danes et al. 1999). In university settings, more educators are using a pre- and post-test approach to assess program clarification; unfortunately, these approaches are often presented and shared as evidence of program impact. For example, a pre- and posttest approach can show changes in knowledge or attitude on finances due to some sort of treatment, but it leaves us short of establishing the link between a treat-ment (education program widely defined) and an outcome, such as less financial stress, reduced reliance on consumer credit, or better management of student financial aid.

In the progress-toward-objectives phase of evaluation, the focus moves to desired outcomes and the more summative measures. Ultimately, this is where university and college administrators will become most interested. During this stage, program evaluators obtain objective measures of the impact of a program on students. Information collected during this stage measures the effect of the program on the student's life, whereas the accountability stage described earlier simply highlights program use and participation (Jacobs 1988). In most cases, it is unclear how to best measure progress toward objectives if the earlier three stages of evaluation are short circuited. For example, workplace financial education programs are frequently designed with the clear intent of increasing rates of participation and savings among employees in qualified retirement plans. With such clear and measurable outcomes, it is not surprising that workplace financial education programs show the most con-sistent and compelling evidence of progress toward objectives (Braunstein and Welch 2002; Todd 2002). The clearly defined targeted needs of the workers, along with ease in accountability by employers, make the measurement of progress toward objectives in workplace programs much easier than in other programs with more loosely defined goals and objectives. In university settings, showing progress toward objectives may present the biggest challenge. Institutions of higher learning are in the business of just that, higher learning, without a consistent record of linking the learning to specific outcomes. Financial education and counseling programs that more narrowly focus on a handful of outcomes in students' financial lives are more likely to be considered successful in terms of progress toward objectives. For exam-ple, if a financial counseling center has a set measurable goal of increasing aware-ness of grant and scholarship programs, then the proportion of students on a grant or scholarship becomes a natural measure of progress toward objectives.

The most common approach to gathering information on progress toward objec-tives is through some form of continued follow-up contact attempting to identify actions being taken that are in congruence with program goals. In the workplace, it is evident to the employer whether the employee decided to increase retirement contributions or begin participation in a retirement program. In a typical college financial literacy program, the outcome goals are typically more wide ranging, and measuring progress toward objectives becomes a challenge. Narrowing the scope of a college or university program will help in its definition as an effective program.

If grants and scholarships are all that the office is about, then measurement becomes clear.

The differential effects of programs are also examined during the progress-toward-degree stage of the evaluation (e.g., whether a financial education program has a greater impact on males than on females). This type of information assists in the improvement of programs. An external evaluator is often contracted to conduct this evaluation stage, particularly when new program-specific measures need to be developed (Jacobs 1988). Information from this stage of evaluation is important for programs planning to replicate and broaden their support (e.g., funders and stakeholders) because it provides the evidence needed to show effectiveness (Jacobs 1988).

The goal of the final evaluation tier, program impact, builds on the progress-toward-objectives tier and entails the measurement of both short- and long-term impacts of a financial education program (Jacobs 1988). This stage of evaluation again reflects the goals and objectives of a program, making it difficult to compare programs that do not have the same focus and nearly impossible to identify the impact of programs with vaguely defined goals. At this stage, measurable levels of differences in treated and non-treated populations are reported. This stage of the process requires a formal experimental, or quasi-experimental, approach to analysis of those receiving some form of financial education and contrasting this group with a similar sample that has not participated in the financial education program (Jacobs 1988). Only through such an experimental approach can the independent impact of the program itself be identified. Once again, colleges and universities are perfectly positioned to contribute to the development of effective financial education through the ability to conduct and report on such controlled experiments. Though significant ethical questions can be raised, in some circumstances, it is reasonable to randomly assign some students into a program with a financial training session and some into a program without and then to observe differences in outcomes, especially if this program is new and experimental.

At this point, there is scarce evidence of such program impact in the financial education literature. Bernheim et al. (2001) provide one of the few examples of research contrasting a financially educated group with a non-educated group, showing the benefits of financial education mandates to be linked to the increased incidence of financial education in high schools and then to higher savings rates and wealth accumulation. The differences between those receiving financial education and those who did not receive education were isolated to individuals who came from households where parents provided poor models of financial management (Bernheim et al. 2001), yet even this study suffers from a selection problem. Similarly, Tennyson and Nguyen (2001) found higher scores for high school seniors on the Jump$tart survey where specific financial education was mandated by states. While the above studies draw on national samples, the approach to program impact evaluation for localized programming efforts is decidedly more focused and straight-forward, and colleges and universities can take the leading role in this work.

Selection of a control group from the same population targeted in the needs analysis provides the necessary baseline for comparison. If the control group cannot be drawn from an identical population, then control variables measuring known determinants of the desired outcomes must be collected for both the treatment group and the control group. For example, if the desired outcome is increased personal savings, then information on income, wealth, household status, education, age, employment status, parenting practices, and financial goals needs to be collected and controlled for by evaluators in the program impact analysis. It is in this final stage where the independent impact of a financial education program is identified. At this point, there are too few examples of financial education evaluation research that have reached this fifth and conclusive tier. Because of this simple fact, definitive statements on the impact of financial education are premature. At the same time, the importance of college financial education is magnified. With the unique ability of student affairs officials to target at-risk student populations, select appropriate control groups, provide potentially effective treatments, and follow-up with program participants, colleges and universities have a unique opportunity to push the *science* of financial education forward.

Summary

Colleges and university administrators know very well that the strength of their institutions is inextricably linked to the finances of their students and alumni. Realizing this, in conjunction with reported low levels of college student financial literacy, institutions are rededicating their efforts toward financial programming and education. Such an investment in personal financial education comes with the expectation of demonstrated benefits to students and subsequently the institution. Without reliable, valid, and relevant information collected from well-designed program evaluations, universities cannot know if their investments are worthwhile.

Currently, university financial education programs often omit evaluation as an integrated component of their program design. While most report some sort of activity, the most effective evidence of program impact is typically an anecdotal account of a program participant. While such stories are important, and often effective in convincing stakeholders of the merit of a program, they fall short of the standards of sound program evaluation. The research and publication record is deeper when it comes to establishing the need for financial education among college students.

Building on these needs assessments, we have described and outlined (see Table 11.1) a comprehensive evaluation framework for college program administrators in the hope that programs will make a commitment to the evaluation process. Not only is Jacobs' five-tiered approach to program evaluation easy to understand but the framework has the advantage of offering great flexibility in its application. It is designed to address the needs of all financial education programs: those programs in the design and development stage as well as programs that are well established and ready to measure effectiveness. The framework is flexible since it addresses a myriad of program goals and objectives regardless of the program's stage of development.

Table 11.1 Jacobs' (1988) five-tiered approach to program evaluation

Evaluation tier	What is the purpose of the evaluation?	Who will use the information collected from the evaluation?	What tasks should be undertaken by the program evaluator?	Application to a financial education program
Preimplementation—information justifying a need for the program	To collect information that documents the need for the program within the community	Members of the community Potential funding agents	Outline characteristics of the program Conduct the needs assessment Adjust the program according to the needs assessment	Collect community-based financial statistics (e.g., debt delinquency, bankruptcy, and savings rates) Interview community leaders regarding causes and effects of financial illiteracy and/or financial troubles Locate local press coverage on financial topics, such as bankruptcy, financial stress Write a description of the financial education program (e.g., target audience, thoughts about changing literacy levels, details regarding program delivery, cost to program participant, who will deliver program, benefits of program)

Accountability—information justifying program viability and utilization	To collect information about program users and program utilization	Funding agents Media sources Leaders in the community	Profile participant characteristics (e.g., background information) Describe program utilization data (e.g., numbers served by program) Estimate cost per unit of service (participant, course, class, etc.)	Provide descriptive profile of individuals who used the program (e.g., demographic information, personal finance data) Be able to report over a certain time frame (e.g., a year) how many individuals went through the program and at what cost
Program clarification—information to fine-tune the program	To collect information used by program developers and personnel to improve the program	Participants of the program Implementers of the program (administration and staff)	Revisit and restate program goals, objectives, teaching methods (e.g., is the program reaching the original target audience or does the audience need to be redefined based on information from the previous evaluation stage) Explore program assumptions	Survey program participants about their satisfaction with the program (e.g., questions regarding satisfaction with the educational sessions, whether the financial education program met expectations) Staff feedback (e.g., program staff receives feedback from participants regarding future financial topics)

(continued)

Table 11.1 (continued)

Evaluation tier	What is the purpose of the evaluation?	Who will use the information collected from the evaluation?	What tasks should be undertaken by the program evaluator?	Application to a financial education program
Progress toward objectives—information demonstrating effectiveness	To collect information that documents the effectiveness of the program and to provide information that the program staff and administration can use to make program improvements	Participants of the program Implementers of the program (administration and staff) Funding agents	Gather information about how the program is administered and operated, who uses the program, which staff members deliver the program Formulate measurable indicators based on the short-term program objectives (e.g., what outcomes does the program wish to impact?) Combine several measurement strategies (e.g., measures that are program specific and measures that are more general) Assess differential program effects based on participant characteristics (e.g., age, race)	Describe how the program operates (what topics are taught, who teaches them, who uses the program, what components do they use) Design and collect objective measures of program success (e.g., if desired program outcome is to increase financial literacy, administer a pre- and posttest of financial knowledge) Several, simple, and advanced behavioral indicators should also measure program outcome (e.g., participant reports activities to reduce debt during a 3-month period) Collect other types of data related to financial behavior (e.g., decision making, feelings of efficacy)

Program impact—program information relative to the big picture	To provide information that contributes to an area of knowledge and/or evaluation and to document program effectiveness in comparison to other programs	Administrators, staff, evaluators, and developers of other programs	Determine method of data analysis; Disseminate program and evaluation information	Analyze the indicators of success relative to the participants' characteristics (e.g., does financial literacy score vary by gender or age?); Publish findings of the effect of the financial education program
		Federal, state, and local policymakers; Research community; Academic community; Potential funding agents; Potential program adapters (including directors); Citizens of program and other communities	Implement experimental or quasi-experimental methodologies (random assignments and/or control groups) to measure program effectiveness (short and/or long term)	Engage in advanced methodological data collection (e.g., implement random assignment of "treatment" of financial education program; construct a control group of individuals who do not participate in program)
			Continue to collect and compile data from program users and staff about program utilization and implementation; efforts in this stage are contingent upon data collected at earlier stages	Evidence regarding the financial education program should (a) be tailored to specific audiences (e.g., community leaders vs. funding agents), (b) be evaluated relative to other programs, (c) be critiqued in terms of strengths and weaknesses of study design and methodological design (e.g., measures and techniques)

Adapted from Jacobs (1988, pp. 52–55)

This program evaluation approach attempts to make good evaluation less difficult for educators while providing a foundation to those who want to evaluate their program but are not sure how. It is our hope that sharing this framework will encourage student affairs professionals and university administrators to think about and integrate evaluation from program inception through eventual identification of program impacts. As mentioned, Jacobs' approach is comprehensive in that it addresses programs regardless of the stage the program is in. This approach does not expect a program to cover all five stages in the initial offerings. The evaluation process will most likely evolve and grow with the program and the resources dedicated to the evaluation. Given the intensity and long-term commitment inherent in the five-tiered approach to evaluation, we argue that university settings are the ideal grounds for conducting methodologically sound assessments of financial education.

There are many benefits to be reaped by incorporating a well-designed program evaluation within your program of financial education. Benefits of data collected through integrated and systematic financial education program evaluation include, but are not limited to, (a) sharing best practices, (b) improving effectiveness of existing programs, and (c) keeping the attention of university leaders, students, faculty, and external funders. Still greater strides can be made in the arena of financial education programs, and evaluation in particular, if more systematic, consistent, and uniform data collection occurs. Universities and colleges seem ideally positioned to make these strides and deliver the program impact evidence that is missing in the financial education literature. Doing so means following Jacobs' (1988) model of evaluation where evaluation of financial education programs is an integrative part of the programming process, not an independent procedure used only to identify the benefits of undertaking the process. The assumptions underlying this framework are a strength, as they state that evaluation should be collected and analyzed in a systematic manner and as an essential component to every program (Jacobs 1988). The evaluation process described herein, and recommended for all financial education programs, is interwoven with the programming itself, making good programming a part of good measurement and vice versa.

References

Amromin, G., Ben-David, I., Agarwal, S.,Chomsisengphet, S., & Evanoff, D. (2009). Financial Literacy and The Effectiveness of Financial Education and Counseling: A Review of the Literature. Retrieved March 14, 2012, from http://www.chicagofed.org/digital_assets/others/region/foreclosure_resource_center/more_financial_literacy.pdf.

Avard, S., Manton, E., English, D., & Walker, J. (2005). The financial knowledge of college freshmen. *College Student Journal, 39*(2), 321–339.

Bernheim, B. D., Garrett, D. M., & Maki, D. M. (2001). Education and saving: The long-term effects of high school financial curriculum mandates. *Journal of Public Economics, 80*, 436–466.

Borden, L. M., Lee, S., Serido, J., & Collins, D. (2008). Changing college students' financial knowledge, attitudes, and behavior through seminar participation. *Journal of Family and Economic Issues, 29*(1), 23–40.

Bowen, C. F., & Jones, H. M. (2006). Empowering young adults to control their financial future. *Journal of Family and Consumer Sciences, 98*(1), 33–39.

Braunstein, S., & Welch, C. (2002). Financial literacy: An overview of practice, research, and policy. *Federal Reserve Bulletin, 88*, 445–458.

Chen, H., & Volpe, R. P. (2002). Gender differences in personal financial literacy among college students. *Financial Services Review, 11*, 289–307.

Chui, M. S. (2009). An elective course in personal finance for health care professionals. *American Journal of Pharmaceutical Education, 73*(1), 1–7.

Cleveland Saves. (2002). *One-quarter of U.S. households are wealth poor*. Retrieved October 29, 2011, from http://www.clevelandsaves.org/back_page/wealth_poor.cfm.

Danes, S. M., Huddleston-Casas, C., & Boyce, L. (1999). Financial planning curriculum for teens: Impact evaluation. *Financial Counseling and Planning, 10*(1), 25–37.

DeLaune, L. D., Rakow, J. S., & Rakow, K. C. (2011). Teaching financial literacy in a co-curricular service-learning model. *Journal of Accounting Education, 28*(2), 103–113.

Doll, K. (2001). *Student provided financial planning on campus: A market analysis*. Unpublished master's thesis, Ohio State University, Columbus, OH.

Durband, D. B., & Britt, S. L. (2011). *Perspectives on university financial education programs: Research survey highlights*. Unpublished raw data.

Goetz, J., Cude, B. J., Nielsen, R. B., Chatterjee, S., & Mimura, Y. (2011). College-based personal finance education: Student interest in three delivery methods. *Journal of Financial Counseling and Planning, 22*(1), 27–42.

Hendrickson, L., Jokela, R. H., Gilman, J., Croymans, S., Marczak, M., & Zuiker, V. S. (2010). The viability of podcasts in extension education: Financial education for college students. *Journal of Extension, 48*(4). Retrieved October 29, 2011, from http://www.joe.org/joe/2010august/a7.php.

HigherOne. (2011). College students' financial literacy slipping despite increase in national attention. *PR Newswire US*. Retrieved October 29, 2011, from http://www.higherone.com/index.php?option=com_content&view=article&id=383:college-students-financial-literacy-slipping-despite-increase-in-national-attention-&catid=13:press-releases&Itemid=79.

Hopley, V. (2003). Financial education: What is it and what makes it so important? Community reinvestment report. *Federal Reserve Bank of Cleveland*, 1–12.

Hung, A. A., Mihaly, K., & Yoong, J. K. (2009). *Federal financial and economic literacy education programs, 2009*. Arlington: Rand Corporation.

Jacobs, F. H. (1988). The five-tiered approach to evaluation: Context and implementation. In H. B. Weiss & F. H. Jacobs (Eds.), *Evaluating family programs* (pp. 37–68). New York: Aldine DeGruyter.

Jariah, M., Husniyah, A. R., Laily, P., & Britt, S. (2004). Financial behavior and problems among university students: Need for financial education. *Journal of Personal Finance, 3*, 82–96.

Julian, D., Jones, A., & Deyo, D. (1995). Open systems evaluation and the logic model: Program planning and evaluation tools. *Evaluation and Program Planning, 18*(4), 333–341.

Knox, A. B. (2002). *Evaluation for continuing education*. New York: John Wiley and Sons, Inc.

Lalonde, K., & Schmidt, A. (2011). Credit cards and student interest: A financial literacy survey of college students. *Research in Higher Education Journal, 10*, 1–14.

Lucey, T. A. (2005). Assessing the reliability and validity of the Jump$tart survey of financial literacy. *Journal of Family and Economic Issues, 26*(2), 283–294.

Lyons, A. C. (2004). A profile of financially at-risk college students. *Journal of Consumer Affairs, 38*, 56–80.

Lyons, A. C., Palmer, L., Jayaratne, K. S., & Scherpf, E. (2006). Are we making the grade? A national overview of financial education and program evaluation. *Journal of Consumer Affairs, 40*(2), 208–235.

Mandell, L. (2008). *The financial literacy of young American adults: Results of the 2008 national Jump$tart coalition survey of high school seniors and college students*. Washington, DC: Jump$tart Coalition.

Masuo, D., Kutara, P., Wall, R., & Cheang, M. (2007). Financial information project: Assessing the financial interests of college students. *Journal of Family and Consumer Sciences, 99*(3), 29–36.

Nellie Mae Corp. (2007). *Graduate students and credit cards, Fall 2006, an analysis of usage rates and trends*. Retrieved October 29, 2011, from www.nelliemae.com/pdf/ccstudy_2006.pdf.

Peng, T., Bartholomae, S., Fox, J. J., & Cravener, G. (2007). The impact of personal finance education delivered in high school and college courses. *Journal of Family and Economic Issues, 28*, 265–284.

Prochaska, J. O., & DiClemente, C. C. (1983). Stages and processes of self-change of smoking: Toward an integrative model of change. *Journal of Consulting and Clinical Psychology, 51*(3), 390–395.

Richter Norgel, E., Hauer, D., Landgren, T., & Kloos, J. R. (2009). *Money doesn't grow on trees: A comprehensive model to address financial literacy education.* Retrieved October 29, 2011, from https://www.noellevitz.com/upload/Student_Retention/RMS/Retention_Success_Journal/RetScssJrnlStCatherineU0909.pdf.

Rosacker, K. M., Ragothaman, S., & Gillispie, M. (2009). Financial literacy of freshmen business school students. *College Student Journal, 43*(2), 391–399.

Sabri, M. F., & MacDonald, M. (2010). Savings behavior and financial problems among college students: The role of financial literacy in Malaysia. *Cross-Cultural Communication, 6*(3), 103–110.

Scriven, M. S. (1981). *The logic of evaluation.* Inverness, CA: Edgepress.

Seyedian, M., & Yi, T. D. (2011). Improving financial literacy of college students: A cross-sectional analysis. *College Student Journal, 45*(1), 177–189.

Stolle, R., & Dumpe, E. (2009). Developing the personal financial literacy of college students. *Proceedings of Academy of Business Education.* Retrieved October 29, 2011, from http://www.abe.sju.edu/proc2009/stolle.pdf.

Student Lending Analytics. (2010). *SLA 2010 financial literacy survey finds 49% of colleges offer financial literacy program; budgeting, credit cards, loan repayment are top subject areas.* Retrieved October 29, 2011, from http://studentlendinganalytics.typepad.com/student_lending_analytics/surveys-and-research-reports/.

Tennyson, S., & Nguyen, C. C. (2001). State curriculum mandates and student knowledge of personal finance. *Journal of Consumer Affairs, 35*(Winter), 241–263.

Todd, R. M. (2002). Financial literacy education: A potential tool for reducing predatory lending? *The Region (Federal Reserve Bank of Minneapolis), 16*, 6–13.

University of Virginia. (2007). *Supplement to the 2007 ACCESSUVA Suvey's report: financial literacy surveys.* Office of Institutional Assessment and Studies. Retrieved October 29, 2011, from http://www.web.virginia.edu/iaas/survey/portal/2006-07/0607financial.shtm.

University of Wisconsin Extension. (2011). *Evaluation.* Retrieved October 29, 2011, from http://www.uwex.edu/ces/pdande/evaluation/index.html.

Vienne, K., & Slate, J. R. (2009). A college financial management center: What do students think? *International Journal of Educational Leadership Preparation, 4*(2), 1–8. Retrieved October 29, 2011, from http://cnx.org/content/m20960/latest/.

Vitt, L. A., Anderson, C., Kent, J., Lyter, D. M., Siegenthaler, J. K., & Ward, J. (2000). *Personal finance and the rush to competence: Personal financial literacy in the U.S.* Middleberg: The Fannie Mae Foundation.

Weiss, H. B. (1988). Family support and education programs: Working through ecological theories of human development. In H. B. Weiss & F. H. Jacobs (Eds.), *Evaluating family programs* (pp. 3–36). New York: Aldine DeGruyter.

Zhu, H. (2011). Teaching OOP with financial literacy. *IEEE Transactions on Education, 54*(2), 328–331.

Chapter 12
Certifications in Financial Education Programs

Angela L. Mazzolini, Mary M. Bell, and Timothy Griesdorn

Introduction

While there are currently no federal laws requiring financial counselors or planners to be certified, there are several benefits to becoming certified. When professionals obtain certification, they have proven they have the required knowledge to perform their chosen professions. This is true with electricians, teachers, plumbers, doctors, lawyers, and also financial professionals. There are educational components to becoming certified that give professionals a better understanding of how to do their job effectively. Most certification programs also require continuing education to keep professionals up-to-date on important subject matter in their fields. Because of the knowledge and current information certifications provide, professionals are better able to serve their clients.

Three certifications that are available to financial professionals include the Accredited Financial Counselor, Certified Financial Planner™, and the Certified Retirement Counselor®. While there are many other certifications available, these three certifications make the most sense for college financial education program staff members. While obtaining these certifications, staff will learn enhanced communication skills, which are vital for relaying information on personal finances.

A.L. Mazzolini, M.S. student (✉)
Department of Personal Financial Planning, Texas Tech University,
15th Street & Akron, Room 262, Lubbock, TX 79409, USA
e-mail: angela.mazzolini@ttu.edu

M.M. Bell, Ph.D. candidate
School of Family Studies and Human Services, Kansas State University,
245 Justin Hall, Manhattan, KS 66506, USA
e-mail: marybell@k-state.edu

T. Griesdorn, Ph.D.
Department of Human Development and Family Studies, Iowa State University,
62 LeBaron Hall, Ames, IA 50011, USA
e-mail: tgriesdo@iastate.edu

D.B. Durband and S.L. Britt (eds.), *Student Financial Literacy:*
Campus-Based Program Development, DOI 10.1007/978-1-4614-3505-1_12,
© Springer Science+Business Media New York 2012

With these certifications, staff members will have the knowledge about financial topics that can then be passed on to students, parents, other college staff and faculty members, and perhaps even to the community.

Accredited Financial Counselor

History of Association for Financial Counseling and Planning Education (AFCPE). The Accredited Financial Counselor (AFC) certification is offered by the AFCPE. The idea for AFCPE began in Kansas City in the winter of 1983 when two colleagues, Drs. Tahira Hira and Jerry Mason, discussed the need for an organization that promoted financial counseling. AFCPE was formally launched at a conference held at Iowa State University in 1984 (Mason and O'Neill 2003). The organization has grown quite rapidly from 60 members in attendance at the first conference to over 500 members attending in 2010. In addition to offering networking opportunities between personal finance professionals, AFCPE also offers two certification programs: the AFC and the Certified Housing Counselor (CHC). The CHC focuses on the legal aspects of the housing market in addition to the AFC component. For the purposes of this chapter, we will be focusing on the AFC because of the focus on money management and counseling skills, which are relevant to campus financial education programs.

The AFC was first offered in 1992 when a need to certify financial counselors became evident to the members of AFCPE. The purpose of the AFC is to give personal finance professionals the skills needed to "assist individuals and families in the complex process of financial decision making, including the ability to:

- Educate clients in sound financial principles.
- Assist clients in the process of overcoming their financial indebtedness.
- Help clients identify and modify ineffective money management behaviors.
- Guide clients in developing successful strategies for achieving their financial goals.
- Support clients as they work through their financial challenges and opportunities.
- Help clients develop new perspective on the dynamics of money in relation to family, friends and individual self-esteem" (AFCPE n.d.).

AFCs are employed in Cooperative Extension, the military, credit counseling, academia, private practice, or other university locations, such as financial aid.

Requirements

The fees associated with the AFC are $900: a one-time $50 registration fee and a $425 course fee for each of the two courses, which also includes self-study materials. There may be additional fees associated with having the exams proctored at a local college or university or learning center. The two courses focus on different aspects of financial counseling. The first course focuses on financial management and covers topics such as budgeting and cash management, credit cards, insurance, retirement planning, and estate planning. The second course focuses on financial counseling techniques and debt management with topics such as communication, listening skills, counseling skills, problem solving, credit reports, identity theft, reducing debt, housing and student loan debt, and bankruptcy. For a full list of topics and the course materials, please visit www.afcpe.org. A score of 70% or better is required to pass each exam, and exams are offered year round.

There is also a work experience requirement of 1,000 hours in the financial counseling field and can include any of the following:

- Working in a related financial or counseling field
- Offering one-on-one counseling or advising services for clients
- Developing and conducting education and training for clients
- Developing education and training programs for financial counselors
- Education and training financial counselors
- Serving as an education director for a financial counseling organization
- Supervising financial counselors

Every person wishing to acquire the AFC must subscribe to the AFCPE code of ethics, which focuses on professional conduct, competency, integrity, and confidentiality. Letters of reference are also required.

Once a candidate has paid the fees, passed the exams, completed 1,000 hours of financial counseling work experience, signed the code of ethics, and supplied references that have been checked, he or she will earn the AFC certification. An AFC is then required to pay $45 yearly membership dues and complete 30 continuing education units (CEUs) every 2 years. Conveniently, the yearly AFCPE conference typically offers 15–17 CEUs every year, and AFC membership dues can be paid at the same time as conference registration. For more information about the AFCPE conference, please visit their website at www.afcpe.org.

Advantages

There are several advantages to becoming an AFC. The study materials are easily obtained and the self-study component allows sufficient time to complete the exams. Once the study materials are ordered, a candidate has 36 months to complete the final exam. Another advantage of the AFC is that anyone is eligible to sit for the exam; no specialized degree is required. Also, the Bankruptcy Abuse Prevention and Consumer Protection Act of 2005 requires all persons wishing to file bankruptcy to first seek credit counseling. Any financial counselor who plans to offer credit counseling in that capacity will need to obtain approval from the Department of Justice (Federal Trade Commission 2006). The AFC program complies with the requirements of the aforementioned act and should be pointed out when applying to the Department of Justice (AFCPE n.d.).

Students who wish to become AFCs will have even more advantages. Instead of the $425-per-exam fee, undergraduate students pay $125 and graduate students pay $175. If a student is involved in an organization or program that offers financial counseling and/or education, the student may use those hours toward the required work experience. Your program can contact AFCPE if you are interested in obtaining a campus agreement for students to enroll in the AFC program.

The knowledge gained through the AFC certification process will enable a financial counselor to more effectively assist clients with formulating and reaching their financial goals. This is especially important in the ever-changing financial world.

Certified Financial Planner®

History of Certified Financial Planner Board of Standards, Inc. (CFP Board)

The concepts and ideas that eventually formed the Certified Financial Planner Board of Standards, Inc. (CFP Board) began to emerge in the late 1960s. After World War II, there were many financial products and services that began to appear on the marketplace to meet the demands of an ever-growing economy. This led to a very fragmented financial services industry. It was on December 12, 1969, in Chicago, Illinois, that 13 founders, primarily from the insurance and securities fields, met to discuss the steps needed to integrate these new services and create a new profession called financial planning. They formed the International Association for Financial Planners (IAFP) as well as created the College for Financial Planning.

In 1972, the first class of students enrolled for the Certified Financial Planners (CFP) course offered by the College for Financial Planning. There were 35 graduates of that first class in October 1973, and they created the Institute of Certified Financial Planners (ICFP) upon their graduation (CFP Board 2011a). In 1985, the College transferred its ownership of the CFP® marks and the responsibilities associated with administering the exam and enforcing the standards to an independent, nonprofit certification organization known as the International Board of Standards and Practices for Certified Financial Planners, Inc. (IBCFP). It was later renamed Certified Financial Planner Board of Standards Inc. (CFP Board) in 1994. CFP Board's certification program became accredited through the National Commission for Certifying Agencies (NCCA) of the National Organization for Competency Assurance (now the Institute for Credentialing Excellence) in 1995. For their 20 years of operations, the headquarters was located in Denver, Colorado, until December 2007 when CFP Board moved its office to Washington, DC. The new location offers close proximity to legislators, regulators, and other organizations that influence policy and debate. CFP Board has been granted 501(c)(3) status by the Internal Revenue Service to engage in appropriate lobbying and legislative activities. CFP Board has established itself as a well-respected organization that advocates personal financial planning matters for the public interest (CFP Board 2011a).

The CFP® certification program grew interest among individuals and organizations around the world. In 1990, CFP Board created the International CFP Council to "promote the professionalism of individuals and organizations offering financial planning services and to ensure that such services are offered in an ethical and competent manner throughout the world." In 2004, the Financial Planning Standards Board (FPSB) was created to administer the certification program outside of the USA. The FPSB is also a nonprofit that "manages, develops and operates certification, education and related programs for financial planning organizations so that they may benefit and protect the global community by establishing, upholding and promoting worldwide professional standards in personal financial planning" (CFP Board 2011a). By 2010, FPSB had members and associate members in over 23 territories globally and over 126,000 individuals using the CFP marks in their respective countries and regions (CFP Board 2011a).

Purpose

The mission of CFP Board of Standards is to "benefit the public by granting the CFP® certification and upholding it as the recognized standard of excellence for personal financial planning" (CFP Board 2011a). The CFP® credential is the most recognized credential in the field of financial planning. Currently, there are over 61,000 CFP® professionals in the United States. This is a huge growth when compared to the 42 CFP® professionals in 1973. Now, according to the Bureau of Labor Statistics, there are more than 149,000 "personal financial advisors." As of the end of 2009, there were 126,016 CFP® professionals worldwide (CFP Board 2011e).

Requirements

The CFP® certification requires that a person meets strict standards in four areas: education, examination, experience, and ethics. The education standards are "designed to provide individuals with the core knowledge needed to practice personal financial planning" (CFP Board 2011a). In order to sit for the CFP® exam, an individual must complete the education requirements in seven areas of financial planning:

- General principles of financial planning
- Insurance planning and risk management
- Employee benefits planning
- Investment planning

- Income tax planning
- Retirement planning
- Estate planning

Recently, CFP Board required that a new Financial Plan Development Course be added to the program, which enhances the education standards for the certification. This new course will require students to "demonstrate their ability to prepare and deliver a comprehensive financial plan through completion" (CFP Board 2011e).

As of 2010, there were a total of 348 educational programs at 221 educational institutions in the USA that offer curricula that meet the requirements for the education experience necessary to sit for the exam (CFP Board 2011e). A list of registered programs can be found at www.cfp.net. Once an individual has taken and passed the required coursework from a CFP Board-Registered Program, the individual is then eligible to sit for the exam. An individual with a specific degree or credential may also meet the educational requirement by challenging the exam. A list of the degrees or credentials that allow an individual to challenge the exam may be obtained from CFP Board. There are certain requirements that must be met for those degrees or licenses (CFP Board 2011e). To find out more about the challenge status, see the CFP Board website for detailed information on the challenge status.

Often, even after taking a comprehensive course of study, most students prepare for the exam by taking an intensive review course. The exam is a pass/fail exam with an average pass rate of 57% (CFP Board 2011f). The CFP® exam is offered three times a year, usually during the months of March, July, and November. Applications are usually requested at least 6 weeks before the test date, and the exam is offered in various locations. For more information, go to http://www.cfp.net/become/exam-details.asp. After passing the exam, an individual must still meet the requirements in education, ethics, and experience before using the CFP® marks.

Some courses of study offer degrees, such as a bachelor's or master's degree in financial planning, but others are only certificate programs. Therefore, after passing the exam, a CFP® candidate must show they have earned a bachelor's degree or higher from an accredited college or university. The individual is also required to complete 15 hours of continuing education each year, which includes at least one hour of continuing education in a CFP® Board certified program of ethics (CFP Board 2011b).

In order to use the CFP® marks, a CFP® certificant must agree to adhere to the professional code of conduct known as CFP Board's Code of Ethics and Professional Responsibility and to Financial Planning Practice Standards. The individual also acknowledges CFP Board's right to enforce the standards through its Disciplinary Rules and Procedures. The standards require a fiduciary duty, which means that a CFP® certificant "must act in the client's best interest when suggesting or recommending investments or financial planning advice" (CFP Board 2011c). When the certification is renewed, the CFP® certificant must sign a disclosure statement indicating if the individual has been "involved in any criminal, civil, self-regulatory organization or governmental agency inquiry, investigation or proceeding" (CFP Board 2011c).

A CFP® candidate must complete 3 years of work experience within a 10-year period prior to the exam and/or up to 5 years after the exam. This experience must come in "the supervision, direct support, teaching or personal delivery of all or part of the personal financial planning process to a client" (CFP Board 2011d, p. 3). The work experience must be a job that directly delivers the financial planning process to a client. Work experience needs to fit within one or more of the following six categories: (1) establishing and defining the relationship with the client; (2) gathering client data, including goals; (3) analyzing and evaluating the client's financial status; (4) developing and presenting financial planning recommendations and/or alternatives; (5) implementing the financial planning recommendations; and (6) monitoring the financial planning recommendations (CFP Board 2011d). Additional information on these areas may be obtained from www.cfp.net.

Advantages

As the world of personal finance continues to grow more complex with an ever increasing amount of financial products, there will continue to be a need for financial experts, especially CFP® professionals. As individual risk increases, consumers will seek out a financial professional who can help them make sense of this complex market place. CFP® professionals are trained in specific areas to help individual consumers reduce risk while maximizing their reward. The CFP® mark is the most publically recognized certification in the financial planning industry (CFP Board's 25th Anniversary 2011e).

Certified Retirement Counselor®

History of International Foundation for Retirement Education (InFRE)

Estimates of the baby boomer population indicated that approximately 78 million baby boomers will retire sometime in the next 18 years. The 2010 Employee Benefits Retirement Institute retirement confidence survey indicates that approximately 50% of all American workers have less than $50,000 saved for retirement (Helman et al. 2010). The International Foundation for Retirement Education (InFRE) was founded in 1997 to address the challenge of helping retirement counselors and administrators increase the retirement preparedness of the American worker (CRC Certification 2010). One of InFRE's goals is to help people know when to retire and how to make their money last. In addition, InFRE strives to help people establish a plan that will help them stay engaged for a healthier, happier, and more productive retirement. InFRE's primary way of educating the American worker about retirement is through the Certified Retirement Counselor (CRC®) designation. By supporting and educating thousands of CRC®'s, InFRE can help retirement counselors and administrators provide non-biased education materials for the American worker. The CRC® is gaining in popularity; approximately 2,000 people have earned the CRC® designation. The CRC® certification program completed the accreditation process of the NCCA in September 2009, and it is one of three financial designations that are registered with the NCCA, the first one being the CFP® designation, which was registered in 1995, and the second one being the Certified Senior Advisor (CSA), which was registered in 2008.

Accreditation is also an indication to employers and clients that those who hold an accredited certification possess a minimum level of knowledge and competency pertaining to their profession. In order to be an accredited program, an institution must meet high standards regarding governance, responsibility to stakeholders, exam process, and recertification. Evidence of compliance with these standards must be submitted along with other required documentation.

Independent accreditation is an important way to distinguish between a "certification" (designed to help prepare retirement counselors to competently address retirement issues) and a "designation" (may only indicate completion of a course). Striving to ensure that all consumers, especially seniors, receive competent retirement planning guidance, many organizations offering financial services to seniors are requiring their employees to become certified.

Purpose

A certification like the CRC® can provide additional assurance to employers and clients that certain minimum qualifications of retirement-specific knowledge and experience have been met. The knowledge required to earn the CRC® indicates that candidates have a strong grasp of retirement and can be helpful in communicating retirement information to the public.

A retirement counselor job focuses on helping people understand the various issues surrounding retirement. A CRC® designation is a good foundation upon which to build if you have the desire to help others understand retirement-related principles of asset accumulation, retirement readiness and strategies for managing retirement income, the impact of inflation on purchasing power, how much to save, the different types of retirement plans, the fundamentals of investments, counseling and communication techniques, and the fundamentals of retirement planning.

Requirements

To earn the right to use the CRC® certification mark, InFRE requires passing a comprehensive exam, completing a minimum period of industry experience, and adhering to a code of ethics. Exams are offered at set intervals throughout the year: January, April, July, and October. Exams are typically administered at colleges or universities as close as possible to the candidate. The exam consists of 200 multiple-choice questions, and candidates are given 4 hours to complete the exam. The application deadline is 6 weeks prior to each exam date. The fee to sit for the exam is $450 for private sector employees and $380 for government employees. InFRE also offers a set of four study guides to help candidates prepare for the exam. The study guides can be purchased for $450 a set, or $125 each, for private sector employees; or $360 a set, or $100 each, for government employees. There is also a student rate for the CRC® exam: $50 to sit for the exam and $100 for the set of training books. Pass rates for this exam have not been published.

In order to complete the certification process, a candidate must have completed a bachelor's degree in any discipline and have a minimum of 2 years of relevant retirement-related experience, or they must have earned a high school diploma or its equivalent and have 5 years of relevant retirement-related professional experience (within the past 7 years). A background check will be conducted upon meeting the educational and experience requirements, and the candidate must agree to abide by the CRC® code of ethics and annual continuing education requirements.

CRC® certificants are required to complete 15 hours of continuing education each year. In addition, a $125 annual renewal fee is required as well as continued adherence to the code of ethics.

Advantages

The CRC® is unique in that candidates do not have to have a specialized degree; high school graduates can obtain certification with additional experience requirements. Study materials are easily obtained, with a reduced rate for government employees. The self-study nature of the exam allows sufficient time to prepare. There is only one exam to pass with just 200 questions, and it is offered four times per year. Finally, it is one of only three certifications in financial planning to be nationally accredited by NCCA. For more information, please refer to the InFRE website, www.infre.org, or call them at 1-847-756-7350.

Summary

Whether choosing the AFC, the CFP®, or the CRC®, it is important for financial professionals to become certified. Knowledge, experience, and credibility are all advantages to becoming certified and will help financial professionals better serve their clients. Setting goals, reducing debt, managing risk and reward, and focusing on specific areas, such as retirement planning, are all important roles of financial professionals. While new students and parents will be filtering through the college or university, it is important for staff to be consistent in their knowledge of the changes in the financial world. Certifications offer the opportunity to stay abreast of the changes through continuing education. Being certified as an AFC, CFP®, or CRC® as part of a campus financial education program will also enable staff to effectively communicate necessary information to students, parents, other campus faculty and staff, and the community.

References

AFCPE. (n.d.). *Certification, Accredited Financial Counselor.* Retrieved April 1, 2011, from http://www.afcpe.org/certification/programs/accredited-financial-counselor.php.
CFP Board. (2011a). *CFP Board mission and history.* Retrieved April 10, 2011, from http://www.cfp.net/aboutus/mission.asp.
CFP Board. (2011b). *Why are the CFP® certification requirements important?* Retrieved April 10, 2011, from http://www.cfp.net/Learn/knowledgebase.asp?id=11.
CFP Board. (2011c). *Ethics.* Retrieved April 11, 2011, from http://www.cfp.net/become/ethics.asp.
CFP Board. (2011d). *Experience.* Retrieved April 11, 2011, from http://www.cfp.net/become/experience.asp.
CFP Board. (2011e). *CFP Board's 25th anniversary: Talking points.* Retrieved April 12, 2011, from http://www.cfp.net/aboutus/anniversarycampaign.asp.
CFP Board. (2011f). *CFP® certification exam statistics.* Retrieved April 12, 2011, from http://www.cfp.net/media/survey.asp?id=9#link4.
Federal Trade Commission. (2006). *Before you file for personal bankruptcy: Information about credit counseling and debtor education.* Retrieved April 10, 2011, from http://www.ftc.gov/bcp/edu/pubs/consumer/credit/cre41.shtm.
Helman, R., Copeland, C., & VanDerhei, J. (2010). *The 2010 retirement confidence survey: Confidence stabilizing, but preparations continue to erode. EBRI issue brief, 340,* 1–44. Retrieved April 17, 2011, from http://ebri.org/publications/ib/index.cfm?fa=ibDisp&content_id=4488.
International Foundation for Retirement Education. (2010). *Certified Retirement Counselor (CRC) certification.* Retrieved April 1, 2011, from http://www.infre.org/CertifiedRetirementCounselor.shtml.
Mason, J., & O'Neill, B. (2003). Letter to the reader. In J. Ladouceur (Ed.), *Association for Financial Counseling and Planning Education celebrates 20 years* (p. 3). Upper Arlington, OH: AFCPE.

Appendix A
For Clients

Basic Money Management

CashCourse (www.cashcourse.org)—This online program is sponsored by NEFE (National Endowment for Financial Educators) and offers online workshops for students. The enrollment process is more involved than most sites. Students need to complete an online enrollment form. After this form is completed, CashCourse emails an agreement which students sign and send back through the postal system. After this process is completed, students can login to CashCourse and sign up for workshops. These workshops cover a wide range of topics, such as budgeting and planning, spending behaviors, debt and credit cards, educational expenses, setting financial goals, and saving.

CNNMoney (www.money.cnn.com)—This website is a partnering of *Money* magazine, *Fortune* Magazine, and the CNN media group. Under the Personal Finance tab, readers will find numerous articles, tools, and guides on how to handle many topics related to personal finance. Although this resource is not repeated under the other topic subheadings in this appendix, there are helpful resources available on tax, retirement, and investing from CNNMoney. There is also an Ask The Expert tab where users can email questions concerning their individual issues.

Consumer Action (www.consumer-action.org)—Consumer Action strives to make heard the voices of underrepresented consumers. Consumer Action is a nonprofit organization that offers educational resources as well as action resources to help those seeking justice. The organization has dedicated its resources to financial literacy and advocating consumer rights with the media as well as lawmakers to sustain justice among the underrepresented groups. Consumer Action offers multilingual publications on many financial topics as well as a Consumer Action newspaper (*Consumer Action News*) and a newsletter (*Consumer Action Insider*).

Federal Citizen Information Center (FCIC) (www.Publications.USA.gov)— Readers can obtain information several ways from this site. Publications can be received by mail or viewed online and most are free of charge. The FCIC also offers

D.B. Durband and S.L. Britt (eds.), *Student Financial Literacy: Campus-Based Program Development*, DOI 10.1007/978-1-4614-3505-1, © Springer Science+Business Media New York 2012 a free consumer information catalog which lists titles, descriptions, and ordering information for more than 200 free and low-cost publications distributed by the center. The center also offers a *Consumer Action Handbook* which is full of information including how to file complaints against businesses, prevent identity theft, and understand credit. Readers will also find information on how to file for bankruptcy, find an attorney, and plan a funeral.

Federal Reserve Board (www.federalreserve.gov/consumerinfo)—This website serves as a great resource for financial topics. Readers will find articles on bank accounts and banking services, credit cards, credit reports and scores, identity theft, leasing, and mortgages. They also offer a *What You Need to Know* series that offers updated rules concerning consumer topics. The site also offers a *5 Tips* series, which provides five tips on personal finance topics such as credit cards, identity theft, and home mortgage issues.

Federal Trade Commission (FTC) (http://www.ftc.gov/bcp/consumer.shtm)—The FTC offers educational materials on a variety of topics such as credit cards and loans, purchasing automobiles, identity theft and internet fraud, as well as basic investment concepts. Each category has a drop-down menu that features articles on specific topics for that particular subject. For example, under the credit and loans category, a person can learn about fair credit practices or consumer rights as well as find articles that offer tips on credit management.

Fin Aid (www.finaid.org)—This site offers a plethora of information on all issues related to financial aid. A particularly interesting resource on the website is the list of common errors on financial aid applications. Reading through this list will enable students to sidestep common mistakes and allow their applications to process quickly. This site also offers loan calculators, a list of preferred lenders, information on interest rates, and consolidation options. This site is a must for those applying to colleges who are also in need of financial aid.

Housing and Urban Development (HUD) (www.hud.gov)—HUD is the US government's department for all topics related to housing. This website offers many educational resources for potential and current homeowners. Mortgage calculators, loan-estimation calculators, and a buying-versus-renting calculator are a few of the resources offered. Also, publications and forms for various homeownership topics are located here as well.

Internal Revenue Service (IRS) (www.irs.gov)—This website is the official website for the Internal Revenue Service. The site houses all forms and guidelines for filing taxes, offers an FAQ tab for possible issues, and lists all of the updated rules and laws for the current tax year. Under the Retirement Plans Community tab, readers will find current forms for retirement planning and the tax system. Also, readers will find articles and guides for common retirement planning issues. This site also lists the different types of retirement plans available through employers as well as individual plans.

Love Your Money (www.loveyourmoney.org)—Love Your Money is an educational resource that is funded by a grant from the Financial Industry Regulator Authority (FINRA) and coordinated through the University of Tennessee. Participants are required to create an account to login to the system. The site contains seven modules and a quiz. Modules cover topics such as spending, budgeting, basic investing, and fraudulent schemes concerning money. After a participant has completed all modules and summaries, a certificate of completion is available for printing.

Money Habitudes (www.moneyhabitudes.com)—This card-style, game-like tool aids people in understanding their habits and attitudes towards money. It also highlights the how, when, and why people use money, especially concerning saving and spending. Packs of Habitudes cards can be ordered from the website. Habitudes cards come in English and Spanish; there is a teen version available as well.

Yahoo! Finance (http://finance.yahoo.com/personal-finance)—This website offers a plethora of information on all topics related to personal finance. Readers can locate articles on banking and budgeting, retirement, personal insurance (life, property, and casualty), as well as planning for college expenses. Each area offers how-to guides and calculators to make planning easier.

Credit Management

Annual Credit Report (www.annualcreditreport.com)—This site is the only website that offers a free credit report to consumers. Individuals select the state in which they reside and fill out an information sheet which requests personal information, including a Social Security number. Correct answers to security questions are also required. Once a person provides correct information, they are able to view their credit report. A person can choose to review reports from all three of the major reporting agencies or select to view only one report. Consumers are eligible for one free report from each agency every 12 months.

Bankrate (www.bankrate.com)—This site contains many tools and informative articles concerning mortgage loans. Readers can track current mortgage rates, use calculators to determine mortgage payments, and view amortization schedules on loans. Bankrate also offers tools and articles on auto loans. Readers can compare rates for new and used cars as well as read articles on current events surrounding mortgage and auto loans. Bankrate also offers information on checking and savings accounts, credit cards, and personal insurance.

Credit Card (www.creditcard.com)—This website allows viewers to search for the best credit card based on the viewer's individual needs. Viewers are able to search for credit cards based on credit score, length of credit history, annual percentage rates, reward cards, and travel and airline cards, and there is a specific search for the best credit cards for college students. This site is easy to use and offers direct links to each credit card's website. There is also a compare option if a viewer has several cards from which they are selecting.

Experian™ (www.experian.com/credit-education/credit-information.html)— Experian™ is one of the three national credit reporting agencies. In addition to being able to access your credit report, Experian™ also provides information on why a credit score is important, tips on how to avoid fraud, and ideas on how to build and maintain good credit.

PowerPay (www.powerpay.org)—This free online program allows users to develop plans for paying off debt and create spending plans. After creating login information, users are directed to the PowerPay homepage. It is here that users enter creditor information. After all credit accounts are entered, the software creates a payoff plan for the individual. Users can use the payment calendar and calculator features to know how their payment schedules will change if payments are increased. PowerPay also offers an education center which houses several articles on budgeting, credit, debt management, identity theft, and insurance.

Saving and Investing

America Saves (www.americasaves.org)—This site focuses on saving money and paying off debt. Participants need to have an understanding of their goals to enroll; an amount to be saved is required on the enrollment page. Members receive a free copy of *The American Saver* newsletter, email access to free financial planning advice, and access to other members who have achieved success with their savings goals. This site also offers educational information related to saving such as compound interest, savings strategies, and savings estimators.

The Choose to Save® Program (www.choosetosave.org)—This national public education program raises awareness about the need to save and plan for long-term financial security through multimedia materials and outreach efforts aimed at the general public. Developed by the Employee Benefit Research Institute (EBRI) and its American Savings Education Council (ASEC) program, the program promotes the idea that saving today is vital to a secure financial future.

Software and Apps

MINT (www.mint.com)—MINT offers an Android or iPhone application that allows users to sign up for a Mint.com account, add banks, and track accounts right from a phone. Information is updated in real time, allowing the user to view up-to-date accounts, check budgets, and edit information on the app. For added security, the app is password protected.

Mvelopes® (www.mvelopes.com)—This online system allows people to create spending plans that can be managed online. System fees depend on which plan subscription is selected. Mvelopes also offers online bill paying for subscribers as well as applications for smart phones and other portable electronic devices. Mvelopes tracks spending on all entered accounts and downloads account information onto one screen for easy viewing.

Appendix B
For Educators and Practitioners

American Council on Consumer Interests (ACCI) (www.consumerinterests.org)—ACCI strives to connect professionals with current consumer advocacy topics, education, policy development, and research. ACCI offers an annual conference in the spring of each year.

American Savings Education Council (ASEC) (www.choosetosave.org)—ASEC is a national coalition of public- and private-sector institutions committed to making saving and retirement planning priorities for all Americans. ASEC is linked with the Choose to Save program, a national public education and outreach program that is dedicated to raising awareness about the need to plan and save for long-term personal financial security.

Association for Financial Counseling and Planning Education (AFCPE) (www.afcpe.org)—This organization is a nonprofit, professional organization that offers education resources and training opportunities to financial counselors and educators. AFCPE also certifies practitioners as Accredited Financial Counselors and Certified Housing Counselors. AFCPE offers an annual conference in the late fall of each year.

Center for Responsible Lending (www.responsiblelending.org)—This organization strives to protect consumers from abusive financial practices. The website offers many articles and videos on mortgage lending, credit cards, overdraft loans, and payday lending. The site also offers many tools and resources that enable consumers to better understand their individual financial situations.

Certified Financial Planner Board of Standards, Inc. (CFP Board) (www.cfp.net/)—The mission of this organization is to benefit the public by granting the CFP® certification. CFP Board increases public awareness of and preference for CFP® certification as the standard for financial planning.

Cooperative Extension (http://www.nifa.usda.gov/financialsecurity.cfm)—Working through land-grant universities and other partners, the Cooperative Extension targets programs for youth, financially vulnerable populations, and consumers making financial decisions throughout their lifetimes. The overall goal is for people to acquire the knowledge, skills, and motivation to build financial security. Programs focus on behavioral change, starting with achieving financial self-sufficiency, then leading to financial stability. The ultimate goal, financial security, is the cornerstone of prosperous communities, nurturing neighborhoods, and strong families. For Cooperative Extension resources, go to http://www.extension.org/personal_finance.

Department of the Treasury Financial Education (www.treasury.gov/resource-center/financial-education/Pages/default.aspx)—This website serves as a resource center for national efforts focused on internal and external financial education programs, grants, and research.

Federal Reserve Education (www.federalreserveeducation.org)—This website is supported by the Federal Reserve and offers many tools and resources for educators and the general public. For educators, the website offers lesson plans and classroom activities concerning personal finance. Under the Public Resources tab, consumers will find articles and helpful tools concerning topics such as credit, banking, personal finances, and consumer protection.

Financial Therapy Association (FTA) (www.financialtherapyassociation.org)—This organization supports the ideology that financial health is made up of positive emotional, behavioral, and economic decisions. FTA offers an annual conference in the early fall of each year. Here educators, researchers, and practitioners join together to share practice methods, current research, and experiences.

Investor Protection Trust (IPT) (www.investorprotection.org)—The Investor Protection Trust provides independent, objective information to help consumers make informed investment decisions. Founded in 1993 as part of a multistate settlement to resolve charges of misconduct, IPT serves as an independent source of noncommercial investor education materials. IPT operates programs under its own auspices and uses grants to underwrite important initiatives carried out by other organizations.

Jump$tart Coalition for Personal Financial Literacy® (www.jumpstart.org/)—Jump$tart is a coalition of organizations from corporate, academic, nonprofit, government, and other sectors that share an interest in advancing financial literacy among students in prekindergarten through college.

National Endowment for Financial Education (NEFE) (www.nefe.org)—NEFE is a nonprofit organization that promotes financial well-being. The organization's website is full of information for researchers, educators, and consumers. Educators will find an enormous amount of information for students in grades K-12 as well as for higher education students. A Financial Education Evaluation Toolkit is provided to help educators measure program success. NEFE also offers grants concerning financial education for groups interested in creating an education program in their area.

The Stock Market Game (www.smgww.org/)—The SIFMA Foundation's Stock Market Game™ provides students the chance to invest a hypothetical $100,000 in an online portfolio. Using a game format, students learn economic and financial concepts for life.

US Securities and Exchange Commission (SEC) (www.sec.gov/investor/students/tips.htm)—The SEC gives a series of questions and answers for parents or teachers to cover with students concerning saving and basic investing. Questions covered include the following: Why invest and save? What is compound interest? What is risk and return? What is diversification? This website offers clear and concise answers that novice investors will understand. This site also offers a financial literacy quiz as well as a savings calculator, plus they provide a list of questions and answers about buying a new home.

Index

CPSIA information can be obtained at www.ICGtesting.com
Printed in the USA
LVOW070219200412

278411LV00006B/27/P